D1134706

Managing Multinationals in the Middle East

Managing Multinationals in the Middle East

Accounting and Tax Issues

WAGDY M. ABDALLAH

QUORUM BOOKS
Westport, Connecticut • London

NORTHWEST MISSOURI STATE
UNIVERSITY LIBRARY
MARYVILLE, MO 64468

Library of Congress Cataloging-in-Publication Data

Abdallah, Wagdy M. (Wagdy Moustafa)
   Managing multinationals in the Middle East : accounting and tax issues / Wagdy M.
Abdallah.
     p. cm.
   Includes bibliographical references and index.
   ISBN 1–56720–267–5 (alk. paper)
    1. Corporations—Middle East—Accounting.   2. Corporations—Middle East—Taxation.   3.
International business enterprises—Middle East—Management. I. Title.
   HF5686.C7A287   2001
   657'.96'0956—dc21   00–023932

British Library Cataloguing in Publication Data is available.

Copyright © 2001 by Wagdy M. Abdallah

All rights reserved. No portion of this book may be
reproduced, by any process or technique, without
the express written consent of the publisher.

Library of Congress Catalog Card Number: 00–023932
ISBN: 1–56720–267–5

First published in 2001

Quorum Books, 88 Post Road West, Westport, CT 06881
An imprint of Greenwood Publishing Group, Inc.
www.quorumbooks.com

Printed in the United States of America

The paper used in this book complies with the
Permanent Paper Standard issued by the National
Information Standards Organization (Z39.48–1984).

10 9 8 7 6 5 4 3 2 1

657.96
A13m

Dedicated to
my wife and my mother
for their love, support, and understanding,
and to the memory and soul of my father

JAN 2 8 2002

Contents

1.   Introduction   1

I.   **Managing Multinational Companies in the Middle East**   **17**

2.   The Economic, Political, and Legal Characteristics of Middle
     East Countries and Their Accounting Systems   19

3.   The Effect of Culture and Religion on Accounting in the
     Middle East and the Harmonization of International
     Accounting Standards   39

4.   Investing in the Middle East   61

II. **Financial Reporting and Performance Evaluation in the
     Middle East**   **85**

5.   Accounting Systems and Practices of Selected Middle East
     Countries: Comparative Analysis with U.S. GAAP and IAS   87

6.   International Accounting Standards and Their Impact on
     Accounting Practices and Principles of Selected Middle
     East Countries   123

7.   Performance Measurement and Evaluation of Foreign
     Subsidiary Managers in the Middle East   149

III. **Tax Systems in the Middle East and Transfer Pricing
     Strategies**   **169**

8.   Tax Systems of Selected Middle East Countries   171

 9. Transfer Pricing Policies for Multinationals Operating in the
     Middle East   197

10. Objectives and Strategies of Transfer Pricing Policies in the
     Middle East   217

11. Transfer Pricing Techniques in the Middle East and Section
     482 of the IRC   237

IV. Looking Ahead   **261**

12. The Future of the Business Environment and Its Effect on the
     Future of Accounting Development in Middle East Countries   263

Index   273

Chapter 1

Introduction

As with many aspects of Middle East business history, the study of both Arab and Israeli businesses has tended to remain isolated from broader trends in business history and the social sciences. While there exist a number of research studies conducted on other areas, there is a deficiency on the Middle East. Most writing on accounting and tax issues in the Middle East has drawn either on Arab countries, the State of Israel, or the political conflict between Arab countries and Israel. This book is unique because it covers four interrelated issues from the point of view of multinational corporations (MNCs). The issues are management, finance, accounting and financial reporting, and taxation of Middle East countries, including Arab countries and Israel.

Unlike other areas of the world, the Middle East has been suffering with major conflicts and problems that go beyond disagreements over territory or fears concerning a rival's geopolitical and economic strategies. Making long-term peace agreements or settlements may look like an impossible mission because it requires not only carefully drawn compromises backed by international powers but also fundamental changes in the attitudes of people toward their enemies. Whether the Middle East will be a more stable and peaceful political and economic environment in the twenty-first century is definitely uncertain.

The Middle East countries are completely different from others in many aspects. They range from very rich oil countries with a high per capita income, such as Saudi Arabia and Kuwait, to underdeveloped and poor countries, such as Sudan and Yemen. Some countries are overpopulated, such as Egypt and Jordan, while others are sparsely populated, such as Saudi Arabia and Oman. However, they share such common features as culture, social life, religion, language, and, above all, the lack of economic development and advanced technology of their own.

As global business and economic expansion continues, Middle East countries witness a gradual move from state-owned and family-owned enterprises to international joint venture participation and ownership; from small business firms to large-scale multinational manufacturing companies from all over the world with more competitive global markets; from short-term financing requirements to long-term credits and capital investments. Combining all of these changes with the continuing need for the efficient utilization of scarce resources (both oil and non-oil), there is an urgent need for a more relevant, timely, comprehensive, and sophisticated management accounting system for both MNCs and local partners.

For MNCs, the Middle East region has a significant level of global trade, as represented by the existence of over 1,000 different MNCs of different nationalities investing approximately over $30 billion in the region. There are more than 100 million people living in the area in more than 10 countries. To managers in these MNCs, the Middle East region's major international advantages include: the presence of major oil and natural gas, major international airports, ports along the Gulf, high per capita income in some countries, a highly skilled educated labor force at a very low cost, and a growing tax-free zone to be used as an industrial base (Kavoossi 1995: 5). The Middle East countries have long been interconnected to the rest of the world through international trade and several economic agreements.

THE MIDDLE EAST BUSINESS ENVIRONMENT

For American, Japanese, British, German, and all other MNCs, understanding the business and people of the Middle East is essential to grasping some of the economic, cultural, legal, and political factors of the area. These environmental factors have a significant impact on MNCs indirectly through their effect on the perception and behavior of outside participants. They also affect MNCs directly through their effects on the behavior of internal participants as they manage and operate their Middle East operations, which include accounting and management control systems.

Economic, Political, and Legal Factors in the Middle East

In general, MNCs invest in the Middle East to take advantage of economic differences, such as taxation, financial markets, product costs, and product-selling markets. Inflation, tariff barriers, fluctuating exchange rates, trade barriers and restrictions, balance-of-payments disequilibrium, and restrictions of foreign trade policies are the most significant economic factors affecting MNCs' success. MNCs invest particularly in Middle East countries for many reasons. These reasons include: (1) improving their competitive position, (2) exploring new markets, (3) maximizing profits, (4) meeting the tariff and quota restrictions of Middle East countries, (5) securing otherwise unobtainable raw materials, such as crude oil, for their home country, (6) exploring the scarce economic resources in Middle East countries, (7) choosing countries with low income taxes on foreign companies or foreign investments, and (8) manufacturing their products in the lowest cost–producing Middle East countries and selling the products in the best-selling markets, such as Europe (Abdallah 1989: 1).

One of the most important economic factors in the Middle East is the energy reserves. Almost two-thirds of the oil reserves and one-half of the natural gas reserves are in the Middle East (Diller and Moore 1994: 156). Middle East oil producers enjoyed a seller's market between 1973 and the early 1980s. However, in the mid-1980s, it became a buyer's market as the supply exceeded the demand. The downward pressure on oil prices and declining economic and political leverage significantly affected oil-rich countries, especially Kuwait and Saudi Arabia. Oil prices dropped by almost 70% (from nearly $40 a barrel in 1981 to only $12) by the summer of 1986. The unexpected results of the oil market forced the oil-producing nations to cut back on expensive social and economic projects and to start to diversify in their economic activities and search for new sources of income (Diller and Moore 1994: 151). In the 1990s, most Middle East countries consumed their own resources as a result of war efforts and the construction of advanced weapons. Currently, other economic problems face Middle East countries, such as a huge foreign debt, the scarcity of water resources, and an overpopulation problem in several poor countries (ibid.).

Now, even though the future is uncertain, the Middle East oil countries are considered vital to the national security and economic interests of the United States and other industrial countries. Moreover, the four biggest Gulf states (Kuwait, Saudi Arabia, the United Arab Emirates, and Iraq) could supply almost 60% of the world's oil needs (Diller and Moore 1994: 167–168).

As the global market expands, a keen competition against Middle East countries comes from different directions, including the European Union (EU), the Association of Southeast Asian Nations (ASEAN), India, China, and Eastern Europe. At this point, some Arab countries felt that they had to make a long-term commitment to increase the Gulf region's international competitiveness and develop an integrated strategic power through new economic and political blocs. In 1981, five Gulf states (Bahrain, Kuwait, Oman, Qatar, and the United Arab Emirates), along with Saudi Arabia, the most powerful and dominant force in the area, formed the Gulf Cooperation Council (GCC) (Mansfield 1981: 193).

The GCC's main objective was to realize cooperation in all economic, political, educational, and informational fields. At the present time, the main purpose of its activities is the harmonization of matters relating to imports and exports, especially to protect its local industries (Cole 1991: 29). In order to reduce uncertainty and provide greater economic stability, the GCC countries have attempted to diversify their economies. Moreover, to respond to the threat of the EU, the GCC's main idea was to integrate the demand and supply for goods and services in the separate states into a common market (Cole 1991: 30).

Another important factor regarding the region is that we, as global businesspersons, are obligated to pay more attention to it than before: this factor is referred to as "Political Islam" or the "Political Economy of Islam," because it has significant implications on the economies, international business, and politics of the Middle East. Islam, in its real context, is not just a religion, it is a way of life. Its true tenets and rules permeate almost everything, including socio-economics, politics, and government. It is not wise for executives of MNCs to disagree or to deny the fact that Islam has a significant impact on the Middle East. Even though most of the local governments of the Middle East may try to pretend that Islam does not have an impact on international business in the area, we have to understand its roots, rules, applications, boundaries, and re-strictions and must consider them when establishing international joint ventures or wholly owned subsidiaries or when striving to continue successful business relationships there.

Religious, moral, and legal values may not have a direct impact on economic theories as pure social science, but they have an impact on the behavior, policies, and principles which make up real-world economics, including economic sys-tems. Consequently, religious values affect consumer behavior, consumer values, preferences, and the allocation of resources. They also affect producer behavior, choices, and pricing decisions for both internal transfers and final products, and affect the role of the country in designing its economic policies, especially if it is a Muslim country, on the basis of Islamic regulations. In conclusion, religion may have a significant impact on designing economic policies and systems. It is obvious, from the above analysis, that Islam is "a religion and state" and a belief system with rules (El-Mahjoob 1986: 3–4).

Understanding the accounting implications of Islam is a new issue that all MNCs operating in the Middle East should consider when setting up their busi-nesses. It is completely different from the prevailing Western perspective. Now, it is important to know the relationship between accounting and Islam. It may affect the management, control, accountability, and social responsibility of Mid-dle East subsidiaries or joint ventures. Many issues might show the impact of Islam on international business, for both accounting and management in the Middle East and other Islamic countries as well. These issues include: (1) work-ing hours, (2) interest, (3) relationship between debtor and creditor, (4) business contributions or monetary donations, (5) taxation, (6) bankruptcy, (7) business ethics, (8) equality, and (9) liabilities or obligations.

Success in achieving the highest profits and creating the best-motivated work teams in the Middle East, as in many aspects of international business, depends on how MNCs are going to accommodate the Islamic concepts in their man-agement strategy. By looking at the situation from a businessperson's viewpoint, Middle East subsidiary or joint venture managers can turn the business around to their company's advantage and obtain the needed production results in the most efficient way at the lowest cost with the least restrictions.

The foregoing trends suggest that financial and management accounting tech-niques and methods should be more responsive to changes in economic conditions in the Middle East. They should be ready to meet the major trends and changes that are expected to prevail in the twenty-first century in the Middle East. In the developed countries, the accounting function is more likely to be responsive to economic and social changes and will continue to be adaptable and dynamic. However, for Middle East countries, the accounting function is not responsive to the economic changes in the local environment (Farag 1991: 246).

In general, the practice of accounting and the development of its tools and related financial and economic reports have been closely (or somewhat) inter-related with the economic and political developments in several countries (Farag 1991: 247). The accounting profession in Middle East countries has not yet made much response to the economic and political developments.

From the perspective of Middle East countries, domestic policy reforms should be redesigned to promote and support the demand for more accounting information to help managers make decisions relevant to the Middle East environment, and to place more emphasis on shaping the accounting profession to make it more relevant and more flexible to report and disclose the necessary financial and economic information that will help both MNCs and their countries to meet the significant economic challenges in the twenty-first century.

The Cultural Influence of the Middle East on Accounting

Another important environmental factor in the Middle East is culture. It includes religious mores, attitudes toward growth and stability, values, traditions, and customs. Some of these variables might have an impact on MNCs operating in different Middle East countries, and each may affect the nature and degree of success of MNC accounting and management control systems required in each country. The feelings and attitudes of people in a country are reflected in the regulations and rules established by that country with respect to MNCs' activities. Abdallah (1984) concluded in his empirical research that cultural variables have a more significant impact on MNCs' financial performance operating overseas than on economic environmental variables.

Many accounting scholars have addressed the issue of the influence of culture on the development of accounting systems. The earliest one included a list of environmental variables and explained the differences in accounting practices (Mueller 1968; AAA 1977). Radebaugh (1975) extended the approach and made a comprehensive framework in an attempt to incorporate the Farmer and Richman model of business environment into a preliminary accounting model.

However, the impact of culture on accounting has yet to be established. Most of the research endeavors in this area (Hofstede 1980; Gray 1988; Perera 1989; Nobes 1983, 1984; Violet 1983; Belkaoui and Picur 1991; Fechner and Kilgore 1994; Doupnik and Salter 1995) have been the acknowledgment of the significance of environmental factors and, in particular, cultural factors in shaping a nation's accounting systems and practice. Violet (1983) argued that accounting is determined by culture, and Hofstede (1980) emphasized that the lack of consensus in accounting practices between countries is because their purpose is not technical but rather cultural. Therefore, there is a general agreement that the culture of a country influences the choice of accounting systems and practices.

Most of the prior research has claimed that national systems are determined by environmental variables. Gray (1988) made a significant attempt to develop a model by identifying the mechanism by which societal level values are related to the accounting subculture, which directly influences accounting practices. Gray used Hofstede's culture-based societal value dimensions as the basis for his analysis. He also identified four value dimensions of the accounting subculture, which are also related to societal values: Professionalism, Uniformity, Conservatism, and Secrecy. Furthermore, he classified accounting systems on the basis of each of the four values. Perera (1989) stressed the relationship between cultural values and the accounting subculture. He proposed a number of hypotheses, as did Gray, on the relationship between cultural values and accounting values.

Doupnik and Salter (1995) made a preliminary empirical test of the general model by examining the relationship between countries' accounting practices and a set of environmental factors and cultural dimensions hypothesized as relevant elements of the model. The results of their research lend support for the general model and provide insight into the importance of various factors in explaining existing accounting diversity.

For MNCs to know how to manage their business successfully and how their accounting systems and practices would work in the Middle East, it is essential for them to understand the culture of Middle East countries and how it affects the business practices there and accounting systems as well. Obviously, any efforts to examine and analyze Middle East cultural influence on accounting should identify (1) a set of specific cultural factors which are likely to be directly associated with accounting systems and practices and (2) the manner by which the association between cultural factors and accounting systems and practices in the Middle East occurs (Perera 1989: 43).

The Unique Culture of the Middle East and Accounting

The question is: How do you make your joint ventures abroad or your wholly owned subsidiary in the Middle East not only more profitable but also more successful in both the short and the long run? To be successful, you have to know how your Middle East customers think, behave, and make decisions, and you must understand their unique culture and social life. This unique culture is not just a part of life, it is a way of life. It has a significant effect on daily decisions, such as eating, sleeping, dressing, working, planning, managing, financing, and investing, among many others. This unique culture is not only for individuals, it is also for businesspeople, business entities, and government.

Therefore, it is vital for MNCs that are willing to or are already investing in the Middle East to understand the unique culture of Islam and to adjust their business, marketing, managing, and financing strategies to fit the particular environment accordingly. In trying to explore how Islam affects MNCs in managing, financing, and accounting for their overseas activities, in this book I present an overview of Islam and how it affects the various businesses operating in the Middle East. The effect of religion on accounting systems and practices also will be discussed. Because there are almost 1.2 billion adherents to Islam in the world today (Webb 1994: 298), it may also be important to stress the global aspects of Islam.

Many management scholars emphasize that religion is the most distinctive factor and the mainspring of culture. Educational systems, political organization, and social relations (such as the role of women) are all significantly affected by the religion of the society in which we live. Religion also has a significant impact at the practical level and ethics of the business firm (Gomez-Mejia and Palich 1997: 317).

It is important to understand what the word "Islam" means. The word "Islam" means submission to the will of God, or the surrender of the believer to one God, or submission of one's heart and actions to the one and only God. The Muslim is thus one who gives himself or herself entirely and exclusively to one God. This is the basic idea of the religion started in 609 by the prophet Mohammed (Peace Be Upon Him—PBU): Muslims believe that Judaism and Christianity prepared the way for Islam and that Mohammed (PBU) revealed the final true religion.

Islam is not just one component of its believers' lives, a set of beliefs remembered on special occasions. Rather, for the devout, it is a way of life. Its tenets and rules permeate almost everything, often including politics and government. Islam is an ancient religion with profound historical and theological ties to Judaism and Christianity. All three religions worship the same God, acknowledge large parts of the same Bible, and revere Adam, Noah, Abraham, and Moses. And, as do Christians, Muslims regard Jesus as the Messiah (Ruff 1998: B1).

In fact, Islam teaches that it represents the modern mainstream of a primordial, monotheistic religion that began with the earliest humans. Over millennia, the religion took form with the early Jewish prophets, was modified significantly by Jesus, and was finally shaped by Mohammed (PBU), the final prophet, who died in 632 (Ruff 1998: B2).

Because of its powerful, cross-cultural appeal, Islam has won the hearts and minds of an estimated 1.2 billion people around the world, making it the second largest religion (Christianity has about 2 billion adherents, and Hinduism is the third largest, with about 800 million). Today, Islam is the fastest-growing religion in the United States, with at least 5 million believers. Approximately 700 mosques are located in major cities of the United States (Webb 1994: 298).

There is much truth in the assertion that "Islam is an egalitarian religion." If we compare both the principles and practice of Islam at its advent with the societies that surrounded them, the Islamic religion really did bring a message of equality. Not only did Islam not endorse such systems of social and tribal discrimination, it explicitly rejected them (Lewis 1995: 205).

A common mistake is to look on the religion of Islam as a separate entity, in the way that other monotheistic religions do. Islam is both the state and the society, and its followers embrace it completely and wholly as a way of life. It is based on the fact that God has created all of us, as humans, to worship him, and that God has created everything—food, life, health, work, children, and money—and it is not fair to be so busy with what has been created for us that we forget the creator.

MULTINATIONAL COMPANIES IN THE MIDDLE EAST

In the 1990s, American MNCs witnessed the erosion of their market shares with the invasion of large numbers of Japanese, British, German, and many other competitors into many domestic and international markets that were traditionally American. As a matter of survival, over the past two decades, many American MNCs entered into international markets. Large MNCs, such as AT&T, Toyota, General Motors, and Chrysler, are joining their European or Japanese rivals to create global manufacturing and distribution, research and development, and telecommunications ventures.

As they enter a Middle East country, managers of MNCs have to cope with local competitive conditions, different laws, different business and cultural practices, and different accounting standards and practices. To meet all of these challenges, American MNCs found that joining with companies or governments that were familiar with local practices and culture was the only way to be successful in doing business in Middle East countries.

Accountants have to proceed with their companies in the same direction. They have to meet the challenges and accurately account and report all activities of international joint ventures in the Middle East. The accounting systems of MNCs are required to report on the performance of Middle East subsidiaries and their managers. The MNCs' reporting system must inform not only the management of risk exposure but also the stockholder, potential investors, and creditors (Spagnola and Brannan, 1994). This book will discuss the theoretical framework of accounting for international joint ventures and the related complex reporting issues associated with American MNCs investing and operating in the Middle East area.

The greater the extent to which corporate headquarters and subsidiaries differ in their cultural distance, the more difficult it becomes to effectively supervise the various units. In other words, as cultural distance increases, the challenges for the organizational control system increase proportionately, because complete and accurate information about unit performance becomes more difficult and expensive to obtain (Gomez-Mejia and Palich 1997: 313).

In the Middle East, every Arabian country runs joint ventures for the purpose of expanding economic and technical cooperation with other countries, absorbing foreign capital, introducing advanced technology and equipment and advanced managerial experience, and recruiting qualified trained personnel to speed up modernization programs. Most of the countries have designed laws, regulations, and practices to attract foreign investors to participate in the development of the local economy, especially in those areas that require the use of their advanced technology, through the transfer of technology.

In some Middle Eastern countries, joint ventures with local partners are allowed without restrictions on minimum or maximum percentage of ownership for local or foreign partners, such as in Egypt. However, in other countries, such as Kuwait, the United Arab Emirates, and Saudi Arabia, a foreign company, even a branch of a foreign company, is not permitted to do business without associating itself with a local partner or a local agent.

Although there is an unavoidable, unpredictable uncertainty of foreign investments and a hostile international business climate in the Middle East, interest in joint ventures has never been keener. Moreover, for more than three decades, many changes have been taking place in Europe, Eastern Europe, Russia, and the United States, the most important being the rapid internationalization of medium- and large-size businesses. U.S. manufacturers, for instance, can no longer rely exclusively on domestic market to sell their products. While maintaining dependence on their domestic resources, these companies can systematically seek out joint ventures in other countries for expansion and larger international market share.

FINANCIAL REPORTING AND PERFORMANCE EVALUATION

American MNCs, which are publicly held, are required by the Financial Accounting Standards Board's (FASB) Statement of Financial Accounting Standards (SFAS) No. 14 to disclose in the notes to financial statements information on their foreign operations. MNCs, under SFAS No. 14, are required to report certain information by geographic area. The statement requires MNCs to present information on foreign operations by significant geographic areas (1) if revenues generated from total foreign operations are 10% or more of consolidated total revenues, or (2) if identifiable assets of total foreign operations are 10% or more of consolidated total assets.

MNCs have two choices for reporting information on their geographic areas: individual countries or groups of countries. It is up to the management to determine the geographic area. SFAS No. 14 includes the factors which should be considered in deciding whether individual countries or groups of countries should report information. The factors include economic affinity, proximity, similarities in business environment, and the interrelationship of the MNCs' operations in different countries.

SFAS No. 14 provides some guidelines to be used for implementing the statement; however, it is up to management to decide on the degree of aggregation to be reported to help financial statement users in assessing the riskiness of MNCs' foreign operations (Doupnik and Rolfe 1990). The management of MNCs who invest in the Middle East should be required to provide disclosure on less aggregated geographic areas. It is correct to say that relatively large investments in high risk areas such as the Middle East do make a difference in risk assessment, therefore, by further desegregating geographic areas into groups such as the Middle East, it will be a better way to reflect differences in investment risk (Doupnik and Rolfe 1990: 267).

MNCs face another accounting problem when they prepare their consolidated statements of cash flows: without disaggregation, stockholders, potential investors, and analysts evaluating MNCs' performance are not able to determine where in the world the cash is generated and used.

In the Middle East, there has been a growing recognition of the urgent need of enforcing the use of International Accounting Standards (IAS) developed by the International Accounting Standards Committee (IASC). The main objective is to ensure that the information upon which investors, creditors, and other users base their investing and financing decisions is comprehensive, reliable, consistent, and internationally comparable.

If every country in the Middle East has the choice to decide on using local, U.S., or IAS standards this will result in the creation of different financial statements. Local accounting standards in the Middle East were originally developed when the world market was not as global as it is today. Under the threat of further financial crises, and with world recession widely predicted, Arab governments, intergovernmental agencies, and global financial institutions now have a real fear that the crisis in Asia will be repeated elsewhere and on an even greater scale. Now it is more important than ever for Arab countries to enforce a core set of internationally recognized accounting standards. Currently, Arab countries have no choice but to follow IAS until they can adopt their own regional accounting standards.

Another important issue facing all MNCs around the world is how to measure foreign subsidiary managers using objective and practical tools. Unfortunately, traditional management accounting techniques are inadequate to appropriately solve the problem, and MNCs are unable to achieve satisfactory and desired levels of performance evaluation. Management accounting techniques have not adequately considered the distinct characteristics of the environment within which MNCs operate and manage their businesses.

The author will suggest an appropriate performance evaluation system to be used for Middle East subsidiary managers of American and non-American MNCs. The proposed system estimates foreign subsidiary managers' relative performance after considering the effects of non-controllable Middle East environmental factors on the measured performance of Middle East subsidiaries.

This book will look at the accounting systems and practices and their cultural, legal, and economic environment in Middle East countries, including four selected Arab countries and Israel. They are of interest for four different reasons:

(1) They represent great varieties in accounting systems and practices; (2) They have the best investment opportunities in the world; (3) They are representative countries from the Middle East, with different economic, political, cultural (including religion), and other important environmental factors; and (4) American readers most often associate them with the Middle East, therefore they are important to the executive officers of American MNCs and U.S. foreign policy.

The countries selected for consideration in this book are Egypt, Israel, Jordan, Kuwait, and Saudi Arabia. It is hoped that the countries selected for inclusion will provide MNCs with some understanding of the role of economic, legal, political, and cultural environmental variables of Middle East countries and their impact on managerial concepts and accounting practices in the Middle East region.

Egypt was selected because of significant changes in its economic affairs in the 1990s, from state-owned to privately owned medium- and large-size companies. By far the largest Arab country in population, it is in the heart of the Middle East and boasts a reasonably well-educated, English-speaking labor force. Moreover, Egypt is a market that is opening wider to American exporters and manufacturing companies.

Israel, according to the U.S. Department of State (1997), has enjoyed rapid economic growth since the beginning of the decade, which has made it an increasingly attractive market for U.S. MNCs. Economic growth averaged 6% annually between 1990 and 1995, as Israel's imports of goods and services surged by approximately two-thirds to $40 billion. While Israel's growth rate slowed to approximately 4% in 1996, its per capita income neared the $17,000 mark.

The accounting profession in Israel has changed substantially since its origin. Even though the profession originally had British antecedents, given the economic and sociopolitical ties between the United States and Israel, it has moved closer to the American accounting practices (Murtuza and Abdallah 1997).

Jordan is developing as an emerging market in the region, according to the U.S. Department of State (1997). In 1996, the Jordanian economy grew at a rate of more than 6%, while inflation was held to under 7%. The International Monetary Fund (IMF) has praised the government's macroeconomic reform program. Despite regional political uncertainties affecting economic development in its strategic sectors, the government of Jordan has reasserted its commitment to continue efforts to open the economy. The anticipated signing of a bilateral investment treaty with the United States demonstrates strong interest in attracting multinational business and foreign investment to Jordan.

Jordan enjoys excellent political relations with the United States, a major trading partner. Increasing numbers of U.S. firms are showing interest in investing and opening branch and regional offices in Jordan. More than 250 U.S. firms have sent representatives seeking business opportunities in Jordan since the signing of the peace treaty with Israel. U.S. firms are attracted to Jordan because of its geographic position, stability, and potential to serve as a regional trade hub.

Kuwait is known for its oil. Its commercial production started in 1946 and peaked at 3.3 million barrels a day by 1972. The oil fields, among the world's largest, are concentrated in a small area, and production costs are extremely low. The level of production at the time of the Iraqi invasion in 1990 was about 2 million barrels a day against an installed capacity of 2.5 million barrels a day; at this rate, Kuwait can continue to produce oil for at least another 200 years (Ernst & Young 1993). The Kuwaiti government encourages foreign investments, especially American, and it treats foreign capital in the same way as local capital, apart from the taxation of profits. To encourage local industrial projects, exemptions from various taxes and duties may be given to foreign companies for up to 10 years, provided that Kuwaiti participation is at least 51%.

At the present time, there are many American–Kuwaiti joint ventures, and they take several forms. Examples are Bechtel International, Environmental Chemical Corporation, Foster-Wheeler Energy Group, Hughes Aircraft International Service Company, and Dyncorp, among many others now in Kuwait. Although each has different corporate goals to be achieved in Kuwait, their overall goals are compatible with those of the Kuwaiti government and people.

The accounting systems and practices of Saudi Arabia provide a good example of how local accounting standards and practices are compatible and conform to the IAS. Saudi Arabia also has been selected for several reasons. First, it is one of the richest countries in the world, with the highest per capita income and the largest amount of proven oil reserves in the world. Second, Saudi Arabia is the birthplace and religious center of Islam; therefore, it is the most representative of Islamic countries in terms of the effect on business environment of the cultural or social differences. Finally, Saudi Arabia has experienced a phenomenal rate of development within the last few years. As a result, international companies have been doing business in the country.

INTERNATIONAL TRANSFER PRICING

For the past two decades, MNCs have not had any business function that goes as deep into most international operations (i.e., manufacturing, marketing, management, and financing) as has transfer pricing. International transfer pricing decisions have a great impact on the international operations of MNCs, directly affecting their global revenues and profits, and can help or limit MNCs' ability to operate, manage, and utilize their economic resources on a global basis to achieve their ultimate goals.

A transfer price is set and used by MNCs to quantify the goods transferred from one subsidiary domiciled in a Middle East country, such as Egypt or Jordan, to a subsidiary in another country, such as the United Kingdom. The dynamic growth of most MNCs going abroad and exploring more and more business opportunities in Middle East countries necessitated more delegation of authority and responsibility with more autonomy for foreign subsidiary managers, which opened the door for further decentralization and intracompany pricing problems (Abdallah 1989).

Since the transfer price for a product or service has an important effect on the performance evaluation of individual Middle East subsidiary managers, their motivation, divisional profitability, and global profits, top management should devote special attention to designing international transfer pricing policies. A soundly developed policy could lead to better goal congruence, better performance evaluation measures, less taxes and tariffs, more motivated managers, less exchange risks, more optimistic relations with host governments, and better competitive positions in Middle East countries and international markets (Abdallah 1989).

COUNTRIES SELECTED FOR THE STUDY

To help MNCs plan, manage, finance, account for, and control their Middle East business activities, it was essential to identify representative countries from the Middle East with different economic, political, cultural (including religion), and other important environmental factors. This book concentrates on the countries American readers most often associate with the Middle East, those that are important to the executive officers of American MNCs and U.S. foreign policy. The five countries selected were Egypt, Israel, Jordan, Kuwait, and Saudi Arabia. These countries are not only relevant representatives for the environmental variables and executive officers of MNCs, but they also represent areas of the world where international companies are doing business.

AN OVERVIEW OF THE BOOK

This book covers four main themes. In Part I, the issue of how to manage MNCs in the Middle East is covered in Chapters 2 through 4. Part II focuses on three issues: (1) the financial reporting and disclosure issues of Middle East countries, (2) International Accounting Standards and their effect on the accounting systems and practices of Middle East countries, and (3) performance evaluation of Middle East subsidiary managers. All three issues will be discussed in Chapters 5 through 8. In Part III, I stress three major issues: (1) tax regulations and rules of the selected Middle East countries; (2) international transfer pricing strategies of MNCs; and (3) Section 482 of the Internal Revenue Code and the new developments related to transfer pricing standards. They will be covered in Chapters 9 through 11. Finally, in Part IV, the future outlook will be explored in Chapter 12.

In Part I, I will introduce a general background on the history of the Middle East, the characteristics or environmental variables of the Middle East, and their impact on MNCs in managing, financing, and controlling their activities. In Chapter 2, I examine the main characteristics or environmental variables of the

Middle East countries. The effect of the environmental variables on accounting systems and practices will be discussed briefly. Chapter 3 offers a discussion of the significant effect of culture (including religion) on MNCs and on accounting systems and practices in the Middle East. The effect of the culture on harmonizing accounting standards will be covered in the last part of the chapter. In Chapter 4, I focus on the importance of the Middle East area for MNCs' investments and joint ventures. I discuss the costs, problems, and benefits of international joint ventures in the Middle East, and I conclude with a discussion of financial, managerial, accounting, and cultural issues that should be considered.

In Part II, I focus on the financial reporting and performance evaluation of Middle East subsidiary managers. In Chapter 5, I present the accounting systems and practices of the five selected countries of the Middle East: Egypt, Israel, Jordan, Kuwait, and Saudi Arabia. The chapter also includes comparisons of the accounting principles of the five selected countries against International Accounting Standards and U.S. Generally Accepted Accounting Principles (GAAP). In Chapter 6, I explore the development of IAS and their impact on the accounting principles and practices of Middle East countries. Chapter 7 features a discussion of performance evaluation techniques and how MNCs can evaluate their Middle East subsidiary managers based on objective, relevant, and operation measures.

In Part III, I cover the taxation systems of the five selected countries of the Middle East, including tax rates, tax regulations, tax treaties, taxation on international transfer pricing, the appropriate transfer pricing policies, Section 482 of the Internal Revenue Code and the Advanced Pricing Agreement program. In Chapter 8, I stress the tax systems and tax regulation of the five selected countries. In Chapter 9, I discuss the characteristics of international transfer pricing systems for MNCs and the factors that should be considered in establishing the correct system.

Chapter 10 offers a discussion of the objectives of establishing international transfer pricing for Middle East operations. Chapter 11 handles different transfer pricing techniques that can be used by MNCs in managing their Middle East business activities. Section 482 of the Internal Revenue Code, dealing with the taxation of intracompany transactions and Advanced Pricing Agreement program, is examined.

Part IV includes the future outlook of doing business in the Middle East in the twenty-first century. In Chapter 12, I include a summary and conclusion of the book and discuss the future of the business environment in the Middle East. I extend the discussion to include the future of accounting systems and practices in the region.

REFERENCES

Abdallah, Wagdy M. *Internal Accountability: An International Emphasis*. Ann Arbor, Mich.: UMI Research Press, 1984.

————. *International Transfer Pricing Policies*. Westport, Conn.: Quorum Books, 1989.

American Accounting Association (AAA). "Report of the 1975–76 Committee on International Accounting Operations and Education." *Accounting Review* (Supplement, 1977), 65–132.

Belkaoui, Ahmed Riahi and Ronald D. Picur. "Cultural Determinism and the Perception of Accounting Concepts." *The International Journal of Accounting* 26 (1991), 118–130.

Cole, Simon. *The Gulf States: A Business Handbook*. Oxford: Blackwell Business, 1991.

Diller, Daniel C. and John L. Moore (eds.). *The Middle East*, 8th ed. Washington, D.C.: Congressional Quarterly, 1994.

Doupnik, Timothy S. and Robert J. Rolfe. "A Geographic Area Disclosure and the Assessment of Foreign Investment Risk for Disclosure in Accounting Statement Notes." *The International Journal of Accounting* 25 (1990), 252–267.

Doupnik, Timothy S. and Stephen B. Salter. "External Environment, Culture, and Accounting Practice: A Preliminary Test of a General Model of International Accounting Development." *The International Journal of Accounting* 30 (1995), 189–207.

El-Mahjoob, Rafaat. *Islamic Economic Studies*. Cairo, Egypt: The Institute of Islamic Studies, 1986. In Arabic.

Ernst & Young. *Doing Business in Kuwait*. New York: Ernst & Young International, 1993.

Farag, Shawki M. "Accounting in the 1990s: An International Perspective." *The International Journal of Accounting* 26 (1991), 243–251.

Fechner, Harry H. E. and Alan Kilgore. "The Influence of Cultural Factors on Accounting Practice." *The International Journal of Accounting* 29 (1994), 265–277.

Financial Accounting Standards Board. *Financial Reporting for Segments of a Business Enterprise*. Statement of Financial Accounting Standards No. 14. Stamford, Conn.: FASB, 1976.

Gomez-Mejia, Luis R. and Leslie E. Palich. "Cultural Diversity and the Performance of Multinational Firms." *Journal of International Business Studies* (2nd Quarter 1997), 309–335.

Gray, S. J. "Towards a Theory of Cultural Influence on the Development of Accounting Systems Internationally." *Abacus* 24, no. 1 (1988), 1–15.

Hofstede, G. *Culture Consequences*. Beverly Hills, Calif.: Sage Publications, 1980.

Kavoossi, M. "Improving International Competitiveness in the Gulf Region: An Assessment." *International Journal of Commerce and Management* 5, no. 3 (1995), 5–16.

Lewis, Bernard. *The Middle East: A Brief History of the Last 2,000 Years*. New York: Scribner, 1995.

Mansfield, Peter. *The New Arabians*. Chicago: J. G. Ferguson Publishing Company, 1981.

Mueller, G. G. "Accounting Principles Generally Accepted in the United States versus Those Generally Accepted Elsewhere." *International Journal of Accounting Education and Research* (Spring 1968), 91–103.

Murtuza, Athar and Wagdy Abdallah. "Acceptance of International Accounting Standards Will Not Create Credible Global Financial Reporting." Working Paper, 1997.

Nobes, C. W. "A Judgemental International Classification of Financial Reporting Practices." *Journal of Business Finance and Accounting* (Spring 1983), 1–19.

————. *International Classification of Financial Reporting.* London: Croom Helm, 1984.

Perera, M.H.B. "Toward a Framework to Analyze the Impact of Culture on Accounting." *The International Journal of Accounting* 24 (1989), 42–56.

Radebaugh, L. H. "Environmental Factors Influencing the Development of Accounting Objectives Standards and Practices in Peru." *International Journal of Accounting Education and Research* (Fall 1975), 39–56.

Ruff, Carolyn. "Islam Is a Way of Life." *Staten Island Advance*, August 1, 1998, B1–B2.

Spagnola, Bob and Rodger Brannan. "International Joint Ventures: A Perspective on Organizational and Accounting Implications of Global Partnering for US Multi-nationals." *The International Journal of Accounting* 29 (1994), 34–54.

U.S. Department of State. *Economic Policy and Trade Practices: Israel.* Country Reports on Economic Policy and Trade Practices, July 21, 1997.

————. *Economic Policy and Trade Practices: Jordan.* Country Reports on Economic Policy and Trade Practices, August 21, 1997.

Violet, W. J. "The Development of International Accounting Standards: An Anthropo-logical Perspective." *International Journal of Accounting Education and Research* (Spring 1983), 1–12.

Webb, Giesela. "Islam and Muslims in America." In Hussin Mutalib and Taj ul-Islam Hashmi (eds.), *Islam, Muslims, and the Modern State.* Houndmills, Basingstoke, Hampshire: Macmillan Press; New York: St. Martin's Press, 1994.

Part I

Managing Multinational Companies in the Middle East

Chapter 2

The Economic, Political, and Legal Characteristics of Middle East Countries and Their Accounting Systems

The purpose of this chapter is to explore the influence of economic, legal, and political factors in developing countries, in particular, Middle East countries, on accounting systems and practices. Prior research has shown that there are difficulties in harmonizing international accounting standards because of the significant effect of economic, religious, legal, and political variables on the internationalization of accounting standards. Moreover, as international comparisons of accounting practices have revealed differences, research has identified that those environmental variables have a considerable effect on a country's accounting system and practices.

This chapter attempts to investigate and discuss the impact of economic, political, and legal factors on business and accounting systems and practices of the Middle East and develop relevant, appropriate accounting systems and practices to fit Middle East countries' environment. Three different choices of accounting systems are suggested: (1) the use of accounting systems of the developed countries, (2) the use of International Accounting Standards, or (3) the development of their own environmental accounting systems. Many problems face Middle East countries when using either of the first two alternatives. The most appropriate system is the suggested "environmental accounting." Under the new system, standards can be developed either for every single country or for a group of countries of similar environmental conditions. In establishing and implementing the new system, three important issues will be proposed: (1) its objectives, (2) its relevant accounting control subsystems, and (3) the reform of the accounting professional organizations to enforce using it.

Discussions of political factors as they affect accounting are sought for various differences in accounting systems and practices in Middle East countries. The expansion of securities markets and the need for reliable, timely, and relevant financial information will be explored. A new environmental accounting system based on Middle East environmental variables will be proposed, and the reform of the accounting profession will be recommended.

HISTORICAL AND GENERAL BACKGROUND

The diversity of the Middle East has always made it a difficult region for unbiased scholars to define and treat politically and objectively. It is a region in which the political has dominated the economic and where the interests of the state have often eclipsed those of society. It is a region in which states and governments, preoccupied with war and peace, survival, and basic democratic currents and constant challenges to their power and authority, have often included accounting and economic issues at the bottom of their lists of priorities.

The five countries chosen—Egypt, Kuwait, Israel, Jordan, and Saudi Arabia—are unquestionably dissimilar in many respects, including levels of development, workings of the market, integration with the world economy, and systems of governance and legitimization. However, they all have had to confront the difficult choices involved in readjusting an economy that showed signs of serious deterioration and stagnation.

Understanding the economic, legal, and political history of the Middle East is extremely important for accountants, corporate executive officers, and local managers. For accountants, it is the environment in which the accounting systems, practices, and profession have been developed and grown, therefore, the environmental variables are the basis for the accounting systems and practices in the Middle East. To corporate executive officers and managers in MNCs, keeping pace with the most recent economic, cultural, and political developments is indeed crucial for the success of their Middle East operations, competition, and investments.

The Middle East region is very important in the strategy of MNCs. First, it occupies a strategic part of the world; the land stretches from the Atlantic Ocean in the west to the Indian Ocean in the east, and from the Horn of Africa in the south to the Northern Tier in the north. Second, it is always troubled by continued political instability. Any military, political, or social actions in the area affect economically and politically not only local business firms and managers but also the rest of the world. Third, Middle East countries are located at the crossroads of three continents, and they control many important waterways: the Suez Canal, Bab Al-Mandeb, the Gulf of Aqaba, the Persian Gulf, and the Straits of Hormuz. Moreover, they perform significant roles in Islamic, African, and nonaligned economic and political councils. Finally, and most importantly, they possess the majority of the world's proved reserves of oil assets, especially in Kuwait and Saudi Arabia.

Unlike other areas, the Middle East has been suffering with major conflicts that look like an impossible mission. Conflicts between Arabs and Israelis, Iranians and Iraqis, and Iraqis and Kuwaitis, as well as other problems, go beyond disagreements over territory or fears concerning a rival's geopolitical and economic strategies. Whether the twenty-first century will produce more stable, peaceful political and economic conditions in the Middle East depends on the intentions, efforts, and actions of both the international community and all of the nations directly involved (Diller and Moore 1994: 1).

Oil wealth has helped some Middle East countries to accumulate significant financial resources that are influential in formulating their foreign policies. Oil still maintains its importance in the production process, despite the discovery of new alternative sources of energy, such as solar and nuclear. As a source of energy, oil has led to a revolution in industrial production in the West; as a source of wealth, oil has led to superficial changes in the Arab world, such as the consumption of expensive, high-quality consumer goods. It also strengthened the power of ruling groups in Arab, oil-producing countries (Dessouki 1991: 93).

From the 1960s to the 1980s, the Middle East enjoyed rising prosperity. It led all other developing regions except East Asia in per capita income growth. By the second half of the 1980s this growth had collapsed. The economic growth barely kept pace with the population increase in specific countries, such as Egypt. In the Gulf Cooperation Council (GCC) countries, per capita income declined (Page 1998: 133–134). Oil export countries such as Saudi Arabia and Kuwait, which used to generate unlimited wealth during the early 1970s, suddenly were forced to make cuts in budgets, governmental services, and aid sent to poor Arab countries. In the 1990s, most countries consumed their own economic resources through their war efforts and the use of advanced weapons. Other economic problems included massive foreign debt, the scarcity of water resources, and a population boom in several poor countries (Diller and Moore 1994: 4).

It is also essential to know the common characteristics of Middle East countries. Similarities include (1) a free enterprise economic system; (2) the Arabic language; (3) the cultural and social tradition, with the significant effect of religion; and (4) similar political and legal systems, also with the significant effect of religion. All of the above variables are very important for accountants, because the greater the similarities among the countries, the better the chance to establish a harmonized accounting system in the region (AlHashim 1985: 4).

A number of important international forces create significant changes in the global market, especially in the Middle East, including international economic/ political interdependence, foreign direct investment and multinational corporate strategy, new technology, international financial markets, the growth of business services, and the activities of international regulatory organizations. Economic groupings, such as the European Community (EC) and the GCC, have been a major influence in promoting economic integration through the free movement of capital, goods, and people between countries.

In 1981, the GCC was formed at the height of the Iran-Iraq War. It consists of six Gulf countries—Bahrain, Kuwait, Oman, Qatar, Saudi Arabia, and the

United Arab Emirates. Saudi Arabia is the most dominant power in the council. The fundamental common factors are the Arabic language, Islam, the similarity among societies and social structures, and shared cultural backgrounds. In addition, the Gulf countries share almost the same level of economic development, which gives them considerable advantage over the European Economic Community (EEC). This advantage may well prove an obstacle to more countries joining the GCC (Cole 1991: 28–31).

The GCC region still holds an important international position in the oil and gas sectors, as indicated by the reserves and production of all GCC countries. Total GCC crude oil reserves increased in 1991 to about 45% of the world reserves. However, the GCC countries are still contributing a smaller percentage to world production compared to their world share reserves (20% of world crude oil production and 6% of world natural gas production). In 1991, the Gulf War caused a decline in the production of refined products.

Similarities exist between the GCC and the EEC. The opening up of the borders of the EEC in 1992 pushed the GCC countries to ensure that their trade would not be adversely affected; to this end, cooperation among the GCC countries has been on the rise (Cole 1991: 28–31).

The GCC's highest authority, the supreme council, which is comprised of the heads of the six countries, usually meets annually in November. At the end of each meeting, the chairmanship of the council passes from country to country, in alphabetical order. The council's role is to lay down broad guidelines of the general policy for the organization. However, the Ministerial Council, the actual policy-making body, meets four times a year to formulate the proposals that are finally sent to the Supreme Council for approval (Cole 1991: 29). The GCC's administration, which is carried out by the Secretariat General, is based in Riyadh, Saudi Arabia. As in the EEC, the GCC establishes committees and subcommittees to formulate the proposals, project feasibility studies, and documents (28–31).

The objective of the GCC was to "realize cooperation in all economic, political, educational, and informational fields." Practically, at the present time, the main purpose of its activities is the harmonization of matters relating to imports and exports, especially to protect local industries (Cole 1991: 28–31). To reduce uncertainty and to provide greater economic stability, the GCC countries have attempted to diversify their economies. Moreover, to respond to the threat of the EU, the GCC's main idea was to integrate the supply and demand for goods and services in the separate states into a common market (28–31). The GCC has been successful in implementing its policy in the areas of economic, financial, and trade issues. Dropping the border controls between EU countries has given the activities of the GCC a strong push.

Japan, with pressure to restrict its imports to the EC and the United States, holds normal unilateral negotiations with the GCC with the view of lending its expertise and setting up joint venture projects in the region (Cole 1991: 28–31).

Arab countries need foreign investment and technology to enhance their ability to attract and absorb and to become globally competitive.

International organizations such as the United Nations (UN) are also involved in the development of global business. The UN is responsible for the emergence of organizations such as the World Bank Group, the International Monetary Fund, the UN Conference on Trade and Development, the Conference on the Law of Sea, the General Agreement on Tariffs and Trade (GATT), and the Economic and Social Council (ECOSOC). ECOSOC includes the Commission on Transnational Corporations (UNCTC), designed to promote an effective international framework for the operation of MNCs and monitor the nature and effects of their activities. The UNCTC is involved, among other activities, in initiatives to develop international standards of accounting and reporting.

The Organization for Economic Cooperation and Development (OECD), unlike the UN, is focused on the development of the industrialized countries of the world. Its main objective is to foster international economic and social development. To this end, a code of conduct, including information disclosure guidelines, has been issued relating to the operation of MNCs to encourage them to develop positive relationships with host countries and their governments.

Because we are moving increasingly toward a world economy, a society's economic well-being and survival depends on its international competitiveness. To become more competitive, Third World countries have found that their choices are increasingly limited by the dynamism of not only their industrialized and developed counterparts but also by their more successful newly industrialized neighbors, such as Israel. Another factor in favor of greater competitiveness is the increasingly free trade–oriented international trade regime institutionalized through GATT and other agreements (Barkey, 1992: 2).

In a world of growing global relationships of a political, social, and economic nature, it has become essential to recognize the importance of international accounting. The issue of using common accounting standards in the global market has come under attack. The extent to which a firm's securities can be issued and traded in a foreign country while adhering only to the home country's accounting standards magnifies the issue. A global environmental and cultural framework was proposed by Gray (1989) as a basis for identifying international forces for change and their impact on accounting systems and practices at the national level.

THE IMPACT ON MULTINATIONAL COMPANIES

The activities of MNCs and their economic significance continued to grow in the 1980s, despite the slowing down of world economic growth, increasing instability in foreign exchange rates, inflation, and interest rates, and growing tendencies toward the protection of local or national products. MNCs were major forces for change, and new forms of business relationships emerged, including

international joint ventures among MNCs and subcontracting arrangements between MNCs and host countries' corporations in Middle East countries.

The relative importance of MNCs from different home countries changed.
The importance of U.S. MNCs declined in the 1980s, whereas it increased for
Japanese and Western European MNCs. Japanese MNCs established themselves
as manufacturers in the United States and Western Europe, and Western European MNCs also made large investments in the United States. On the other
hand, foreign investment by U.S. MNCs expanded at a much slower pace than
in the past, with more concentration on Egypt and Israel (Gray 1989: 295–296).

Although the large MNCs account for a sizable share of the world economy,
smaller companies are now just as likely to invest abroad. However, the 600
largest MNCs still account for one-fifth of the world's total value added activity
in manufacturing and agriculture. MNCs account for well over three-quarters of
their home countries' trade flows. However, half of all the world's companies
investing abroad are small and medium sized. The 1980s also saw an increasing
number of MNCs from developing countries, involved mainly in the extractive
and mineral-processing industries, and from centrally planned socialist countries
with state corporations expanding into services, especially marketing and trade
(Gray 1989: 296).

MNCs responded to the slow growth and uncertain economic conditions of
the 1980s by developing global strategies to strengthen their position, both in
their home markets and in the major developed market economies, especially
the United States. More specifically, there was a trend toward concentrating on
core and related business activities and on diversifying geographically, thus
product consolidation was preferred to product diversification. As a major part
of this strategy, there was a dramatic wave of international mergers, acquisitions,
strategic alliances, joint ventures, with corresponding divestment, and management buyouts (UN 1988). Most of this activity involved MNCs in both the
United States and the United Kingdom, but Japanese MNCs began to take an
increased interest. In addition, there was a trend toward cooperative arrangements with respect to both research and development and the implementation
of new technology (Gray 1989: 296).

In developing countries with very small, limited securities markets, government policy makers need to watch and control the economic and business activities of business firms to design and implement certain public policies.
Constituencies other than foreign investors, such as government, trade unions,
and public interest groups, seem to have a great interest in the affairs of MNCs.
These groups can make decisions and take action, which might significantly
affect the way in which MNCs operate their businesses in the country.

In Middle East countries, MNCs have reacted to the general worsening of
economic conditions and the instability of such countries by reducing foreign
investment and increasingly preferring non-equity arrangements. In doing so,
they used different techniques, including licensing agreements, management

contracts, franchising, international subcontracting, and joint ventures, to reduce their exposure to business and political risks.

MNCs, in general, are interested in maximizing their overall benefits and profits from total global operations; the main interest of their host countries is to maximize national economic benefits. A potential conflict of interest exists between a MNC and the countries in which it operates (Rahman 1990: 87). Middle East countries need to design and implement certain policies to control MNCs' activities and ensure that they are generating benefits compatible with their national goals.

Political groups, on the basis of allegations that they take out of the country more than they invest, often attack MNCs. MNCs can avoid this kind of political risk by showing their contributions to the host economy. Preparing a local social responsibility (or accountability) statement as a supplementary report to the conventional financial statements can accomplish this. This statement provides valuable information about the activities that generate added value and the activities to which the added value is distributed.

The social responsibility statement is be useful to many Middle East countries, including government policy makers, local employees, trade unions, political groups, and other social groups. The distribution of this social responsibility statement allows MNCs to reduce conflicts with host countries and thereby receive favorable treatment from the political groups whose decisions might affect their business operations (Rahman 1990: 96).

GLOBAL STOCK FINANCIAL MARKETS NEED RELEVANT ACCOUNTING INFORMATION ON INVESTMENTS IN THE MIDDLE EAST

Internationally, the scale of financial activities has increased even more strongly in the 1980s and 1990s. A global capital market is in the process of being formed with a high degree of integration and cooperation between national centers. This is the result of the erosion of national barriers in financial markets arising from the growing deregulation of national markets, listing of foreign companies' securities, innovations in financial instruments, and improved communications through the intensive use of computer technology (Gray 1989: 297). The need for relevant financial information to compare investment opportunities of different character is greater than ever.

Several organizations are working to expand their international trade and investment. At the political level, dramatic changes are creating the need for economic changes, which are restructuring the landscape of international business. Further, the growing trend toward the deregulation of markets and the privatization of public-sector corporations in many developing countries, such as Egypt and Jordan, have opened up new opportunities for international investment and joint ventures.

At the international financial markets level, significant efforts have been made to harmonize several accounting and tax issues, which are considered barriers to the globalization of securities markets. These issues include differences in tax rules, foreign currency exchange restrictions, official restrictions on foreign investments, and financial reporting and disclosure requirements. There are some advantages to the harmonization of financial reporting rules. If all countries implemented and used the same rules to construct their accounting standards, it would greatly enhance comparability. Financial analysts and potential investors would be able to compare the financial statements of companies in different countries without the need to make complex adjustments for the differences in accounting principles.

The OECD has been influential here in its efforts to harmonize the minimum requirements for the admission of securities to listing and the content of prospectuses. Moreover, both the International Federation of Stock Exchanges (IFSE) and the International Organization of Securities Commissions (IOSCO) are trying to promote the internationalization and integration of securities markets on a global basis (Gray 1989: 299).

Recognizing this trend, the International Accounting Standards Committee (IASC) and the International Federation of Accountants (IFAC) have recently been involved in the harmonization efforts and provided a private professional counterpoint to the activities of intergovernmental organizations such as the UN, the OECD, and the EC.

The expansion of securities markets in Middle East countries can be a major source of invested capital for economic growth and development in Middle East countries. A positive, significant correlation has been found between the gross domestic products of developing countries and the securities market activities, including the number of companies listed, market capitalization either in local currency or U.S. dollars, and trading value in either local currency or U.S. dollars (Sedaghat, Sagafi-Nejad and Wright 1994: 297).

In Middle East countries, the important question is, does the release of corporate annual financial reports have an effect on securities markets' activities? The answer depends on the size of the securities markets. In small ones such as in Egypt, Saudi Arabia, or Kuwait, the effect of the release of financial reports might not be significant. However, in major stock markets, such as the New York Stock Exchange (NYSE) and the Tokyo Stock Exchange (TSE), the release of corporate annual financial reports causes a change in investor expectations, thus significantly changing trading volume.

Abdelsalam and Satin (1991) conducted empirical research on a Middle East country, Saudi Arabia, and found that it had a very small, fairly new securities market, and that no measurable reaction occurs for the release of financial information (311). One obvious reason is the smallness of the Saudi market, both in number of firms and in number of investors. Another factor is government intervention. The government subsidizes or partially owns some firms, which reduces both individual investor reaction and total market reaction to earnings news. Investors in subsidized firms are not as concerned with their profits; the government as a shareholder has more interest in aiding its own economy than in receiving dividends (ibid.).

Corresponding to the growth in the number and size of Middle East corporations was the demand for equity investments, which gave rise to the development of securities markets where the raising of investment and finance could be facilitated. Another trend is the growth of emerging markets in Europe and in the Middle East, such as the EC and the GCC. Securities markets are fundamental elements of the transition to a global economy, including the privatization of government-owned business entities and the need to attract foreign investments.

A key factor influencing accounting systems and practices is the emergence of securities markets and the need for reliable, relevant financial information to help investors and creditors make the right decisions. The expansion of securities markets is well recognized by Middle East countries as a major key in economic growth and development. Therefore, international accounting harmonization is a major step for the success of any newly developed securities market.

In concluding this section, four major issues may have a significant impact on the effectiveness of securities markets in the Middle East (Sedaghat, Sagafi-Nejad and Wright 1994: 297):

1. The impact of the transition from public to private ownership of business entities on the development and expansion of securities markets;
2. The importance of financial accounting and reporting criteria and standards in securities markets of Middle East countries;
3. The need for public education to reduce the negative impact of a newly established securities market on the economy and to increase the public trust in a free market economy; and
4. The link to other major international capital markets, such as the NYSE and the TSE.

ENVIRONMENTAL FACTORS AND ACCOUNTING IN THE MIDDLE EAST

Accounting is considered the measurement and communicator of relevant economic information about a business entity to decision makers. In the past two decades, the accounting function in the United States has undergone significant changes, such as inflation, the use of convertible securities, financial reporting for oil- and gas-producing companies, warrants in mergers and acquisitions pension plans, financial instruments, and financial derivatives.

As a tool for control, analysis, and decision making in every environment, the accounting system is the only way for a government to determine which part of its economy is efficient and productive and to allocate economic resources effectively. This was the reason behind the push for Egypt and other Arab countries to use uniform accounting systems (AlHashim 1985: 2).

Like other human activities and disciplines, accounting is a product of its social, economic, political, and legal environment. It plays a significant role in measuring and communicating the results of the economic, social, legal, and managerial performance of a business entity. It provides corporate executive officers, managers, employees, shareholders, governments, the public, and professional organizations with information for the reevaluation of financial, economic, social, legal, and political objectives and activities.

In the United States, the United Kingdom, and Japan, the accounting function is responsive to environmental changes and will continue to be flexible and dynamic. However, in Middle East countries such as Egypt, Kuwait, Jordan, and Saudi Arabia, the accounting systems and practices are very slow in responding to economic, social, or political changes in the local environment.

Changes in environmental factors affecting national economic and human cultural and behavioral differences have created new global challenges for international accounting systems and research. In particular, the significant growth of market globalization and corporations, coupled with the stimulus for economic integration and development in Europe, Asia, and the Middle East, creates many problems which have yet to be resolved (Gray 1989).

MNCs face a new dilemma of global competitiveness. As they compete for a larger market share of the Middle East, they attempt to focus on two major issues: (1) the least production cost and the best-selling markets and (2) higher-quality products and increased customer satisfaction. In doing so, their chief executive officers (CEOs) rely on both accounting and non-accounting information in making their investment and financial decisions. If accounting systems and practices, as one of the major inputs for their decisions, of the Middle East countries, were identical, there would be no problem in understanding the published financial statements of domestic corporations and MNCs operating in the Middle East countries. Unfortunately, this is not the case for international accounting and reporting systems.

Financial statements and reports of national or foreign-owned firms should include a better set of indicators of the contributions of those firms to the economy of the host country, which will encourage new investors to become interested in Middle East countries and to ensure that the operating policies of managing their investments are not conflicting with the objectives of the economy of the host country (Farag 1985: 13).

The financial statements of the MNCs of Egypt, Israel, Kuwait, and Saudi Arabia, for example, are not directly comparable because of the use of different accounting practices and principles. There are key differences in accounting principles among Middle East countries. However, if accounting principles and practices were the only differences among Middle Eastern countries, then the straightforward transformation of the accounting information of one country's principle to another's would be sufficient to make financial statements of different Middle Eastern countries comparable. International accounting researchers have been examining two important questions: (1) What differences and similarities exist across national accounting systems? (2) What environmental factors explain these differences and similarities? (Doupnik and Salter 1995: 190). Unfortunately there have been limited research efforts to develop theories to explain how different environmental variables affect national accounting systems and practices.

In general, accounting systems and financial reporting have been closely interrelated with the economic, legal, and political changes in several countries. Until now, the accounting profession in Middle East countries has not significantly responded to these environmental developments, for several reasons (Farag 1991: 246–247):

1. The nature of business entities was basically in production and services, especially for commodities of the agriculture and mineral sectors. Manufacturing, marketing, and finance functions were not among priorities for local investors.

2. Large public and private ownership of most economic resources was concentrated in the hands of a few entities or individuals.

3. Capital securities markets (a) do not function at all, (b) operate in very small activities not much affected by annual corporate financial reporting, or (c) do not exist.

4. Economic or political unexpected negative movements or actions may erode the confidence of local investors and the link between savings and investments. Most rich Arab people have been investing all of their savings abroad, however, foreign investors finance most local projects and enterprises.

Now it is obvious that Middle East countries have social, economic, political, and legal differences that prevent accounting numbers from being interpreted in the same way, even if they were generated using the same accounting concepts and principles. Those differences make international harmonization of accounting neither practical nor valuable.

However, for Middle East countries to make their accounting systems and practices more responsive to environmental factors, they have three different choices, as can be seen in Figure 2–1. These are:

1. To use the accounting systems in the developed countries and make some modifications to fit their economic, social, political, and legal needs.

2. To use the international accounting standards as developed by the International Accounting Standards Committee (IASC).

3. To develop their own accounting systems and practices based on their own economic, social, political, and legal environmental factors, in other words, to use the accounting systems that are specially designed for their own environmental factors. This new system may be called the "environmental accounting" system.

The Accounting Systems of Developed Countries

For Middle East countries to use (or borrow) accounting systems of developed countries may not be relevant because different social, cultural, economic, and

Figure 2–1
The Three Alternatives of Accounting Systems in the Middle East

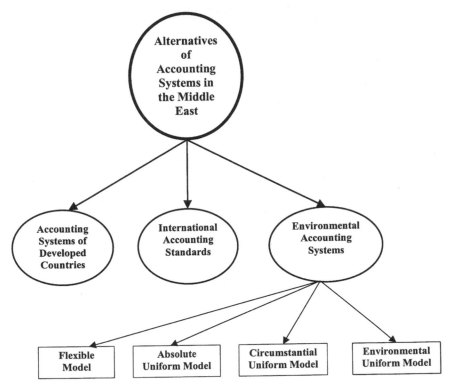

political factors require them to have different accounting systems and standards. Besides being an alien system to the country's environment, the imported accounting systems from industrial countries will not be the right ones for several reasons. First, Middle East countries have a high priority for economic and social developments and a low priority for profit motives. Second, the advanced accounting systems of developed countries need to be significantly modified to fit the economic and social needs of Middle East countries. Third, harmonizing accounting standards between countries with similar environmental factors is considered the best chance for Middle East countries to participate in the growing trend of global financial markets and to improve the performance of their securities markets (Hassan 1985: 93).

The International Accounting Standards

This alternative requires the use of International Accounting Standards (IAS), as developed by the IASC. The accounting system can be a simplified version of International Accounting Standards. It may be a proper short-run solution in Arab countries; however, it may only be used during a transition period.

The best-known examples of this alternative have occurred in Saudi Arabia and Kuwait. In Saudi Arabia, the accounting principles and practices are compatible and in conformity with the IAS. Abdallah (1997) compared the standards developed by the IASC with the Saudi accounting standards. He concluded that the latter are compatible with the IAS because of the importance of international markets to the Saudi economy.

In Kuwait, until 1990, no accounting standards or regulations were followed. Public firms had borrowed the British standards, and in some cases they used U.S. Generally Accepted Accounting Principles. Because the British controlled Kuwait until its independence in 1961, the British accounting standards, due to their popularity, were expected to be used in the 1970s and 1980s.

The lack of accounting and auditing standards was among the main reasons for the 1982 stock market crash in Kuwait. The auditors were charged with not having done a credible job, even though a lack of appropriately audited financial statements has been blamed for the crash. In general, the majority of Kuwaiti investors, when making investment decisions, do not pay much attention to the information contained in financial statements issued by the public firms.

Currently the financial statements of Kuwaiti companies generally follow the usual international presentation. Unlike Saudi Arabia, Kuwait has no accounting standards of its own. Compliance with the standards promulgated by the IASC is mandatory for shareholding and for limited liability companies for accounting periods starting on or after January 1, 1991. Prior to that date, there was compliance only with the format of the IAS.

In recent years, there have been many unsuccessful efforts to harmonize both regional and global accounting systems, for example, through the EEC and the IASC, mainly because of the environmental differences among countries. In the Middle East, even though common similarities exist with social, economic, and political factors, there have never been any attempts to harmonize the accounting and auditing standards of Middle East countries.

Now, the most important question is, who sets accounting or auditing standards in Middle East countries: professional accounting bodies, private or public organizations, or the government? In fact, different accounting standards are the product of different sets of cultural, social, legal, political, and economic variables in each country. To be successful, it is essential to ensure that there are enough similarities in environmental factors among the countries to try to harmonize accounting and auditing standards (AlHashim 1985: 1–12). Moreover, the IASC has done an excellent job in bringing together accounting and standards-setting bodies from around the world to deal with the accounting standards problems. However, we also must look carefully at factors that impair its ongoing effectiveness. First, its authority in imposing its standards is limited. Second, the IASC is composed primarily of representatives from national professional accounting bodies of developed countries rather than from national standard-setting bodies of both developed and less developed countries.

Environmental Accounting Systems

This alternative suggests the development of the Middle East's own accounting and auditing systems and standards based on its economic, social, political, and legal environmental factors. The specially designed accounting and auditing standards for a single country or for a group of countries with similar environments should be the best-fitted system. Let us call the new suggested accounting and auditing standards the "environmental accounting and auditing systems."

Again, the appropriate environmental accounting and auditing systems can be designed for one Middle East country or a group of countries. Three major issues must be addressed in establishing the new system as a basis for setting accounting and auditing standards and for resolving financial reporting disputes. They are: (1) determining the objectives for which particular environmental accounting and auditing systems are to be used, (2) choosing the relevant accounting control subsystems to be used as a basis for implementing the standards and concepts, and (3) developing the profession needed to enforce the use of the new environmental accounting systems.

In Middle East countries, the objectives of financial statements and reporting are to provide useful financial and non-financial information about economic and social resources to investors, creditors, and other groups such as the government, employees, and customers to help them make the correct decisions. To meet the needs of the intended users of environmental accounting systems, three main objectives are suggested, as seen in Figure 2–2.

1. To provide useful information to investors, creditors, and governmental organizations about economic resources and to management to make the correct allocation decisions.
2. To provide useful information to users to help them in assessing entities' and their managers' performance.
3. To provide useful information in assessing products and/or services and the ability to continue providing them in the most efficient, effective ways.

In Middle East countries, there exists basically a market economy, which places more emphasis on earning a profit and on achieving a higher rate of return on investment; therefore, financial accounting for a business enterprise is relevant in the Middle East economy. However, there is a lack of empirical evidence regarding the impact of economic, political, and cultural factors in Middle East countries on accounting systems and practices.

Islamic beliefs and rules have had a significant impact on Middle East attitudes and behavior with respect to economic activities, such as interest, bankruptcy, the relationship between debtor and creditor, Islamic banking, and more. The profit concept or capital maintenance approaches are accepted in Islam.

Figure 2–2
Objectives of the Environmental Accounting System

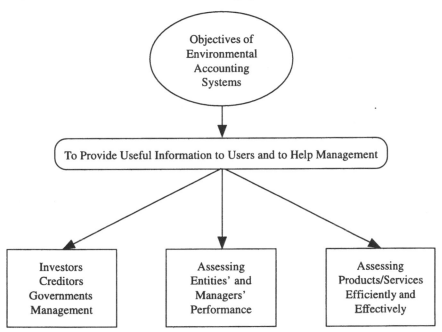

Some believe that since accounting is a social science and has a dynamic nature in meeting most of users' needs, there is a need for an Islamic accounting system as part of the IAS, which might be perfected for use in Arab and Islamic countries as well (Hassan 1985: 93).

Under the current accounting systems, the financial information in the annual corporate reports of most Arab countries does not disclose sufficient details on related party transactions, accounting policies, contingent liabilities, and many other important issues, therefore, they are not achieving the above-stated objectives. Any current or potential investors, by relying on up-to-date conventional accounting systems, may not be able to compare different corporate annual reports because of the lack of consistent and comparable accounting and auditing standards.

The success of managing private and public business entities depends on the relevancy and reliability of financial information provided by the appropriate environmental accounting systems and practices to help management make the correct financial capital and operating decisions. To ensure that those decisions are rational, financial reporting and disclosures should not be based on a system imported from a foreign environment.

Because of the difficulties that both governments and accounting firms face, no significant efforts have been made to develop appropriate environmental accounting or auditing standards, or a code of professional ethics to be used in the region. Unfortunately, no private professional organization exists in any country in the region, except Israel. However, some countries, such as Saudi Arabia, began to head in this direction in the 1990s.

For economic, cultural, and social developments, Middle East countries require the new environmental accounting systems and practices to be tailored to their social, economic, and political needs. The development of the new accounting systems and practices should match the high rates of economic and social growth and provide relevant, timely, and reliable information to help entrepreneurs, investors, and MNCs make the right decisions.

In the Middle East, as countries begin to choose a relevant accounting control subsystem to be used as a basis for implementing new environmental accounting and auditing standards of their own, they can choose from among four subsystems of accounting control models. AlHashim (1985: 4–6) suggested the use of a flexible, an absolute, or a circumstantial uniform system. The fourth, the environmental uniform model, is suggested for the Middle East environment. The four subsystems, as seen in Figure 2–1, are outlined and discussed next.

The Flexible Model

With this model, different accounting methods and reports can be selected. Free choices with the same circumstances or facts may be used to translate the same set of economic events or transactions. This model is of limited use, because it encourages the practice of different accounting methods to manipulate financial results. It needs a high level of accounting education, which may not be available in most Middle East countries. A lack of right and effective accounting education and financial issues in Arab countries is an obvious important factor in rejecting this model.

The Absolute Uniform Model

This model requires the use of one set of accounting methods and reports, regardless of circumstances or needs. It is used for pricing inventory and for administrative ease and control. However, it is too radical and inflexible. The best-known example is the Egyptian uniform accounting system that was developed in the 1960s and is still used in state-owned business entities. It has been proven that it is not a good accounting system for investors.

The Circumstantial Uniform Model

Different accounting methods can be used for different economic events, facts, or circumstances, such as the Straight Line (SL) and the Double Declining Balance (DDB) methods for depreciating the cost of a machine. Under this accounting system, the accounting and auditing standards may not be acceptable.

The Environmental Uniform Model

Under this model, accounting and auditing methods, standards, and reports are responsive to users' environmental needs. There are different accounting standards for different users' social, economic, or political needs. However, the greater the similarities among Middle East countries' environmental factors, the better the chance to establish an environmental, harmonized accounting system in the region.

Under the fourth suggested model, the accounting standards and procedures should be derived from the local economic, social, and political environment, should fit into the home environment to be successful, and should be modified to meet any new circumstances or changes in the local environment.

The lack of accounting organizations or professional bodies in Middle East countries makes it difficult, in the beginning, to implement the new environmental system, and it necessitates the use of international accounting standards as a short-run temporary solution. In general, the level of accounting education in Arab countries is low and does not allow accountants to make their own judgments on accounting issues. However, since the late 1980s, most Arab countries, including Saudi Arabia, have strengthened their accounting educational systems and actually started to develop their accounting professional organizations in the early 1990s (AlHashim 1985).

Unfortunately, many governments in Arab countries have chosen to intervene in the economic affairs and developments of their countries to stimulate the national rate of economic growth. AlHashim (1985: 8–9) suggested that the GCC should abandon the use of the flexible accounting system and move to a similar system such as the environmental uniformity model to help organizations direct their scarce economic resources toward achieving a higher rate of economic growth. It is the most appropriate accounting system for the Middle East countries at the micro, macro, and regional levels.

The domestic economic and financial policy reform of Middle East countries should be designed to promote and support the demand for environmental accounting information. Increased emphasis should be placed and pressure should be applied on shaping the accounting profession in Middle East countries to be more relevant and flexible to report and disclose necessary financial and economic information to help meet the significant economic challenges of these countries in the twenty-first century.

The environmental accounting system is the only way a government can determine which part of its economy is efficient and productive to allocate the economic resources effectively. This was the reason behind the push for Egypt and other Arab countries to use uniform accounting systems (AlHashim, 1985: 2).

However, the accounting profession in most Middle East countries either does not respond to economic changes or is not competent in supporting relevant information to help identify and solve the problems. For example, financial accounting and reporting on performance evaluation do not present the true picture of the operating results of business enterprises. Therefore, managerial or economic decisions based on such information will not lead to the best allocation of resources and will intensify the imbalances and distortions of the economy.

There will be an urgent need for supplementary information, such as value-added statements, to help decision makers evaluate the performance of entities, subsidiaries, executives, managers, and projects.

Unless the accounting profession will be well developed and the accounting education system will be improved and upgraded, no progress will be made in the Middle East region to serve the operational, financial, and capital needs of the stable economy and business enterprises using the appropriate development projects under the correct economic policy.

SUMMARY AND CONCLUSIONS

This chapter summarizes the historical and general background of the economic, political, legal, and common characteristics of Middle East countries. It discusses and emphasizes the importance of understanding the environmental factors for accountants, corporate executive officers, local managers, and the strategy of MNCs. Also examined were the international forces and organizations that made significant economic changes in the Middle East, such as the EEC, OECD, GATT, and GCC.

In addition, we noted how MNCs react and respond to the economic and political changes in the Middle East. A conflict of interest exists between MNCs' global goals and host countries' national goals. It is suggested that MNCs can reduce their risk and alleviate the conflict with host countries by transforming the conventional income statement and balance sheet to social responsibility statements and presenting their significant economic and social contributions to the host countries in terms of value-added activities.

Corresponding to the growth in Middle East corporations was the demand for equity investments, which gave rise to the development of securities markets where the raising of investment and finance could be facilitated. Securities markets are fundamental elements of the transition to a global economy, including the privatization of government-owned business entities and the need to attract foreign investments. A key factor influencing accounting systems and practices was the emergence of securities markets and the need for reliable, relevant financial information to help investors and creditors make the correct decisions. Therefore, the international harmonization of the accounting systems in Middle East countries is a major step in the success of any newly developed securities market.

Moreover, accounting plays a significant role in measuring and communicating the results of the economic, social, legal, and managerial performance of a business entity. This chapter also examined the three different choices of accounting systems available in Middle East countries: (1) to use the accounting systems of the developed countries, (2) to use International Accounting Standards, or (3) to develop their own environmental accounting systems. Many problems face Middle East countries when using either of the first two alternatives. The most appropriate system is the suggested "environmental accounting." Under the new system, standards can be developed either for a single country or for a group of countries with similar environmental conditions. In establishing and implementing the new system, three important issues must be addressed and implemented: (1) its objectives, (2) its relevant accounting control subsystems, and (3) its profession to enforce using it.

The objectives of the environmental accounting system are to provide useful financial and non-financial information about economic and social resources to investors, creditors, and other groups such as the government, employees, and customers to help them make the right decisions. The new system should match the high rates of economic and social growth and provide relevant, timely, and reliable information to help entrepreneurs, investors, and MNCs make the correct decisions.

Middle East countries should design their economic and financial policy reform to promote and support the demand for environmental accounting information. More emphasis and pressure should be placed on shaping the accounting profession to be relevant and flexible in reporting and disclosing the necessary financial and economic information to help decision makers meet the significant economic challenges in the twenty-first century.

REFERENCES

Abdallah, Wagdy M. "Accounting Standards in Saudi Arabia and International Accounting Standards." *International Review of Accounting* 2 (1997), 27–41.

Abdelsalam, Mahmoud and Diane Satin. "The Effect of Published Corporate Financial Reports on Stock Trading Volume in Thin Markets: A Study of Saudi Arabia." *The International Journal of Accounting* 26 (1991), 302–313.

AlHashim, Dhia D. "Accounting Framework for the Gulf Cooperation Council." In V. K. Zimmerman (ed.), *The Recent Accounting and Economic Developments in the Middle East*. Urbana-Champaign: University of Illinois, Center for International Education and Research in Accounting, 1985, 1–12.

Barkey, Henry J. *The Politics of the Economic Reform in the Middle East*. New York: St. Martin's Press, 1992.

Choi, Frederick D. S. and Richard M. Levich. *The Capital Market Effects on International Accounting Diversity*. Homewood, Ill.: Dow Jones–Irwin, 1990.

Cole, Simon. *The Gulf States: A Business Handbook*. Oxford: Blackwell Business, 1991.

Dessouki, Assem. "Social and Political Dimensions of the Historiography of the Arab Gulf." In Eric Davis and Nicolas Gavrielides (eds.), *Statecraft in the Middle East*. Miami: Florida International University Press, 1991, 92–115.

Diller, Daniel C. and John L. Moore (eds.). *The Middle East*, 8th ed. Washington, D.C.: Congressional Quarterly, 1994.

Doupnik, Timothy S. and Stephen B. Salter. "External Environment, Culture, and Accounting Practice: A Preliminary Test of a General Model of International Accounting Development." *The International Journal of Accounting* 30 (1995), 189–207.

Farag, Shawki M. "Management and Development: The Case of Performance Evaluation." In V. K. Zimmerman (ed.), *The Recent Accounting and Economic Devel-*

opments in the Middle East. Urbana-Champaign: University of Illinois, Center for International Education and Research in Accounting, 1985, 13–24.

————. "Accounting in the 1990s: An International Perspective." *The International Journal of Accounting* 26 (1991), 243–251.

Gray, S. J. "International Accounting Research: The Global Challenge." *The International Journal of Accounting* 24 (1989), 291–307.

Hassan, Naim. "International Accounting Standards: Desirable as a Short-Term Solution in the Case of the Arab Gulf States?" In V. K. Zimmerman (ed.), *The Recent Accounting and Economic Developments in the Middle East*. Urbana-Champaign: University of Illinois, Center for International Education and Research in Accounting, 1985, 69–100.

Page, John. "From Boom to Bust—and Back? The Crisis of Growth in the Middle East and North Africa." In Nemet Shafik (ed.), *Prospects for Middle Eastern and North African Economies*. New York: St. Martin's Press, 1998, 133–158.

Rahman, M. Zubaidur. "The Local Value Added Statement: A Reporting Requirement for Multinationals in Developing Host Countries." *The International Journal of Accounting* 25 (1990), 87–98.

Sedaghat, Ali M., Tagi Sagafi-Nejad, and George Wright. "Economic Development and Securities Markets in Developing Countries: Implications for International Accounting." *The International Journal of Accounting* 29 (1994), 297–315.

United Nations Center on Transnational Corporations. *Transnational Corporations in World Development: Trends and Prospects*. New York: UN, 1988.

World Bank. *World Development Report, 1989*. Oxford: Oxford University Press, 1989.

Chapter 3

The Effect of Culture and Religion on Accounting in the Middle East and the Harmonization of International Accounting Standards

The purpose of this chapter is to explore the effect of culture in general and Islam in particular on the accounting systems and practices of the Middle East and the harmonization of international accounting standards using the Hofstede–Gray theory. Prior research has shown that there are difficulties in harmonizing international accounting standards because of the significant effect of different culture values on the achievability of uniform international accounting standards. Religion, especially Islam, is one of the most significant cultural values that has a considerable effect on a country's accounting systems and practices, and it should not be ignored.

Several cultural issues suggested by Hofstede (1980, 1987, and 1991) and extended by Gray (1988) will be analyzed to explain the effect of Islamic culture on the accounting systems and practices of Islamic countries in South Asia, Africa, and the Middle East. The effect of religion on the accounting systems and practices of selected Middle East countries will be examined, and a modified version of the Hofstede–Gray theory is used to explain the differences in the accounting systems of Middle East countries. In addition, a new approach for establishing Islamic international accounting standards will be recommended.

INTRODUCTION

Most of the research efforts of accounting scholars have addressed the issue of the influence of culture on the development of accounting systems and practices in different countries around the world. The earliest included a list of environmental variables and explained the differences in accounting practices (Mueller 1968). Radebaugh (1975) extended the approach and made a comprehensive framework in an attempt to incorporate the Farmer and Richman model of business environment into a preliminary accounting model.

In the 1980s and 1990s, management and accounting scholars began to look closely at the impact of culture on accounting. Most of the research endeavors in this area (Hofstede 1980, 1987, and 1991; Gray 1988; Perera 1989; Nobes 1983, 1984; Violet 1983; Belkaoui and Picur 1991; Fechner and Kilgore 1994; Doupnik and Salter 1995) have been the acknowledgment of the significance of environmental factors, in particular, the cultural factors that shape a nation's accounting systems and practices. Violet (1983) argued that accounting is determined by culture, and Hofstede (1987) emphasized that the lack of consensus in accounting practices between countries is because their purpose is not technical but rather cultural.

Recently the effect of religion on the concepts and mechanisms of accounting in the Islamic world and its potential influence on the harmonization of international accounting have been discussed by Hamid, Graig, and Clarke (1993). Baydoun and Willett (1995) discussed the issue of the relevance of Western accounting to developing societies, and they concluded that it is not clear exactly what aspects of Western accounting systems are irrelevant to the needs of users in developing countries.

The harmonization of financial reporting rules may have some advantages, such as the comparability of financial statements of companies in different countries without the need for complicated calculations to adjust for accounting differences. However, harmonization entails imposing Western accounting principles on countries whose business and accounting practices are less developed than those in the West (Hamid et al. 1993: 132). It also ignores the fact that accounting is considered a socio-technical activity in any country, including human, non-human, financial, and non-financial resources or techniques as well as interaction between the two. Moreover, Hamid et al. (1993) suggested that cultural inputs such as religion should not be ignored, because religion is a confounding element in harmonizing international accounting standards. Therefore, there is a general agreement that accounting cannot be "a culture free" (Violet 1983; Fechner and Kilgore 1994: 267; Gray 1988; Perera 1989).

Most prior researchers have claimed that national systems and practices are determined by environmental variables. Gray (1988) made a significant attempt to develop a model by identifying the mechanism by which societal level values are related to the accounting subculture, which directly influences accounting practices. Gray used Hofstede's culture-based societal value dimensions model as the basis for his analysis. He also identified four value dimensions of the accounting subculture, which are also related to societal values: Professionalism, Uniformity, Conservatism, and Secrecy. Furthermore, he classified accounting systems on the basis of each of the four values.

Perera (1989) stressed the relationship between cultural values and the accounting subculture. He proposed a number of hypotheses, as did Gray, regarding the relationship between cultural values and accounting values. Doupnik and

Salter (1995) made a preliminary empirical test of the general model by examining the relationship between countries' accounting practices and a set of environmental factors and cultural dimensions hypothesized as relevant elements of the model. The results of their research lend support for the general model and provide insight into the importance of various factors in explaining existing accounting diversity.

One of the most significant developments in the study and analysis of accounting systems and practices in different countries has been an improved awareness of the importance of cultural factors in shaping a country's accounting system and practices. This in turn has led to several attempts to identify both the relevant cultural factors and the way such factors affect and shape accounting systems and practices.

In the Middle East, culture is often considered one of the important environmental factors that shape accounting systems and practices. One can see the impact that culture has had on accounting in the Middle East, in part by comparing the accounting systems and practices with those of major industrial countries. Baydoun and Willett (1995) adopted the Hofstede–Gray framework as an implied definition of cultural relevance and applied it to Lebanon, one of the Middle East countries, to see if the result led to conclusions that may be relevant to its history, environment, and culture.

Again, this chapter explores the effect of culture in general and Islam in particular on the harmonization of international accounting standards. First, the Islamic laws and regulations and their effect on business organization and accounting practices will be stressed. Second, the main characteristics of the culture (including societal and religious variables) of selected Middle East countries will be discussed. Third, the effect of religion on accounting values and concepts in selected Middle East countries will be examined, and a modified version of the Hofstede–Gray cultural accounting framework is suggested. Finally, the study will be extended to the implication of religion on MNCs' accounting systems and practices in the Middle East.

THE ISLAMIC CULTURE

Hofstede (1991: 5) defined "culture" as the collective programming of the mind which distinguishes the members of one group or category of people who share the same social and cultural environment from another. He stressed the fact that culture is learned rather than inherited. This programming is more likely established in an individual by adolescence, but it does evolve from generation to generation in the same social group. In general, culture may include the beliefs, values, and traditions that are shared in a specific society at a specific time. Therefore, religion, education, norms, customs, and history are essential components of the culture of a society (Ralston et al. 1997: 177). One of the most important cultural values for any Islamic country is religion. It has a significant impact on the business practices (including accounting) of 1.2 billion adherents. In the pages that follow in this section, the Islamic culture and its effect on Hofstede's cultural values and Gray's accounting values will be discussed.

Unfortunately, Islam is largely misunderstood, not only by non-Muslims but also by many native-born Muslims. A brief understanding of some of the basic tenets and practices of Islam may help alleviate some incorrect biases that a non-Muslim doing business in the Middle East and/or Islamic countries may have and similarly may generate a sensitivity for other practices that may be encountered or observed in Muslim employees or colleagues (Webb 1994; Szapiel 1998).

Life for any individual, a worker, a manager, or an officer, is often influenced by many variables, and for a majority of people in any Islamic country, including the Middle East, the influence of culture (especially Islam) is apparent in many of their personal and public activities, actions, decisions, and behaviors. Therefore, a businessman or a MNC doing business in the Middle East will undoubtedly encounter this influence during interpersonal interactions with Muslim individuals, both within and outside of the workplace, and a sensitivity to and an understanding of these influences and preferences may contribute to improved personal and business relations.

Islam is an Arabic word that means "peace," "obedience," or "submission" of one's heart to One and Only One God—the Creator. The Arabic word for Him, as revealed in the Holy Qur'an, is *Allah*. Islam is an ancient religion with profound historical and theological ties to Judaism and Christianity. It teaches a primordial, monotheistic religion that began with the earliest human—Adam. Muslims believe in original books revealed to Moses, Jesus, and other prophets (Ruff 1998). Over thousands of years, the religion took form with the early Jewish prophets, was significantly modified by Jesus, and was finally shaped by Mohammed (PBU), the final prophet, who died in 632 (ibid.).

Islam is the fastest-growing religion in the United States and Canada, with at least 6 million followers. Some come from other countries, but many, especially African-American Muslims, have lived in the United States all of their lives (Power 1998; Webb 1994). Because of its powerful, cross-cultural appeal, Islam has won the hearts and minds of an estimated 1.2 billion people around the world, making it the second largest religion (Christianity has 2 billion adherents, and Hinduism is third largest, with about 800 million). Despite its association in the minds of Westerners with Arabs, about 85% of Islam's faithful people are not Arabs. South Asia has the largest Muslim population, with 275 million believers, and Africa is second largest, with 200 million (Ruff 1998).

Islam is not just a religion but a way of life, and if fully realized by the individual and community, it offers guidance not only for a spiritual relationship with the Creator, God, but also for practical, day-to-day living, including business practices, accounting ethics, and decisions (Szapiel 1998; Power 1998). The practice of Islam requires reciting prayers (*salat*) five times a day, giving charity (*zakat*), performing the pilgrimage to Mecca (*hajj*) once in the lifetime, if one can afford it, and fasting (*sawm*) during the month of *Ramadan*. In Islamic societies, unlike in Western societies, religion is taught in public schools and supported by the government; in other words, there is no separation between state and mosque.

A Muslim is forbidden to eat pork or to drink wine or use other intoxicating substances. Modesty in behavior as well as dress is advised, therefore it is considered improper for a Muslim man or woman to look directly into the eyes of someone of the opposite sex when speaking and more appropriate to look down or away. A non-Muslim may consider this impolite, hence the importance in understanding the reason for this behavior.

The space set aside for prayers in a workplace usually consists of an empty room with a floor covered by a clean covering, such as a carpet over which one walks only after the shoes are removed. At one time during the performance of the prayer, one must touch the floor with one's forehead while leaning forward balanced on the hands and knees. Due to this position in particular, women prefer to have a separate room in which to pray, or at least a section in the back of the room where they may maintain modesty during these postures. This is not to be otherwise misinterpreted as a subordinate place for women. In general, in any situations, whether at work or in social gatherings, Muslim men and women prefer to congregate separately when possible, in order to avoid mixing with the opposite sex, which would make observation of modesty more difficult (Szapiel 1998).

Hofstede (1980, 1987, and 1991) developed a commonly acceptable, well-defined, empirically based terminology to describe cultures. He identified four different elements of culture that most strongly affect behavioral work situations in the organizations and institutions of a country. These include Individualism, Power Distance, Uncertainty Avoidance, and Masculinity. One can see the impact the basic tenets and practices of Islam—*salat*, *zakat*, *hajj*, and *sawm*—has had on Hofstede's four cultural values, in part by comparing the social actions of individuals and organizations of Western countries with those of Islamic countries.

The Islamic principle of taxation, including charity (*zakat*) amounts to at least 2.5% per annum of an individual's minimum balance of financial holding for a year, excluding specific exemptions, and is considered sufficient to adequately distribute wealth within a society. Of course, this assumes that all other business transactions are fair and just. God, the Creator, asks everyone nicely and voluntarily to make *zakat* (Qur'an 2: 245). "Who of you will lend Allah a goodly loan which he will return after multiplying it for him manifold? For Allah has the power both to decrease and increase your wealth, to Him you will be returned." In this way, a spiritual incentive to pay taxes voluntarily for the sake of God is one of the best tools for a country. However, the taxpayers should be true believers in God, the Creator.

In Islam, usury is strictly forbidden. Another Islamic principle of business is to not charge interest for loans. Interest is called *riba*, which means "increase." Islamic scholars agree that any increment over and above the amount of capital loaned is *riba* (Hamid et al. 1993: 143). After repayment of the loan, the debtor is also strongly discouraged from offering the loaner any gift in appreciation of the loan, and the loaner is similarly discouraged from accepting any gift. Although there is no true Islamic government in power at the present time, some predominantly Muslim-controlled governments try to provide some interest-free loans.

Most of what is written above regarding Islamic tenets and principles may be found throughout the Qur'an, as are the sayings and practices of the Prophet Mohammed (PBU), frequently quoted by most Muslims. Hart (1992) ranks the Prophet Mohammed (PBU) as the first of the 100 most influential people in world history. Doing business in the Middle East as in any country different than one's own can only be facilitated by a full understanding of the customs and culture of the people of that country, and in the process, one may even find that one's own business philosophy may adapt in a way that may lead not only to increased levels of material wealth, but also to moral and ethical success, and ultimately to an individual's true happiness (Szapiel 1998).

The Islamic culture, as the most essential component of Middle East culture, has a significant effect on the four cultural and accounting values suggested by the Hofstede–Gray theory. The performance of prayers (*salat*) five times a day has an impact on all four cultural values. *Salat* may be performed in two different ways: individually (a person praying alone) or in a group (prayer in a congregation—*salat-al-jama'ah*). It is well known in Islam that congregational prayer has greater rewards and benefits than praying individually. The outcome of this basic pillar of Islam is that the society should have a small Power Distance, should integrate Individuals into a more cohesive group, should have weaker Uncertainty Avoidance, and should have a stronger Masculine society. All of these issues and how they are related to the harmonization of accounting standards will be discussed in more detail later in this chapter.

Similarly, if we take a closer look at other Islamic practices—*hajj, zakat*, and *sawm*—we can identify a strong effect on the four cultural and accounting values under the concept that there is no separation between state and mosque. Based on the Hofstede–Gray theory, discussed in the following sections, Islamic cultural values are obviously related to the accounting subculture, which directly influences accounting systems and practices.

THE MIDDLE EAST CULTURE

It is difficult to adequately describe the Middle East culture because conflicting groups—Arabs and Israelis—existed in the same region. Arab culture draws upon several thousands years of history. The real Arabs originate from Arabia, or the contemporary countries of Saudi Arabia, Yemen, and the Gulf states (Kemper 1998). Not all Arabs are Muslims; Christian and Jewish Arabs live in the Arab countries. Nor is every country in the Middle East Arab. Israel is located in the Middle East, and it is not an Arab country.

The word "Arab" usually brings to mind images of white-robed Bedouins riding across the desert on their camels; however, this is not the true picture. There are almost 200 million Arabs who make up the majority population of 15 countries. They represent the largest, most diverse, and most politically influential Muslim ethnic group in the world (Bethany World Prayer Center 1997). However, a historical link between Arabs and the Islamic religion is still very strong.

Nydell (1996) divided the cultural values of the Arab culture into three important components, which may have a significant effect on both MNCs' business and accounting systems and practices in the Middle East. These include (1) basic values; (2) basic religious attitudes; and (3) basic self-perceptions. Nydell (1996: 21–24) describes them briefly:

I. Basic Values
   1. An individual's dignity, honor, and reputation are very important.
   2. Loyalty to an individual's family has a higher priority than individual needs.
   3. Individual status is a function of one's social class, family background, individual character, and accomplishment.
II. Basic Religious Values
   1. Every individual believes in one God, acknowledges His power, and has a religious affiliation.
   2. Piety is one of the most praiseworthy characteristics in an individual.
   3. Religion should be taught in public schools and supported by governments; in other words, no separation between state and church (mosque/temple).
III. Basic Self-Perceptions
   1. Arabs are generous, polite, humanitarian, and loyal.
   2. Arabs have a rich cultural heritage.
   3. Arabs are a clearly defined cultural group (Arab nation).
   4. Arabs are misunderstood and incorrectly characterized by most Westerners (including Americans).

Culture, in general, may refer to all social, political, and other variables that affect a person's behavior. In the Middle East, religion is an essential component of cultural values. If accounting is a product of both its society and environment, then religious values shape and reinforce local business practices, accounting systems, accounting practices, national accounting standards, and the accounting profession. However, the influence of religion on the development of accounting has not yet been explored in depth (Hamid et al. 1993: 132).

From a cultural point of view, Hofstede (1987) specified four characteristics of culture: symbols, heroes, rituals, and values. He said that the fourth one, the

Figure 3–1
The Effect of the Three Basic Components of Middle East Culture on the Societal Values of the Society

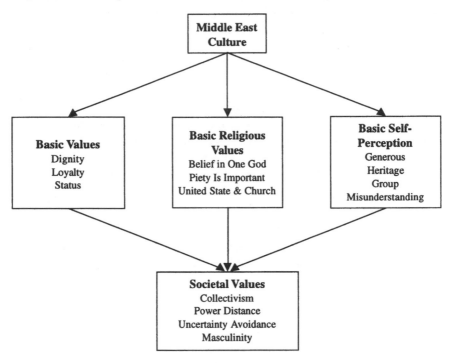

deepest-seated level, is the most difficult to change, and he suggested that differences in institutional behavior between national societies can be explained by differences in four dimensions: large versus small Power Distance; strong versus weak Uncertainty Avoidance; Individualism versus Collectivism; and Masculinity versus Femininity. He considered all of the four cultural dimensions reflective of the cultural orientation of a country.

While many businesspeople might wonder if there is a "Middle East culture," given the diversity, religious, and geographic disparateness of the Middle East, most Arabs are more homogeneous than Westerners and Americans in the way they live, think, behave, and make decisions. The three main cultural values—basic values, basic religious attitudes, and basic self-perceptions—are the major common characteristics of the Arabs of the Middle East (Nydell 1996). However, in the Jewish State, Israel, people have different cultural values, and they behave, live, and make their business decisions differently than Arabs.

In the Middle East, the four defined societal values by Hofstede (1991) are believed to be the outcomes of the three basic beliefs and values suggested by Nydell (1996), as can be seen in Figure 3–1. Arab cultures are more heavily influenced than are American cultures by institutions such as family, religion, and government, which interact to shape the value systems of individuals and groups. These cultural differences have been directly linked to differences in managerial practices and accounting systems and practices that have been witnessed in these two cultures (Yasin et al. 1992: 77).

HOFSTEDE–GRAY THEORY AND THE ISLAMIC CULTURE

The main features of Holstede's (1991) dimensions and some of the issues related to them are discussed next, followed by a consideration of their implications for accounting systems and practices in Middle East countries.

Large versus Small Power Distance

People of a large Power Distance society tend to accept a hierarchical order in which everyone has a place that needs no further justification. People in small Power Distance societies tend to strive for power equalization, and they demand justification for those power inequalities that do exist.

Collectivism versus Individualism

This dimension relates to the degree of integration a society maintains among its members. Individualism is concerned with a preference for a loosely knit social framework in society; everyone is expected to look after himself or herself and his or her immediate family. On the other hand, Collectivism indicates a preference for a tightly knit social framework in which individuals from birth onward are integrated into strong, cohesive groups, where their relatives or others in the group are expected to care for them in exchange for unquestioning loyalty. The fundamental issue here is the degree of interdependence a society maintains among individuals.

Strong versus Weak Uncertainty Avoidance

The fundamental issue involved here is how a society reacts to the fact that the future is unknown (i.e., whether it tries to control its future or simply awaits it passively). In weak Uncertainty Avoidance societies, people have a natural tendency to feel relatively secure and to maintain a more relaxed atmosphere in which practice counts more than principles, and deviance is more easily tolerated. In strong Uncertainty Avoidance societies, people tend to try to manage the future, because the future remains essentially unpredictable, thus there will be a higher level of anxiety. In such societies, institutions try to create security and avoid risk. One important way to create security is through restricted codes of belief, behavior, and law.

Masculinity versus Femininity

This dimension relates to the division of roles between sexes in a society. Masculinity stands for a preference in society to show personal pride through achievement, heroism, assertiveness, financial success, and material success. Femininity, on the other hand, stands for a preference for relationships, modesty, caring for the weaker, and equality of life and preservation of the environment.

Gray (1988) has suggested a theoretical framework showing associations between cultural variables and accounting systems and practices. He used Hofstede's (1980) culture-based societal value dimensions to develop a model that identifies the mechanism by which societal values become related to the accounting subculture, which directly affect the development of accounting systems and practices in a specific country.

In Hofstede's model, societal values (culture) are determined by environmental factors (geographic, economic, demographic, etc.) modified by external influences (forces of nature, trade, conquest, etc.). Societal values have institutional consequences in the form of a political system, legal system, religious values, nature of capital markets, and so on. Gray extends this model to propose that the value systems of accountants (accounting values) are related to and derived from societal values, and these accounting values, along with the institutional structure, affect the accounting systems and practices. Then he identifies four distinguishable value dimensions of the accounting subculture which are also related to societal values (Gray 1988: 8). These accounting subculture values include:

1. Professionalism versus Statutory Control: a preference for the practice of individual professional judgment and the maintenance of professional self-regulation, as opposed to compliance with imposed governmental legal requirements and statutory control.

2. Uniformity versus Flexibility: a preference for the enforcement of uniform accounting practices between companies and for the consistent use of such practices over time, as opposed to flexibility in accordance with the perceived circumstances of individual companies.

3. Conservatism versus Optimism: a preference for a cautious approach to measurement to cope with the uncertainty of future events, as opposed to a more optimistic, laissez-faire, risk-taking approach.

4. Secrecy versus Transparency: a preference for confidentiality and the restriction of disclosure of information about the business, only to those who are closely involved with its management and financing, as opposed to a more transparent, open, and publicly accountable approach.

In order to discuss the cultural values of the Middle East, Gray's framework, using Hofstede's four societal values, is combined with Nydell's three basic beliefs and values of the Arabs, as seen in Figure 3–2. It may be believed that the accounting systems and practices in the Middle East are a product of the

Figure 3–2
The Relationship between Middle East Societal Values, Accounting Subculture,
and Accounting Systems and Practices Using Hofstede–Gray's Accounting Theory
Combined with Nydell's Social Values

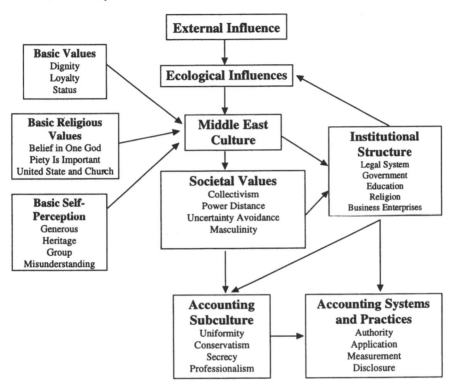

Sources: Radebaugh and Gray 1997; Nydell 1996.

environmental factors, assuming the accounting systems originated from the country itself. However, if the accounting systems were imported from the Western countries, it is not clear whether the system would be appropriate for a specific developing country of the Middle East, the Middle East region, or a cultural group in the Middle East.

The differences identified in the accounting practices and systems between U.S. and Arab countries can be explained in terms of their cultural environments. The growth of economic activity in the United States occurred in an atmosphere of classical liberalism, with a broadly laissez-faire approach to government. It can be described as a society with a highly individualist atmosphere.

In this financial community, investments are promoted by trying to interest people with uncommitted funds in various investment projects. Once prospective investors began to assess investment opportunities on the basis of their expected earnings, financial statements that included some kind of earnings amount became a necessity for the functioning of the entire system. This was a background for the development of capital market activity, which is the main source of funds for investments in the United States. The activities of these markets have resulted in continuous pressure being exerted for the provision of financial information for investors, making investors and creditors the most important recipients of accounting reports from business firms.

The pressure for the disclosure of more financial and non-financial information had a significant effect on the development of accounting principles and practices in the United States, and the requirements of the capital market became a major influencing factor in American disclosure style. Furthermore, financial reporting and capital market activity were so closely related that they became interdependent. Some developments took place in Israel, where it was assumed that accountants, independent of legal or political direction or government intervention, should implement them.

The position in Islamic countries in general, and Arab countries in particular, is quite different from that outlined above. In Egypt, Jordan, Kuwait, and Saudi Arabia, there has been a tradition of state intervention in economic affairs. Moreover, in practice, items such as related party transactions are generally not disclosed in financial statements.

CULTURAL AND ACCOUNTING VALUES OF ARABS AND ISRAELIS COMPARED TO THE UNITED STATES, AND THEIR IMPLICATIONS FOR INTERNATIONAL ACCOUNTING HARMONIZATION

An understanding of how cultural values affect cross-national accounting diversity can be useful in an effort to reduce that diversity and to enhance the comparability of accounting information worldwide. If differences in accounting systems and practices are significantly affected by national differences in culture that do not change or change slowly over time, achieving comparability of accounting across countries might be impossible (Doupnik and Salter 1995: 190).

Now, do different cultures result in different accounting systems? How do the differences in the culture of Arabs and Israelis affect accounting in the United States? To determine if the accounting differences, because of the culture differences, are irreconcilable ones, we need to understand the impact of cultural values on the accounting systems of Arabs and Israelis, as compared to Americans, based on the Hofstede–Gray–Nydel theoretical framework. The four accounting value dimensions of Gray, the four societal values of Hofstede, and some of the issues related to them are discussed below, followed by a consideration of their implication for accounting systems and practices of selected Middle East countries.

There are significant cultural differences between Arabs, Israelis, and Americans. Table 3–1 shows Hofstede's differences in the cultural values of Arab

Table 3–1
Hofstede's Middle East Cultural Value Scores Compared to Those of the United States

	Israel	Arab Countries	United States
Power Distance			
Score Rank	52	H 7	38
Score	L 13	80	40
Individualism			
Score Rank	19	low 26/27	1
Score	54	38	91
Uncertainty Avoidance			
Score Rank	19	H 27	43
Score	H 81	68	46
Masculinity			
Score Rank	29	H 23	15
Score	H 47	53	62

Source: Hofstede 1991.

countries as compared to the United States, and the cultural values of Israelis compared to the United States. Unlike the case of Israel and the United States, no direct assessment of Egypt's, Kuwait's, or Saudi Arabia's four cultural dimensions is available. However, Hofstede (1991) provides data on Arab countries as a group including the three Arab countries, which can be used as the starting point for the analysis. Hofstede's cultural values for the Arab countries compared to Israel and the United States are shown in Table 3–1.

As can be seen in Table 3–1, the Arab countries as a group have higher Power Distance and Uncertainty Avoidance and lower Individualism and Masculinity than the United States. However, Israel has higher Uncertainty Avoidance and lower Power Distance and Individualism and Masculinity than the United States. In the Middle East, Arab countries have higher Power Distance and Masculinity and lower Individualism and Uncertainty Avoidance than Israel.

However, Hofstede's scores may not reflect a specific Middle East country's cultural values. The group of countries Hofstede described as "Arab" consists of great cultural diversity with representatives from the richest (such as Kuwait) and poorest countries (such as Egypt) on a per capita GNP basis (Baydoun and Willett 1995: 76). In this section, the cultural and accounting values will be discussed from the Islamic culture point of view and their effect on accounting practices, hence international accounting harmonization.

Power Distance

The identified attributes of this dimension tend to draw attention to issues such as whether subordinate participation in the planning phase of budgeting is important or paternalistic management style, such as in implementing an imposed budgeting concept, is the accepted style in Middle East countries. In most Middle East countries, such as Egypt, Kuwait, and Saudi Arabia, the Power Distance is large, and the degree of inequality is measured by the extent of Power Distance. The level of Power Distance is related to the extent of centralization of power (authority), such as in most of Egypt and to the degree of autocratic leadership.

Other related issues are income differentials and equitable and fairness tax systems. In countries that have large income differentials and inequitable tax systems, Power Distance tends to be large. As can be seen in Table 3–1, the Arab countries as a group ranked seventh out of 50 national groupings, with a score of 80, compared to a ranking of 38 and a score of 40 for the United States, and a ranking of 52 with a score of 13 for Israel.

In Arab countries, an Arab executive belongs to a culture that is affiliation oriented and government dominated. The American executive belongs to a culture, which is power and achievement oriented, and operates within a free market system (Yasin et al. 1992: 78).

Gray (1988) derived four accounting value dimensions (accounting subculture) which are related to Hofstede's (1991) cultural values. These accounting values are Professionalism, Uniformity, Conservatism, and Secrecy. To what extent can Power Distance be linked to the accounting values of Arab countries? In Islam, the main objective of the performance of the basic tenets of Islam is to reduce the Power Distance to the minimum. However, not all Muslims follow the Qur'an or the Sunna of the Prophet Mohammed (PBU) exactly. The Islamic culture of Shura (team) may have a significant effect on reducing the Power Distance between different classes of people.

From the accounting values point of view, the degree of Professionalism preferred in an accounting subculture would influence the nature of authority for the accounting system. In the Arab countries, the lower the degree of Professionalism, the greater the need for government intervention, and the lower the degree of professional self-regulation. Power Distance is strongly linked to Professionalism, less strongly linked to Uniformity, and weakly linked to Conservatism. However, there is a close relationship with Secrecy. In Saudi Arabia, most international joint ventures with foreign partners involve the disclosure of information at a minimum degree to preserve power inequalities, as seen in Table 3–2.

Table 3–2
Associations between Social and Accounting Values in Arab Countries

	Accounting Values			
Cultural Values	**Professionalism**	**Uniformity**	**Conservatism**	**Secrecy**
Power Distance	Strong	Less Strong	Weak	Strong
Collectivism	Strong	Strong	Strong	Strong
Uncertainty Avoidance	Strong	Strong	Weak	Weak
Masculinity	Strong	Strong	Weak	Weak

Individualism

If executive decision is affected by the cultural values of the country in which it is practiced, then one would expect differences between the Arab and American business cultures with regard to executive managerial and financing decisions. These differences may follow a pattern similar to the differences between the American and Japanese cultures, based on the fact that both the Japanese and Arab cultures are group rather than individual oriented. The Japanese "Kaigi" system of decision making through the group is similar to the Arab culture concept of "Shura," reaching decisions through group consensus (Yasin et al. 1992: 78).

As can be seen in Table 3–1, the Arab countries as a group ranked 26th/27th out of 50 national groupings, with a score of 38 compared to a ranking of 1 and a score of 91 for the United States, and a ranking of 19 with a score of 54 for Israel. Hofstede (1991: 57) concluded that the degree of Individualism in a country is statistically related to that country's wealth.

Accordingly, wealthy countries tend to be more collectivistically oriented. This would seem to indicate an aspect of clear difference in societal values that exists between countries (Perera 1989: 44). In rich Arab countries such as Saudi Arabia and Kuwait, cultural values like loyalty to one's family and the Shura (teamwork) concept come from the Islamic Sharia (regulation), as stated in the Qur'an, and from the teaching of the Prophet Mohammed (PBU). Even though Egypt is presumed to be an Islamic country, the Shura concept is seldom used. The effect on accounting systems and practices would be quite obvious in this case. Most accounting principles are more likely mandated or influenced by government intervention in the majority of Arab countries.

Arab and American cultures are distinctly different. Arab cultures are more heavily influenced by institutions such as family, religion, and government, which interact to shape the value systems of individuals and groups. These cultural differences have been directly linked to differences in managerial decisions, accounting practices, and auditing standards, evidenced in these two cultures (Yasin et al. 1992: 77). To what extent can Individualism or Collectivism be linked to accounting values in Arab countries? Collectivism rather than Individualism can be linked most closely to public regulations/statutory control, a strong link to Uniformity, and a high level of Individualism with a strong link to Conservatism and Secrecy, as seen in Table 3–2.

Uncertainty Avoidance

The Arab countries as a group ranked 27 out of 50 national groupings, with a score of 68 compared to a ranking of 43 and a score of 46 for the United States and a ranking of 19 and a score of 81 for Israel. In Islam, there is a strong belief to plan for one's life as though one is going to live forever, and to be ready for the day of judgment (life hereafter), assuming that one is going to die tomorrow (Authentic Hadeeth of the Prophet Mohammed—PBU). Therefore, certainty is high because of the strong belief in one's heart that God is going to provide one with the best in life, as long as His guidance (the Qur'an) and the Sunna (the teaching of the Prophet Mohammed—PBU) are followed.

Religion, as one of the most important cultural values in the Middle East, the place where all three major religions—Judaism, Christianity, and Islam—are revealed, is an important factor in creating a feeling of certainty. If most religions attempt to produce in the minds and hearts of individuals an expectation of something that is certain, Islam, with the unaltered book of truth (the Qur'an), emphasizes the fact that the more certain one is of expecting that something good is going to happen, it really is going to happen, as long as one fears God— the Only God—the Creator, and no one else.

Certainly the identified characteristics of this dimension tend to draw attention, among other things, to the existence of a need for formal and informal codes to guide ethical behavior, the degree of formalization, the standardization and ritualization of organizations, the extent of tolerance of deviant ideas and behavior, and the willingness to take risks (Perera 1989: 46). The only book that contains those codes is the Qur'an, and it is all-inclusive of what was revealed to Moses, Jesus, and all other prophets as ritual codes. Moreover, it includes the most practical codes of accounting ethics, honesty, bankruptcy, business negotiations, contracts, accountability or stewardship, and banking transactions, among many other things.

To what extent then can Uncertainty Avoidance be linked to accounting values in Arab countries? Given the significant effect of religion on Muslims' managerial decisions, it may be argued that it is linked most closely to Professionalism and Uniformity, because a weak Uncertainty Avoidance would lead to a concern for the application of Islamic law and order and rigid codes of behavior to protect the innocent. However, there is a weak link to both Conservatism and Secrecy, as can be seen in Table 3–2.

Masculinity

The Arab countries as a group ranked 23 out of 50 national groupings, with a score of 53, compared to a ranking of 15 and a score of 62 for the United States, and a ranking of 29 and a score of 47 for Israel. A brief introduction to some of the basic tenets and practices of Islam related to the treatment of women may help alleviate some incorrect biases that a non-Muslim doing business in the Middle East may have, and similarly may generate a sensitivity for other practices one may encounter or observe in a Muslim employee. Szapiel (1998) emphasized that by acquiring some understanding of this particular aspect of the Middle East culture, a successful and meaningful business relationship may be achieved with the businesspeople or business entities of these countries.

The rights of women in Islam are often misunderstood, not only by non-Muslims but unfortunately by many Muslims. This generates incorrect notions about the treatment of women. Surprising to many people, Islam outlines very specific rights for women in society, many of which were not enjoyed by women in Western countries for hundreds of years after Islam advised them and which still today are not realized by women in many countries. For example, as propounded by the Prophet Mohammed (PBU), in the seventh century, women were given the right to vote long before American and English women were in the twentieth century, to own property, and to obtain divorces from their husbands. A married Muslim woman is allowed to retain any private property she held before marriage, and she does not have to transfer it to her husband after marriage, in contrast to early English common law, which was subsequently revised to allow women to retain their property yet permitted the husband to manage it and keep the gains. It was further revised in the nineteenth century to allow women to manage their property. A Muslim woman is also permitted to retain her maiden name after marriage (Szapiel 1998).

Hofstede (1991) placed the Arab country group in the middle range (53) of ranking all countries included in his research. Within the Arab countries, Saudi Arabia is the strongest masculine society, which places it toward the highest end of the Masculinity scale of the Arab countries. In Egypt, Muslim and non-Muslim women have been included in some leading roles in society.

To what extent can Masculinity be linked to accounting values in the Arab countries in the Middle East? Given the Islamic treatment of women in certain countries, but not all of them, it is clear that the link to Professionalism and Uniformity is expected to be strong. However, there is no clear link to either Conservatism or Secrecy, as seen in Table 3–2.

Is Accounting Harmonization Possible with Cultural Differences?

One can see the impact that culture has had, in part by comparing the accounting systems and practices of developed countries to Arab countries. Because of these cultural differences, the harmonization of accounting standards may be difficult, if not impossible. If we look closely at the effect of religion on investing and financing decisions combined with the development of accounting principles and practices to account for global business transactions, we may find that the prohibition of interest (*riba*) in Islam presents only one cultural element that makes the harmonization of accounting standards more difficult (Hamid et al. 1993: 146).

Evidence shows that repealing existing regulations of different countries, rather than piling on additional or new regulation, may help expand capital markets. One example that comes to mind is the Security and Exchange Commission's (SEC's) passage of Rule 144A, which exempts the sale of securities to large institutional investors from the SEC's registration and reporting requirements. Allowing foreign companies to raise capital in the U.S. market without being required to follow SEC rules would undoubtedly make it easier to raise capital, since SEC registration requirements are a high barrier to entry.

Another related issue is business and accounting ethics. Islamic regulations might have a significant impact on accounting practices, which may be in favor of the whole society, but will have conflicts with the business practices in Western countries. This issue might require further research to investigate the ethics in Islam and their impact on global businesses.

If the national cultural values of Islamic societies shape and reinforce both accounting systems and practices, it will be a rational decision to harmonize the accounting standards of those countries as one subgroup of the international community. Therefore, it is time for the IASC to consider not harmonizing International Accounting Standards but rather establishing Islamic International Accounting Standards (IIAS). IIAS will be helpful to South Asian Muslim countries (275 million), African Muslim countries (200 million), Arab countries (180 million), and the remaining Islamic adherents (545 million). IIAS should be based on the Holy Qur'an and on the Sunna of the Prophet Mohammed (PBU).

SUMMARY AND CONCLUSIONS

This chapter discussed the effect of cultural values, including religion, on the accounting systems and practices of developing countries in general and on the Middle East in particular, using the Hofstede–Gray theory. Prior research has shown that there are difficulties in harmonizing International Accounting Standards because of the significant effect that different culture values have on the achievability of uniform International Accounting Standards. Moreover, as international comparisons of accounting practices have revealed differences, research has identified that cultural and religious variables have a considerable effect on a country's accounting systems and practices.

This chapter analyzed several cultural issues originally suggested by Hofstede (1980, 1987, 1991)—Power Distance, Uncertainty Avoidance, Individualism, and Masculinity—and extended by Gray (1988) to explain the effect of cultural values on accounting systems and practices. The effect of culture in general and religion in particular on accounting systems and practices in selected Middle East countries was examined, and a modified version of the Hofstede–Gray cultural accounting theory was used to explain the differences in accounting systems in the Islamic countries.

In conclusion, accounting systems and practices in Islamic countries have been significantly influenced by several Islamic cultural values, with religion being the most significant. It may not be acceptable by those countries to use the IASC as a substitute for their national accounting standards. If the national cultural values of Islamic society shape and reinforce both accounting systems and practices, it will be a rational decision to harmonize the accounting standards of those countries as one subgroup of the international community.

It may not be practical for developing countries to borrow Western accounting systems and to implement them in developing countries because they do not fit into the Middle East environment. Every country's accounting system should be considered its socio-technical system.

If the financial community in general and the accounting profession in particular intend to improve the global business environment and the application of relevant accounting systems in Islamic countries, it is essential to spend time understanding the applicability of ethical and practical codes described in the Holy Qur'an and the Sunna of the Prophet Mohammed (PBU) not only as religious rules for Muslims but also as guidance for non-Muslims in the global business environment for almost every single activity in global business.

The issues that might be of interest to the IASC and the global business environment for consideration when setting up the IIASs include: (1) the relationship between the person, the group, the employer–employee, office mates, the family, and the whole society; (2) the commercial and noncommercial transactions, and whether the transactions are acceptable or forbidden, according to the book of Allah and the Sunna of the Prophet Mohammed (PBU); (3) the limitation of the interpersonal relationship among members, businesspeople, societies, nations, the government, and the public; (4) the clear and obvious answers for several problems in this society; (5) interest; (6) the relationship between debtor and creditor; (7) business contributions or monetary donations; (8) equitable taxation; (9) bankruptcy; and (10) business ethics, including accounting.

REFERENCES

Baydoun, Nabil and Roger Willett. "Cultural Relevance of Western Accounting Systems to Developing Countries." *Abacus* 31, no. 1 (1995), 67–91.

Belkaoui, Ahmed Riahi and Ronald D. Picur. "Cultural Determinism and the Perception of Accounting Concepts." *The International Journal of Accounting* 26 (1991), 118–130.

Bethany World Prayer Center. "The Unreached Peoples Prayer Profiles—The Diaspora Arabs." www.bethany.com, 1997.

Davis, Eric and Nicolas Gavrielides (eds.). *Statecraft in the Middle East*. Miami: Florida International University Press, 1991.

Doupnik, Timothy S. and Stephen B. Salter. "External Environment, Culture, and Accounting Practice: A Preliminary Test of a General Model of International Accounting Development." *The International Journal of Accounting* 30 (1995), 189–207.

Fechner, Harry H. E. and Alan Kilgore. "The Influence of Cultural Factors on Accounting Practice." *The International Journal of Accounting* 29 (1994), 265–277.

Gray, S. J. "Towards a Theory of Cultural Influence on the Development of Accounting Systems Internationally." *Abacus* 24, no. 1 (1988), 1–15.

Hamid, Shaari, Russell Graig, and Frank Clarke. "Religion: A Confounding Cultural Element in the International Harmonization of Accounting?" *Abacus*, 29, no. 2 (1993), 131–147.

Hart, Michael H. *The 100: A Ranking of the Most Influential Persons in History*. Secaucus, N.J.: Carl Publishing Group, 1992.

Hofstede, Geert. *Culture Consequences*. Beverly Hills, Calif.: Sage Publications, 1980.

———. *Accounting and Culture*. Barry E. Cushing (ed.). Sarasota, Fla.: American Accounting Association, 1987.

———. *Cultures and Organizations: Software of the Mind*. London: McGraw-Hill Book Company, 1991.

The Holy Qur'an. Text, Translation, and Commentary by Muhammad Taqi-ud-Din Al-Hillali. Jeddu, Saudi Arabia: Maktabat Dar-us-Salam, 1983.

Kemper, Cynthia L. "Arab Culture Little Understood in West." *The Denver Post Online*, April 29, 1998.

Lewis, Bernard. *The Middle East: A Brief History of the Last 2,000 Years*. New York: Scribner, 1995.

Mueller, G. G. "Accounting Principles Generally Accepted in the United States versus Those Generally Accepted Elsewhere." *International Journal of Accounting Education and Research* (Spring 1968), 91–103.

Nobes, C. W. "A Judgmental International Classification of Financial Reporting Practices." *Journal of Business Finance and Accounting* (Spring 1983), 1–19.

———. *International Classification of Financial Reporting*. London: Croom Helm, 1984.

Nydell, Margaret K. *Understanding Arabs: A Guide for Westerners*. Yarmouth, Maine: Intercultural Press, 1996.

Perera, M.H.B. "Toward a Framework to Analyze the Impact of Culture on Accounting." *The International Journal of Accounting* 24 (1989), 42–56.

Power, Carla. "The New Islam." *Newsweek*, March 16, 1998, 34–38.

Radebaugh, L. H. "Environmental Factors Influencing the Development of Accounting Objectives Standards and Practices in Peru." *International Journal of Accounting Education and Research* (Fall 1975), 39–56.

Radebaugh, L. H. and Sidney J. Gray. *International Accounting and Multinational Enterprises*. New York: John Wiley & Sons, 1997.

Ralston, David A., David H. Holt, Robert H. Terpstra, and Yu Kai-Cheng. "The Impact of National Culture and Economic Ideology on Managerial Work Values: A Study of the United States, Russia, Japan, and China." *Journal of International Business Studies* (1st Quarter 1997), 177–189.

Ruff, Carolyn. "Islam Is a Way of Life." *Staten Island Advance*, August 1, 1998, B1–B2.

Szapiel, Susan. "The Influence of Middle East Culture on the Work-Related Values." Working Paper, October 1998.

Violet, W. J. "The Development of International Accounting Standards: An Anthropological Perspective." *International Journal of Accounting Education and Research* (Spring 1983), 1–12.

Webb, Gisela. 1994. "Islam and Muslims in America." In Hussein Mutalib (ed.), *Islam, Muslims and the Modern State*. New York: St. Martin's Press, 298–315.

Yasin, Mahmoud M., Ronald F. Green, and Tom Zimmerer. "Executive Courage Across Cultures: An Organizational Perspective." *International Journal of Commerce and Management* 1 (1992), 75–87.

Chapter 4

Investing in the Middle East

This chapter introduces guidelines for MNCs on the important financial, managerial, and tax issues of investing, financing, or managing joint ventures in the Middle East. Countries' rules, regulations, facts, and experiences that uniquely affect the management and financial reporting of joint ventures in the Middle East will also be discussed.

The chapter also reviews five major problems that have been encountered in managing American joint ventures in the Middle East, which have a significant impact on managing MNCs and should be considered when making investment decisions. These include: (1) pricing and marketing decisions of products, (2) determining what constitutes fair compensation for labor, (3) designing the appropriate tax and nontax incentive system, (4) keeping a foreign exchange account sufficient to meet foreign obligations, and (5) reducing the risks of expropriation or confiscation.

For financial reporting requirements and tax planning strategies, several unique issues of the five Middle East countries' joint venture income tax will be discussed. The advantages and disadvantages of the local tax practices will be investigated, and their effects on MNCs in designing their tax planning strategies will be briefly evaluated. Finally, several important recommendations will be suggested for MNCs to use in managing, financing, and investing in the Middle East.

BACKGROUND

In the Middle East, every Arabian country runs joint ventures to expand economic and technical cooperation with other countries, to absorb foreign capital, to introduce advanced technology and equipment and advanced managerial experience, and to recruit qualified trained personnel to speed up modernization programs. Most of the countries have designed laws, regulations, and practices to attract foreign investments to participate in the development of the local economy, especially in areas that need their advanced technology, through the transfer of a highly developed technology.

In some Middle East countries, joint ventures with local partners are allowed without restrictions on the minimum or maximum percentage of ownership for local or foreign partners, such as in Egypt. However, in other countries such as Kuwait, the United Arab Emirates, and Saudi Arabia, a foreign company, even a branch of a foreign company, is not allowed to do business without associating itself with a local partner or an agent.

WHY DO MNCs INVEST IN THE MIDDLE EAST?

MNCs are motivated to go to the Middle East by many factors that are different from industry to another, and even from one company to another within the same industry. An American MNC may manufacture its products at home and then export them to any Middle East country, such as Egypt or Israel, and achieve higher profits. It may import from a foreign subsidiary in Saudi Arabia owned by a Saudi national company or a joint venture between a Saudi partner and a British MNC. In this case, it may be cheaper for an American MNC to manufacture its products and establish an American subsidiary or a joint venture where labor costs are the lowest, and sell them where selling prices are the highest.

MNCs may start to look for new markets outside of their home country for many reasons. These include (1) improving their competitive position in both domestic and international markets; (2) exploring new markets; (3) maximizing profits; (4) meeting tariff and quota restrictions in foreign countries; (5) securing otherwise unobtainable raw materials, such as oil and gas, for the home country; (6) exploring the scarce economic resources in the Middle East countries; and (7) manufacturing their products in the lowest cost–producing countries, especially Middle East countries, and selling the products in the best-selling markets (Abdallah 1989: 1).

The growth of MNCs has created new issues for Middle East national economies as well as international economies. These issues include international location of production and distribution territories, their effect on national and international stock and commodity markets, their significant effects on both home and Middle East governments' revenues, and the balance of payments of both foreign and home countries.

One of the major characteristics of a successful MNC is having a highly efficient organizational tool for utilizing scarce economic resources on a worldwide basis. Moreover, if the headquarters is to achieve the goals set out in the strategic plan, the international activities of all of its Middle East and domestic subsidiaries need to be planned, organized, coordinated, and controlled on a global basis.

HOW TO CHOOSE THE BEST INVESTMENT IN THE MIDDLE EAST

Despite all of the talk of recession and a hostile international business climate in the Middle East, interest in joint ventures has never been keener. Certainly U.S. manufacturers can no longer rely on a nearly exclusive domestic market to sell their products. Most medium-sized American companies, therefore, should try to explore the creative strengths of Middle East countries' economic resources. While maintaining dependence on their domestic resources, these companies can systematically seek out joint ventures in Middle East countries for expansion and a larger international market share. If your company has this goal in mind, you must answer two key questions:

1. Should your company, or joint ventures in which ownership is shared with local interests, be wholly owned foreign subsidiaries in the Middle East?
2. If the joint venture approach is adopted, should your firm seek a majority, if it is possible, or a minority participation?

Before considering the second question, CEOs and controllers must determine which type of investment they would seek in the Middle East, joint venture or wholly foreign owned. To illustrate this, let us look at selected countries, such as Egypt, Kuwait, Israel, Jordan, and Saudi Arabia. In the past few years, a number of major foreign companies have decided to set up wholly foreign-owned enterprises, notably in Egypt, rather than enter into a joint venture. This may have advantages, particularly in giving management a freer hand. The obvious benefit of this is having a local partner to smooth over problems in dealing with official local authorities or departments that control all of the elements required to carry on business, including supply of labor, power, water, and raw materials. At the moment, wholly foreign-owned enterprises are taxed under the Foreign Enterprises Income Tax Law, while equity joint ventures receive more favorable treatment under the local Investment Joint Venture Income Tax Law of most Middle East countries.

Joint ventures may involve partnerships with private or state-owned firms in the foreign country and will reduce the investment required by the establishing company. In general, the ownership strategy alternatives are limited in some countries. For other countries, however, the multinational firm has considerable choice. It is important to know that ownership strategies in foreign countries can change investment requirements and other resource commitments for new investments. They also are an important component of overall global strategy. Moreover, they affect the extent to which individual subsidiaries participate in one's company's worldwide strategy (Abdallah 1992).

WHY IS A JOINT VENTURE IMPORTANT FOR ONE'S COMPANY?

If your company decides to go for a majority ownership of local subsidiaries, you will enjoy the greatest flexibility in areas such as intercompany pricing policies, organization, and dividend policy. Yet you will find that divestment of some equity can provide more benefits than what you expect under other options, through protection against controls. The greater the proportion of ownership that is divested, the greater the gain in protection and the greater the loss of parent company control. On the other hand, ownership sharing is the major deterrent to host-country controls in local subsidiaries with nationals. Although the decision to engage in joint ventures involves many issues other than a defensive move against national controls, this strategy can have the triple effect of reducing the apparent threat of foreign domination, securing local allies, and enlarging the role of native enterprise in the local economy.

Although the evidence is still fragmentary, three additional advantages can be gained by joint ventures. First, technical or operational resources can be advantageous when participating with a strong local partner that has access to or controls supplies and resources that are necessary to the company's operations and will ensure that the company receives a supply of such items. Moreover, the local partner will help smooth over problems in dealing with governmental authorities or departments, which control all of the elements required to carry on business.

Second, when the financial resources of your company are limited, joint ventures may allow you to enter into more foreign projects. In some countries, local partners will accept the technological know-how, patent rights, or even the trade name of the multinational firm as a substitute for invested capital in payment for a share of the subsidiary's equity. Moreover, joint ventures lessen the risk of foreign exchange losses by reducing the amount of investment in the foreign country. In most Middle East countries, joint ventures receive more favorable treatment under the Joint Venture Income Tax Law than do foreign subsidiaries.

Third, the most important motivation for joint ventures in several, especially Middle East, countries is the political consideration. Sharing ownership with local or national firms can encourage national identification and reduce the appearance of foreignness, thus the risk of expropriation. Furthermore, local partners may in some cases have some kind of political influence and protection against the possibility of severe national controls or expropriation.

A closer look at Middle East countries reveals that good economic performance in certain countries, such as Egypt, Jordan, Kuwait, and Saudi Arabia, has been achieved in almost all of the joint ventures that have gone into production or operation. The facts over recent years have proven that by absorbing foreign capital and running joint ventures, Egypt and Saudi Arabia have imported advanced technology, have renewed and upgraded products, have promoted the technical transformation of existing enterprises, and have increased export and foreign exchange earnings. Both countries have also learned from advanced foreign managerial experience and have thus improved the management and operation of their own enterprises. It is expected that in Egypt and Jordan more and larger joint ventures will be set up with foreign partners in the near future.

Seen as part of a strategy, both distribution and sharing local ownership can be important. For example, in Kuwait and Saudi Arabia, placing local ownership in the hands of a small number of local partners is an advantage, because such partners are likely to take an active interest in protecting the profitability of their investment from erosion by Kuwaiti or Saudi government controls. So when including local ownership into its strategy, a MNC may be able to retain a greater degree of control, in excess of its ownership share.

In Kuwait and Saudi Arabia, joint ventures are very different from what is normally referred to by the term in the United States. Normally in Middle East joint ventures there is no direct relationship between equity and profits. For example, one could have 51% equity and 75% profits. Such an agreement, and indeed management control, can be ensured either by the articles of incorporation or by a separate management contract. Kuwaiti, Egyptian, or Saudi joint ventures with substantial Saudi equity enjoy government preference as sources; joint ventures of 25% or more have a five-year or 10-year tax holiday. Overall, a Saudi or Kuwaiti joint venture is quite flexible and subject only to one's ability to negotiate a useful agreement.

In Egypt, the government offers attractive incentives for foreign investors, such as reduced import duties, tax exemption, and the elimination of exchange controls, especially in projects that earn foreign currency and reduce the country's imports. Free zones have been established in areas such as Port Said, where foreign projects can be established without Egyptian equity participation.

Egypt is a market that is becoming more open to international exporters, especially for goods ranging from expensive consumer products to competitively priced industrial and agricultural inputs (such as chemicals and industrial equipment) for different segments of the developing industry in Egypt. Egypt's fiscal and monetary reforms since 1991 have created a stable currency and have allowed it to accumulate reserves in excess of its imports.

In January 1996, the Egyptian government made a significant change in the economy by privatizing its extensive public holdings by establishing a new cabinet to sell off state-owned factories and other companies to both Egyptian and foreign investors. It is believed that share sales through the capital market, to both Egyptian and foreign investors, are growing steadily, making investors more confident in the government's reform program.

In 1997, several economic laws were introduced, and some were approved, to facilitate the participation of the private sector and to help foreign companies do business in Egypt. In May 1997, the Investment Incentives and Guarantee Laws were approved by the Egyptian People's Assembly. Recently, American MNCs have been competing for major strategic projects in Egypt, including airports, telecommunications, TV broadcasting, and port projects.

In Israel, foreign financial institutions have begun to consider Israel as a potential market for three main reasons: (1) the rapid growths in the high-tech sector, (2) the country's privatization programs, and (3) a progressive pace in the peace processes. Israel's high-tech sector attracts almost half of Israeli business for investment institutions. The high-tech sector remains one of the strongest sectors of the economy and, with reasonable progress in the peace process with Palestine, Lebanon, and Syria, more foreign investors are willing to increase their investments. Privatization of the government-owned business entities, such as El Al and Israel Electric Company, offers a variety of opportunities for new investors (Mungai 2000: 66). In the meantime, Israel is trying to go into a process of disinflation, resulting from tight monetary policy and lower import prices. It is expected that the average inflation rate should fall from 9% in 1997 to just over 3% by 2002. The growth of export and private consumption should bring about a recovery from 2000 onwards, with GDP growing by an average of 4.4% during 2000–2002 (*Crossborder Monitor* 1998: 7).

The market is sophisticated and highly competitive. Market and legal expertise, partnerships with local firms, reliable local agents, and a commitment to service are critical to successful entry. Market barriers result from differing systems of standards, a complex and often not transparent government tendering system in Israel, and a series of taxes, apart from customs, which raise the final prices of imported goods (U.S. Department of State—Israel, 1997).

Major American sales and investment opportunities are in the area of computers, telecommunications, processed foods and electric power equipment, and electronic components. Investments expected to add major opportunities in the next few years include pollution control, airport ground equipment, medical equipment, and insurance. Israel's high priority on attracting foreign investment, the concentration of private-sector growth in high-tech sectors, and favorable financing conditions all make the country a good investment focus (ibid.).

In Jordan, the Companies Act of 1989 distinguishes between two types of foreign companies: foreign companies operating in the Kingdom and foreign companies not operating in the Kingdom. The former applies to foreign firms seeking to establish branch offices to conduct business in Jordan. The latter applies to representative (i.e., regional) offices that are not permitted to conduct full commercial activities in Jordan, or act as commercial agents and middlemen for business activities. However, they are allowed to serve as liaisons between their head offices and Jordanian or regional clients, and to represent their companies' business interests in Jordan. Regional and representative offices also may be set up to coordinate and direct scientific and technical services for clients in Jordan. Foreign firms qualified to execute contracts in Jordan are encouraged to establish branch offices (U.S. Department of State—Jordan 1997).

American MNCs may establish joint Jordanian–American offices to do business in and from Jordan. However, Jordanian law requires that the Jordanian interest be at least 51%. Joint trading offices may engage in business activity, including trade, contracting, land, maritime, and air transport. Joint offices also are allowed to engage in financial services and stock market operations through registered brokers.

HOW TO START A JOINT VENTURE IN THE MIDDLE EAST

The next decade will be a critical one in fulfilling the long-run potential of the Middle East. For a long time, Arab countries have relied on oil revenues, which are now declining, and have refused market-oriented reforms. Now it is essential to reap the benefits of a changing global economy. Industries and exports must be diversified to secure additional foreign currencies, higher rates of economic growth, and less reliance on imported food and other goods. In the twenty-first century, privatization must take over most state-owned enterprises to participate and push the economies and standards of living to higher levels and to increase international competitiveness. Peace must be achieved to attract more investment for both Arab countries and Israel. Regional and global economic integration should be used as a springboard for development and growth. Any Middle East country that ignores these golden opportunities will be left behind in the twenty-first century (Riordan et al. 1998: 15).

In the 1990s, Middle East countries shifted to a new development strategy, with the main emphasis on industrialization and economic diversification. MNCs involved in exporting to Arab countries and Israel are gradually realizing that the best way to maintain and possibly expand their market share is to establish joint ventures there. Factors that usually increase a foreign investor's success include a willingness to transfer technical expertise and train local nationals for management positions and the ability to develop close business relationships with national counterparts.

Now is the best time for American MNCs to start new joint ventures and increase their global market shares of sales, profits, and investments by choosing the best investments in the region. In establishing a joint venture in the Middle East, certain guidelines should be followed by MNCs, which will be discussed next.

Are Your Goals Compatible with the Middle East Country's Economic Goals?

The common practice in American–Middle East joint ventures is that the American partner provides its share of the needed capital, equipment, and technology, while the local partner provides the remaining share of the capital, the premises, and the workforce and services. The two sides run the enterprise jointly, sharing profits or products and risks and liabilities in accordance with the proportions laid down in the contract under the principle of equality and mutual benefit.

Most Middle East countries, such as Egypt and Saudi Arabia, have two principal economic goals: (1) economic diversification to decrease dependence on oil through the development of industry, agriculture, and mining; and (2) assumption of responsibility by the private sector for the Kingdom's or the country's economic development. To achieve the first goal, the local government encourages joint ventures with foreign participation and management, by assuring them of virtually no restrictions on the entry or repatriation of capital, profits, or salaries, especially joint ventures that will gradually evolve into enterprises with local management and local majority ownership. The government especially encourages foreign investment that transfers technological expertise and provides training opportunities for local managers. The second goal is promoted through round table discussions between the government and the business community.

In Israel, the government encourages foreign investment. Some incentives are provided for export-oriented industries and for job creation in development and other areas. In Israel, there are no restrictions for foreign investors regarding the forms of doing business, except in certain sectors of the defense industry. There is no government assistance or approval for projects in the saturated economic branches.

Kuwait's main goal is decreasing dependence on oil revenues, therefore it has several economic goals, including investing overseas, encouraging the private sector to be responsible for the economic development of the country, and the introduction of a counter-trade offset program (Ernst & Young 1993: 3). In general, foreign companies are encouraged to do business in Kuwait as long as they contribute to broadening the industrial and commercial base of the economy of the country. In other words, foreign investments are expected to assist the country in reducing its dependence on oil revenues.

Kuwaiti businessmen have been famous as traders; therefore, they are given preference by the government. However, many business opportunities exist for foreign companies and investors in Kuwait, which are necessary for it to meet its economic objectives to rebuild and strengthen the economy. Specific activities are not allowed by foreign companies, including government contracts, owning real estate, owning shares in local companies, and banking activities. The oil industry is entirely owned by the government. To encourage local industrial projects, exemptions from various taxes and duties may be given to foreign companies for up to 10 years, provided that Kuwaiti participation is at least 51%.

Is There a Right Local Partner?

In deciding on the right local partner, three important issues should be considered. First, the partner should have a product that perfectly fits your business. Second, management ability is and will be a critical factor in the venture. With the recent influx of Western managers, the great lack of national manpower and management, and the tremendous growth in the national economy, significant changes in the market will undoubtedly occur in the next decades. Third, a local partner must be able to provide a variety of contacts at a high ministerial level. Even though these contacts are necessary from time to time, it is equally important to have appropriate connections at the middle and upper-middle levels, and it is imperative that the joint-venture partner be able to provide such access.

However, one of the major restrictions on foreign investment is that Saudi Arabia's laws do not allow foreign firms to do business there under their own names. They should have a local partner, and the business should be conducted under the Saudi name. In Kuwait, the venture has no legal personality and does not require registration in the commercial register; the joint-venture partners are separately registered in their own names. The joint-venture agreement serves only to define the rights and obligations of the parties and the method of sharing profits and losses. Joint ventures may not issue negotiable shares or bonds.

Is There a Good Location in the Country?

Selecting a new location in any Middle East country is not as simple as it is in the United States. Strong support from the local government is critical to the success of the project. Your location is dependent on what kind of product or service is offered, how close you are to the source of supply, and how your strategy will achieve your goals.

In Egypt, there is a recent development in real estate which provides free land to investors for certain investment projects in the new industrial areas in Upper Egypt. Moreover, free zones have been set up where projects can be established without Egyptian equity participation. The establishment of free zones is intended to capitalize on Egypt's central geographical location in the Middle East and to encourage the use of the country as an export platform to the area and to Europe.

Although physically located in Egypt, the free zones are regarded as being outside of the country. The four types of free zone are (1) storage and warehousing, (2) mixing and repackaging, (3) assembly and manufacturing for exports, and (4) services.

Entities operating in the free zone of Egypt are exempt from all taxes, except for a fee of 1% of the cost, insurance, and freight value of commodities entering or leaving the free zone. Projects that do not involve the entry or exit of commodities are subject to an annual fee of 1% of project revenues. Free-zone projects are exempt from the regulations pertaining to importation and exportation.

The Saudi government provides a wide variety of incentives designed to promote industrial development within Saudi Arabia and, at the same time, to benefit local businesses. Incentives are provided to businesses in industrial cities for industrial expansion. In addition, in various parts of the Kingdom, the government has developed industrial parks where sites are provided for the erection of plants and industrial buildings and the erection of living quarters for the workforce. These sites are leased to industries for nominal rents, and utilities and similar services are provided at subsidized prices.

Israel's borders enclose a total of approximately 8,500 square miles, including the Golan Heights (approximately 463 square miles), but excluding Gaza, Jericho, and the West Bank. In Israel, factories are concentrated in Haifa and Tel Aviv–Jaffa, although an important industrial complex is developing around the new port of Ashdod. On the other side, Kuwait is geographically located between Iraq and Saudi Arabia on the northeast coast of the Persian Gulf. Kuwait has an area of 6,800 square miles.

Jordan is situated in the great land bridge between Europe, Africa, and Asia, covering an area of approximately 34,750 square miles. Its terrain provides a range of landscapes and climates; the Badia Plains lie to the east, with mountains in the center. The port of Aqaba, in the far south, gives Jordan a narrow outlet to the Red Sea. Projects in industrial estates are exempt from real estates taxes. Two industrial estates are currently in operation: one in Sahab (near Amman) and the other in Ibrid (approximately 46.5 miles north of Amman). The estates provide facilities for more than 600 industrial units of various sizes.

Do We Have to Balance Our Foreign Exchange Income and Expense?

In Egypt, because of the economic reforms and agreements reached with the International Monetary Fund (IMF), exchange control has been eliminated. Therefore, there are no restrictions on the repatriation of capital, profits, proceeds of sales, fees, and royalties.

In Israel, there are no exchange controls when foreign companies make investments, however, to avoid unnecessary repatriation problems later, foreign residents should comply with certain formalities that will enable them to repatriate their funds or place them in a freely convertible account (Price Waterhouse 1995: 49).

In Kuwait, the unity of currency is the dinar (KD), which is divided to 1,000 fils. The dinar is freely convertible. Kuwait pegs its dinar to a basket of currencies, although it is significantly weighted toward the U.S. dollar, the currency it receives for its oil exports. Kuwait has no exchange controls.

Saudi Arabia has no exchange controls, no special exchange rates for special transactions, and no emergency rules enabling legislation relative to exchange controls. Also, there are no restrictions or requirements with respect to the use of currency accounts by domestic or foreign investors and traders. If one cannot satisfy these requirements, it may not be worthwhile to open negotiations.

THE MANAGERIAL AND FINANCIAL ISSUES

Middle East joint ventures may limit American MNCs to retain control over the decisions of foreign subsidiaries. This control issue can be the source of many conflicts between MNCs and their local partners. Where the special advantage of the MNC lies in a unification of markets and the rationalization of production, finance, and other functions on a regional or a global basis, the interest of any sub-unit, and local partners owning shares in that sub-unit, is likely to conflict with global objectives and opportunities. As an example, to build volume, the firm might prefer to adopt an appropriate transfer-pricing policy that would leave all profits in the marketing subsidiary only partly owned.

Although experience in conducting Middle East joint-venture projects is still limited, a review of the five major issues that have been encountered in negotiations may be of interest to MNCs considering this type of investment.

Access to and Pricing of Raw Materials and Final Products

Access to and pricing of raw materials and utilities may pose frequent problems in Middle East joint ventures. The Joint Venture Law of Saudi Arabia requires a joint-venture company to give priority to Saudi sources of necessary raw materials and other goods. In their purchase of items such as machinery, equipment, raw materials, fuel, spare parts, vehicles, and office equipment for their own use, joint ventures have the right to decide whether to purchase the goods in Saudi Arabia or abroad. They also have the right to export their products themselves and to determine the export prices of the products themselves.

Because Saudi Arabia is heavily dependent on imports even for certain basic foodstuffs, prices can be high in relation to many Western countries. As a result, price controls have been instituted for basic foodstuffs and commodities, while certain food items are subsidized. Electricity rates and domestic fuel prices also are very low. Persistent overcharging for controlled commodities can result in fines, the closure of premises, and imprisonment.

Pricing products or services may be an essential factor for the success of joint ventures in the Middle East. A MNC may need to understand how it is going to price its products or services to be sold in either the local or international market in its feasibility study. In Egypt, the market is quite sensitive to the price of a product or a service, and quality takes second place to cost. In most cases, the Egyptian government accepts contracts with low bids, regardless of quality. In Israel, price is one of the major factors affecting purchasing decisions by Israeli companies and consumers. Joint-venture companies often use low market penetration pricing during the introduction of a new product, followed by a price increase once the market share and reputation are established. Since most distributors prefer exclusivity, a special pricing clause may be incorporated into the contract.

Labor and Labor Cost Problems

The most important variables of the production and production costs of joint ventures are the availability of a skilled, educated labor force at a low cost. The lack of a skilled workforce is a major problem in Saudi Arabia. Saudi employees comprise only 20% of the total workforce in the Kingdom; the 80% represents foreign employees. The Saudi workforce is small in relation to total population, because women generally are not allowed to work. Religious culture, as it is applied in Saudi Arabia, requires the complete separation of the sexes in both the workplace and in educational places.

Egypt's plentiful labor pool and the availability of a reasonably well-educated, English-speaking, and inexpensive labor force are its major strengths. Labor costs are a fraction of those in industrialized countries such as the United States, Japan, and countries in Western Europe. In 1996, the workforce was estimated to include about 16.4 million workers, of whom 2.87 million, about 17.5%, were unemployed. Underemployment probably affects one-third to one-half of all workers. Approximately 2.9 million Egyptians work overseas (U.S. Department of State—Egypt 1997).

Under the Egyptians' companies law, the number of Egyptian employees should be at least 90% of the total employees, and their wages and salaries should not be less than 80% of the total amounts paid, with the exception of the technical administrative staff, which should not be less than 75% of the employees and 70% of the total amounts paid to such staff (EY Investment Profile—Egypt 1998: 2).

In Saudi Arabia and Kuwait, wage and salary levels vary significantly, depending on the nature of the job, the location of the job, and the nationality of the employee. Foreign employees usually receive a housing bonus in addition to their typical base pay. For the business entity, the payroll costs represent a significant element of total production costs. The Western workforce is paid higher salaries by Western standards, therefore some business firms and government agencies are replacing Western expatriates with Asians and Far Easterners, where possible, to reduce payroll costs. However, the government has imposed some restriction on the employment of non-Saudis/non-Kuwaitis to ensure the use of Saudi or Kuwaiti national employees, respectively. The government does not control wage rates, and there is no legislation to impose a decrease or an increase in wages and salaries.

On the negative side, foreign companies are strictly enforced to meet requirements for employing a minimum number of national employees. This issue is considered one of the most difficult faced in doing business in Saudi Arabia and Kuwait, and procedures and preferences will continue to favor local companies. Minimum legal working conditions, compensations, and benefits apply to all workers. Technical and skilled labor is not widely available.

Domestic Sales versus Exports

In Egypt, foreign MNCs can sell directly within the country, as part of their manufacturing or assembly operations in Egypt, if they are registered to make direct sales. However, most foreign MNCs rely on Egyptian companies for wholesale and retail distribution, ensuring their effectiveness through staff training programs in Egypt and abroad, through a supply of short-term home office personnel to work with the Egyptian company in Egypt, and through frequent visits by marketing and support staff.

In Saudi Arabia, sometimes the Saudi government wants the joint venture to market its products internally in order to meet its domestic needs. More often, however, it is more interested in earning foreign exchange by exporting the product and resisting pressure for entry into the domestic market. For example, at the feasibility report study stage, the Saudi party should be responsible for providing the supply-and-demand information on the products and the trend for future sales of the products. In the joint-venture contract, the provisions on the quantity to be sold on the domestic market should be included, as well as the sales channel and sales method.

In April 1994, Israel and the Palestinian Authority signed an agreement that allowed for the free movement of goods and services between Israel and the West Bank and Gaza Strip, and also established a special customs union between the two sides.

At the feasibility study report stage, joint-venture parties should carefully study the available information on supply and demand in respect to the products intended to be used by the potential joint ventures and the trend of international markets. Based on this data, the parties may then decide on the quantity of products to be exported and where and how to market them. All of this should be clearly provided for in the joint-venture contracts.

Foreign Exchange Control and Regulations

Saudi Arabia does not impose foreign exchange control regulations on the entry or repatriation of cash, funds, profits, or salaries of people working in Saudi Arabia. American firms establishing permanent joint ventures within Saudi Arabia need a foreign capital investment license. Royalties and service fees may be repatriated freely, however, these payments may be subject to withholding tax. The liquidation of investments can involve a lengthy, complex process. The Saudi Riyal is freely convertible through banks or money exchangers, both of which are licensed and regulated by the Saudi Arabian Monetary Agency (SAMA). Guarantees against inconvertibility are unlikely to be required.

The Egyptian government is encouraging the inflow of foreign currency through tourism and exports and reducing its reliance on imports. Moreover, the Egyptian pound is freely convertible through banks or money exchange companies, both of which are licensed and regulated by the Central Bank of Egypt.

The Risk of Expropriation

As a result of the lack of exchange controls in Saudi Arabia, a foreign investor is not restricted to the repatriation of share capital, loans, dividends, and income to the home country, provided that taxation and company tax requirements have been met. However, a portion of profits must be set aside up to a certain limit prior to dividend payments. American MNCs are naturally interested in reducing the risks of expropriation or confiscation by the government, therefore Saudi Arabia is the best market with which to be associated, with the lowest risk of expropriation.

In Egypt, Decree 119 of February 1991 was issued to remove most foreign exchange controls and free exchange control rates to move with market forces. Moreover, in April 1994, the Foreign Exchange Law 79 of 1979 was amended to allow the free transfer of foreign currency into and out of the country. Also, no exchange control regulations or monetary restrictions are imposed on the repatriation of funds, profits, and 50% of salaries pursuant to foreign investments.

Israel is a member of the Multinational Investor Guarantee Agency (MIGA) of the World Bank. In this case, foreign investors may purchase insurance against political and non-business risks with respect to recognized investment in Israel.

ACCOUNTING AND FINANCIAL REPORTING

In this section, accounting and financial reporting requirements as they affect foreign investors in the Middle East countries will be discussed briefly. A more detailed discussion of the accounting systems and practices will be covered in Chapter 5. Special attention will be given to the U.S. Generally Accepted Accounting Principles (GAAP) and information disclosure requirements as compared to those of the five selected Middle East countries.

Egypt

In Egypt, the accounting and financial reporting requirements were taken originally from the British accounting system. There are two different sets of Egyptian GAAPs; the first is required from the public-sector firms owned by the Egyptian government, and it is a uniform accounting system, similar to the French uniform accounting system, applicable to all industries. The second set of GAAPs, discussed below, is applicable to private and foreign companies operating in Egypt.

In general, the Egyptian GAAPs, applicable to private and foreign companies, can be described briefly by the following: (1) Financial statements should be prepared using historical cost concepts; (2) Book and tax accounts are generally the same; (3) Relations with parent and related party transactions must be disclosed; and (4) Accounting principles and practices follow internationally accepted standards.

Egypt does not have an organization that promulgates Egyptian Generally

Accepted Accounting Principles, similar to the Financial Accounting Standards Board of the United States. In response to the growing demand, this situation is changing; the Egyptian Society of Accountants and Auditors is reviewing standards issued by various international bodies with the end goal of promulgating Egyptian standards.

Israel

A joint venture is not organized as a separate legal entity, however, it may be established as (1) a contractual relationship between the participants specific to a particular transaction or activity, (2) a formal partnership in which each participant assumes liability under the terms of the partnerships' ordinance, or (3) a company in which the participants in the joint venture are represented as shareholders.

The only financial statements required by the companies' ordinance are a balance sheet and an income statement. However, under the 1968 Securities Law and the 1993 Securities Regulations, companies offering their securities for sale to the public are required to prepare and publish a complete set of financial statements, including the consolidated balance sheet and income statement, a statement of cash flow, changes in shareholder's equity, and comprehensive notes to the financial statements.

Two main bodies regulate and promote the accounting profession in Israel: the Auditors' Council and the Institute of Certified Public Accountants in Israel (ICPA), established in 1931. The ICPA's pronouncements on auditing and accounting are binding, and its views on related subjects are solicited by the government, the Knesset and various public bodies. In addition, publicly traded companies must issue unaudited quarterly financial statements with a review report.

Jordan

According to the Jordanian Commercial Law, all companies are required to keep a general journal, inventory records, and a correspondence register. All accounting books and records must be kept in Arabic or English. In 1989, the Jordanian Association of Certified Public Accountants passed a resolution adopting the IASs.

Public shareholding companies, limited liability companies, and operating foreign branches must submit audited financial statements to the Ministry of Industry and Trade and Income Tax Department. Unaudited, half yearly financial statements must be submitted to the Amman Stock Exchange and the Central Bank of Jordan. However, regional offices are not required to file financial statements.

Kuwait

All business foreign companies and partnerships doing business in Kuwait are required to keep adequate financial records, including a general journal, inventory sheets, a general ledger, an expenses analysis journal, and a stock record.

An annual audit and compliance with the standards promulgated by the IASC are required for shareholding and limited liability companies.

Foreign contractors are required to present audited financial statements of their Kuwaiti operations in support of their income tax filings. They do not need to be maintained in Arabic. However, for public shareholding companies, the audited balance sheet, the income statement, the directors' report, and the auditors' report, must be submitted in Arabic within three months after the end of the company's fiscal year to the Ministry of Commerce and Industry, to the Kuwait Stock Exchange, and to the general assembly of shareholders.

Saudi Arabia

All companies formed in Saudi Arabia are required to comply with Saudi Generally Accepted Accounting Principles. These companies must have their financial statements audited by an auditor licensed in Saudi Arabia and must file annually with the Ministry of Commerce. All joint ventures are required to maintain the following books in Arabic and keep them in Saudi Arabia: (1) a journal, (2) a general ledger, and (3) an inventory book, including a comprehensive trial balance. The inventory book is similar to a detailed balance sheet and income statement. The final version of the accounting system must be filed with the Department of Zakat and Income Tax (DZIT).

The Standard of General Presentation and Disclosure (SGPD), issued by the Ministry of Commerce on May 11, 1990, is the only form of generally accepted accounting principles. It states the requirements of general presentation and disclosure in the financial statements of profit-oriented entities and consolidated financial statements, and provides pro-forma examples of presentation. The SGPD also determines the treatment of accounting changes and contingent gains or losses. In general, a joint venture, for financial reporting purposes, adopts the international practice of accrual base of accounting. American–Saudi joint ventures use the U.S. dollar as the bookkeeping unit and produce an Arabic version of the accounting statements in Saudi currency.

The SGPD requires that financial statements include a profit-and-loss statement, a statement of appropriation of profits, a balance sheet, and an auditor's report. The statement of source and use of funds are included, but not mandatory. No specific presentation format is imposed, except for banks. A joint venture, with its auditor, can establish its own format.

The accounting profession in Saudi Arabia is controlled by the Ministry of Commerce. It has developed at an accelerated pace, compared to other parts of the world. The Ministry has issued the Saudi Arabian SGPD and the Saudi Arabian Auditing Standards as main guidelines for the profession. It is required that at least 20% of an accounting firm's technical staff consist of Saudi nationals.

FINANCIAL INCENTIVES FOR JOINT VENTURES

In Egypt, foreign investment is governed by Law No. 8 of 1997, the Investment Law. The goal of this law is to offer preferential treatment to foster private-sector investment, including that by foreign MNCs. The government's policy is to offer several incentives, including tax exemptions, for 5, 10, 15, or 20 years, reduced import duties, and the elimination of exchange controls, to encourage foreign investment, particularly in projects that earn foreign currency and reduce the country's reliance on imports. Moreover, free zones have been set up where projects can be established without having Egyptian equity participation. Other financial incentives granted to foreign MNCs include freedom from price controls and guarantees against nationalization and confiscation.

In Israel, the government does not impose restrictions on the level of foreign ownership. Any new or expanded industrial or tourism operations may enjoy any or all of the following incentives: (1) company tax rates of 10% to 25%, which depend on the level of foreign ownership; (2) dividend withholding tax or branch tax of 15%; and (3) loans or grant and loan packages, up to 70% of all project expenditures.

In Jordan, the government encourages industrial investment and offers incentives for certain projects, mainly in the form of tax exemptions. Moreover, certain businesses established in the free zones and industrial sites are eligible for tax and other exemptions. Approved projects may also benefit by importing fixed assets into Jordan without payment of import duties for a period of up to three years. The 1987 Jordanian Encouragement of Investment Law (revised in 1988) accords generous incentives to domestic and foreign investors on an equal basis. For foreign investors, the transfer of profits realized on foreign capital invested in the country and the repatriation of foreign capital invested is guaranteed by law. Interest earned by outside parties on credit facilities extended to the government of Jordan, or to Jordanian financial institutions is tax exempt. For any approved economic project by the committee, a foreign investor enjoys two additional exemptions:

1. Exemption from income tax and real estate taxes for five years.
2. Exemption of fixed assets from customs duties, imports, and other fees.

In Kuwait, to encourage local industrial projects, exemptions from various taxes and duties may be given to foreign companies for up to 10 years, provided that Kuwaiti participation is at least 51%.

The Saudi government provides non-tax incentives, such as loans of up to 80% of fixed assets for agricultural projects under SR 3 million and 40% for projects over SR 3 million. In addition, the government will fund 90% of the cost of new agricultural projects in specified regions, if the projects are designed to help the government meet specified national objectives.

The Saudi Industrial Development Fund (SIDF) grants loans to industrial institutions amounting to 50% of the total cost of the project. These are recovered within five to 10 years after a grace period, usually ranging from one to one-and-one-half years, beginning at production. The fund does not charge interest on these loans, but does charge annual administrative fees amounting to 2.5% of the outstanding loan value.

Foreign investors in Saudi Arabia are allowed access to local sources for credit facility options, including medium- and long-term finance offered by specialized credit institutions established by the government.

JOINT VENTURE INCOME TAX

MNCs should be interested in opportunities for the regional coordination of business and investment activities in the Middle East. The expected benefits of a Middle East plan include not only taxation but also customs duties, centralization of management, and professional training programs, among many others. An obvious and an important trend in the area toward customs duty harmonization is the formation of the GCC. Products manufactured in a GCC country can, in general, be exported to another GCC country without customs tariffs if they are regarded as a national product.

Other regional trends are becoming obvious. Most Middle East countries have amended their tax laws to provide greater incentives for foreign MNCs and to include lowering tax rates to the levels of many developed countries. In the remaining part of this chapter, only one part of tax incentives will be covered in detail, that is, the tax holidays in the five selected countries. Other incentives will be discussed in the chapters that deal with the taxation issues of Middle East countries.

Egypt

In Egypt, the corporate tax system is neutral toward foreign investors. Under the Egyptian Corporate Tax Law, a foreign corporation is taxed only on its Egyptian source income. However, the effect of the Egyptian tax system may be mitigated by bilateral tax treaties. Unfortunately, there is no uniform method of accounting prescribed for foreign joint venture taxpayers. Any approved standard accounting method that clearly reflects the taxpayer's income and conforms to the generally accepted accounting practice of the industry may be adopted.

Under the Egyptian Corporate Tax Law, taxable corporate income is total revenue after deducting all expenses, exempt income, and relief for losses brought forward (allowed for five years only). In general, the business profit of a corporation, for tax purposes, is computed from its profit and loss account (income statement), as determined from its books of account. However, there are several important tax issues multinational companies need to know, and brief guidelines are provided below to help companies planning for Egyptian joint ventures.

1. *Foreign exchange gains and losses* are considered as taxable income and allowable deduction, respectively, in the tax year they are realized or sustained.

2. *Royalties* are treated as ordinary income and are taxed at corporate rates. Royalties that are paid to a foreign entity are subject to corporate tax at a rate of 40% plus 2% development duty tax on taxable amounts exceeding 18,000 Egyptian pounds levied on an amount net of an arbitrary deduction for expenses. This tax is usually withheld at the source.

3. *Depletion of the oil and gas exploration*: Depreciation and amortization of oil and gas equipment and exploration and development expenses is accomplished through a cost recovery formula. Exploration expenditures are recovered over five years, and development expenditures are recovered over a period from five to 10 years, while operating expenses are recovered immediately. Cost recovery (tax depletion) is limited to the value of the cost recovery pool.

4. *Losses*: Operating losses may be carried forward for five years. Loss carry backs are not permitted. Operating losses may not be transferred to other profitable entities within a related group. Loss carry forward is allowed but not on the total company concept. It is allowed only for every separate concession; no carry back is allowed.

5. *Tax holidays* are available to encourage foreign investment in a variety of activities, including land reclamation, cultivation of arid land and the desert, industry, tourism, and housing. However, there are no tax holidays included in the concession agreement between Amoco and Egypt for oil exploration and production.

6. *Tax rates*: The standard corporate tax rate is 42% of taxable income. However, the tax rate applicable to exporting and industrial (manufacturing) activities is 34%. Oil exploration production companies are subject to corporate tax at a rate of 40.55%. An additional 2% development duty tax is assessed on any taxable amount over LE 18,000.

7. *Foreign tax credits*: There are no tax credits for foreign taxes, except as allowed by bilateral tax treaties. However, foreign taxes may be taken as a deduction for Egyptian tax purposes in situations not covered by tax treaties. In general, relief from double taxation is provided to foreign investors by allowing deduction of the tax paid to another country and by treaty.

Israel

The Israeli government imposes no restrictions on the level of foreign ownership, however, the reduced company tax rates on income vary according to the percentage of foreign ownership of the company. Companies with foreign ownership exceeding 25% are considered foreign investors' companies, and they enjoy a maximum of 10 years' tax reduction to 25%.

Jordan

Under the Encouragement of Investment Law No. 11 of 1987, the net profit on approved projects is exempt from income tax for up to five years. This begins on the date of operation. Moreover, all approved industrial, trading, investment, and service projects established in the free zones, Zarqa and Aqaba, enjoy the following incentives:

1. Exemption of the project's profits income taxes for 12 years;
2. Exemption from income and social welfare taxes on salaries and allowances to non-citizen employees working in the free zone;
3. Exemption from custom duty, import fees, and other taxes of goods imported from the free zones; and
4. Exemption of the buildings and structures constructed in the free zones from license, license fees, and property taxes.

Kuwait

Foreign companies may not be able to obtain tax exemption, unless they are government-to-government contracts, such as for defense purposes. In general, there is a 10-year tax holiday for a new industrial project. Investment incentives (e.g., grants, tax deferrals, special access to credit, import quota exceptions, etc.) are available to foreign investors, and special treatment is given to them. At the moment, incentives—in the form of exemptions from import duties and corporate income taxes for periods of up to 10 years—are officially available only for industrial undertakings approved by the Council of Ministers. There is a movement underway to expand the investment incentives available to foreign investors. A special committee was appointed in March 1997 to review the existing obstacles to foreign investment and to propose legislative changes to improve Kuwait's attractiveness to foreign investment (U.S. Department of State—Kuwait 1997).

Saudi Arabia

Saudi Arabia grants a 10-year tax holiday on profits arising from new capital investments in existing industrial joint-venture projects. The tax exemption is granted to foreign companies participating in industrial projects in Saudi Arabia, as stated in the Foreign Investment Law. It is applicable to any future foreign capital investment made in the expansion of an existing industrial joint venture.

The Saudi–American joint venture must qualify for and meet several licensing and administrative conditions set forth in the Foreign Capital Investment Law (FCIL). The main conditions for deciding whether the investment qualifies for tax holiday are: (1) The foreign capital must be invested in development projects (excluding petroleum and mineral extraction projects); (2) The investment must be accompanied by foreign technology, know-how, or expertise; (3) The investment must contribute to the training of Saudi personnel. In addition, the foreign capital must be invested in the following activities: (1) productive industrial development projects, (2) productive agricultural development projects, (3) health development projects, (4) provision of services, and (5) contracting.

For American–Saudi joint ventures to enjoy the benefits provided for in the FCIL, American participation cannot exceed 75%. The major benefits of qualifying under the FCIL are as follows: (1) exemption from income tax and company tax for a period of 10 years in the case of industrial joint ventures, and for a period of five years in the case of non-industrial joint ventures; (2) the joint venture can enjoy other privileges given to national industries (such as exemption of duties in the import of machinery, equipment, raw materials, and so forth); and (3) the ability to acquire any real estate required by the project in accordance with the Law for Non-Saudi Ownership of Real Estate, at a nominal price. Moreover, the FCIL extends the benefits of the 10-year income and corporate tax exemption to capital expansions of existing industrial projects, made through either new capital infusion or the capitalization of undistributed profits held as reserves in the company.

The American companies should note that the income and corporate tax exemption will be applicable only to the profits arising from the capital expansion portion of the project, not including the profits arising from the original project.

In concluding this section, foreign capital investment in an economic project in Saudi Arabia enjoys a tax holiday for 10 years if the project is agricultural or industrial (manufacturing), or for five years, if the project is service oriented. To qualify for the tax holiday, Saudi participation in the business entity must not be less than 25%. Due to local regulations and preferences for Saudi products, it is generally beneficial to have at least 50% to 51% Saudi ownership. In addition, up to 50% government financing and other incentives may be available. Full repatriation of capital and profits is guaranteed.

SUMMARY AND CONCLUSIONS

This chapter introduced, discussed, and analyzed some guidelines on the important issues of managerial, financial reporting, and taxation of American joint ventures in Middle East countries. Countries' rules, regulations, facts, and experiences, which uniquely affect management and the financial reporting of American–Middle East joint ventures, were also discussed.

In most Middle East countries, a good, profitable performance has been achieved in almost all of the joint ventures that have gone into production or operation. All five countries included in the study have been shifting to a new development strategy in the past few years, with the main emphasis on industrialization and economic diversification. MNCs involved in exporting to Middle

East countries are realizing that the best way to expand their market share is to establish a joint venture there.

Five major issues have been encountered in managing American joint ventures in the Middle East. They include: (1) pricing and marketing decisions of products, (2) determining what constitutes fair compensation for labor, which joint ventures will be obligated to pay, (3) designing the appropriate tax and non-tax incentive system that fits the Middle East countries' joint ventures, (4) keeping a foreign exchange account sufficient to meet foreign obligations, and (5) reducing the risks of expropriation or confiscation by American investors, significant issues that should be considered before starting the joint venture.

For financial reporting requirements, American joint ventures should report their financial and accounting activities to both the U.S. parent company and the local partner group. They should design and structure their financial and accounting system in accordance with the relevant laws of the country. Most American joint ventures use the U.S. dollar as the bookkeeping unit and produce an Arabic version of the accounting statements in the local currency.

For tax planning strategies, several unique issues of the five Middle East countries' Joint Venture Income Tax were discussed, including tax holidays, losses, tax on reinvested profits, dividends, royalties, and tax rates. Most local governments provide tax and non-tax incentives for joint ventures, if the projects are designed to help the government meet specified national objectives. American investment in an economic project enjoys a tax holiday for 10 years if it is an agricultural or an industrial (manufacturing) project, or five years if the project is service oriented. Full repatriation of capital and profits is guaranteed. Moreover, customs duties on all imported machinery, equipment, spare parts, and raw materials are waived unless the items are also produced locally. In addition, tariff protection from competing imports will be granted if the local product is of an approved standard.

There are some disadvantages with local tax practices, and American companies should consider these in their tax-planning strategies. They include: (1) The tax law does not recognize loss carryovers; (2) Income from subsidiaries operating in a country cannot be consolidated for tax purposes; (3) A withholding tax is sometimes imposed on the value of services performed outside of the country, such as design or engineering work done in the foreign partner's home country; and (4) Royalty payments for proprietary technology and management fees are taxed on the assumption that they represent 100% profit to the recipient.

Three important recommendations are suggested: (1) opening the Middle East financial and capital stock markets and allowing equity participation in joint stock investment companies for non-nationals; (2) setting up tax- and duty-free zones for industrial development and allowing foreign investors to own commercial real estate; and (3) issuing new regulations dealing with pollution control and environmental protection and industrial safety and security.

In conclusion, American companies that are considering joint ventures in Middle East countries need to balance the advantages and disadvantages of different projects with regard to their companies' global objectives, financial resources, and limitations. The maximum financial and political protection in foreign countries can only be achieved through joint ventures with carefully selected projects, especially Third World countries.

REFERENCES

Abdallah, Wagdy M. *International Transfer Pricing Policies: Decision-Making Guidelines for Multinational Companies*. Westport, CT: Quorum Books, 1989.

———. "What You Need to Know before Entering into a Joint Venture in an LDC." *Corporate Controller* (May–June 1991), 35–38.

———. "Management Accounting Problems in China." *Management Accounting* (April 1992), 58–61.

Azzam, Henry T. "Joint Ventures in the Kingdom." *Middle East Executive Reports* (March 1993), 19.

Brigges, James R. "Joint Venturing in the Middle East." In John D. Carter, Robert F. Cushman, and C. Scott Hartz (eds.), *The Handbook of Joint Venturing*. Homewood, Ill.: Richard D. Irwin, 1988, 303–317.

Cohen, Jerome Alan. "Equity Joint Ventures." *The China Business Review* (November–December 1982), 23–30.

Crossborder Monitor. "Middle East: 1998–2002." New York: The Economist Intelligence Unit, Vol. 6 (September 1998), 7.

Ernst & Young. *Doing Business in Kuwait*. New York: Ernst & Young International, 1993.

EY Investment Profile—Egypt. http://mbendi.co.za/ernsty/eyegeyip.html, June 1998.

Harrington, Kathryn R. *Strategies for Joint Ventures*. Lexington, Mass.: Lexington Books, D.C. Heath & Company, 1985.

———. *Managing for Joint Venture Success*. Lexington, Mass.: Lexington Books, D.C. Heath & Company, 1986.

Mungai, David. "Middle East and Africa." *World Trade* 13 (February 2000), 62–68.

Price Waterhouse. *Doing Business in Israel*. New York: Price Waterhouse, 1995.

Riordan, E. Mick, Uri Dadush, Jalal Jalali, Shane Streifel, Milan Brahmbhatt, and Kazue Takagaki. "The World Economy and Its Implications for the Middle East and North Africa, 1998–2010." In Nemat Shafik (ed.), *Prospects for Middle Eastern and North African Economies*. New York: St. Martin's Press, 1998, 15–46.

Robock, Stefan H. and Kenneth Simmonds. *International Business and Multinational Enterprises*, 3rd ed. Homewood, Ill.: Richard D. Irwin, 1983.

U.S. Department of State. *Economic Policy and Trade Practices: Egypt*. Country Reports on Economic Policy and Trade Practices, August 21, 1997.

———. *Economic Policy and Trade Practices: Israel*. Country Reports on Economic Policy and Trade Practices, July 21, 1997.

———. *Economic Policy and Trade Practices: Jordan*. Country Reports on Economic Policy and Trade Practices, August 21, 1997.

———. *International Trade Administration—Country Commercial Guide—Kuwait—Investment Climate*. October 1997.

Part II

Financial Reporting and Performance Evaluation in the Middle East

Chapter 5

Accounting Systems and Practices of Selected Middle East Countries: Comparative Analysis with U.S. GAAP and IAS

This chapter examines more closely the accounting systems and practices in selected "strategic" Middle East countries: Egypt, Israel, Kuwait, Jordan, and Saudi Arabia. Specific knowledge of accounting in a country is needed when financial statements from that country are analyzed. The five countries selected are all significant economies in the world, and they are home to the vast majority of the world's MNCs. Understanding how accounting rules and standards are established, and the effect on the practice, is important for knowing why, for example, a country requires that accounting be done in a particular way.

BACKGROUND

Corporate executive officers and corporate controllers of MNCs make daily investment and financial decisions by relying on relevant accounting and non-accounting information. Comparable accounting information is essential to ensure the free flow of capital across international borders. In recent years, the growth of cross-border financial transactions has led a number of organizations to work toward harmonizing accounting rules and practices. Among these groups seeking to harmonize global accounting practices is the IASC, which has been the most active group, but not the only one. It is assisted in its efforts by other groups such as the World Bank. The efforts of the IASC and others have led to the adoption of internationally accepted standards in many countries, however, such acceptance varies from one country to another.

If the accounting systems and practices of Egypt, Israel, Jordan, Kuwait, and Saudi Arabia were identical, there would be no problem for international investors, creditors, and capital market regulators in understanding the published financial statements of domestic and multinational companies operating in any one of the five countries. Unfortunately, this is not the case here. Given the lack of accounting comparability and harmonization between accounting systems in Middle East countries, it is not surprising then that investing and financing decisions tend to be risky.

In an attempt to attract higher levels of foreign investment, Middle East countries are responding with several tools, including the following: (1) increasing the flow of economic information to investors; (2) broadening the use of international accounting standards; and (3) improving the efficiency of their capital markets (*Crossborder Monitor* 1997). Due to the fact that the quality of financial disclosure influences the quality of decisions made by investors and creditors, it is essential for foreign investors and creditors to understand the accounting systems and practices of Middle East countries, for several reasons: (1) to compare the financial reports of MNCs operating in Arab countries and Israel; (2) to analyze the differences in financial reporting systems and auditing standards and practices of Middle East countries; (3) to know the effect of accounting differences on asset valuation and income determination of local or joint ventures operating in Middle East countries; (4) to decide where to invest at a high rate of return and a low rate of political risk; and (5) to look for the possibility of designing the appropriate uniform or harmonized accounting systems and practices of the selected Middle East countries.

This chapter presents a brief overview of the economies of the five selected Middle East countries and their accounting principles and practices, including the similarities and differences between their own accounting GAAP, U.S. GAAP, and IAS. Table 5–1 summarizes the economies of the selected Middle East countries. Then the key accounting issues such as investments, inventory, asset valuation, equity method, consolidation, deferred income taxes, foreign currency translation and transactions, and financial reporting requirements will be discussed in detail. The 10 accounting issues are summarized in Table 5–2. Finally, important guidelines and major recommendations to help investors and creditors make investing and financing decisions in the Middle East will be presented.

ACCOUNTING PRINCIPLES AND PRACTICES

Egypt

Overview

Egypt is the largest Arab country by population. It is in the heart of the Middle East, it boasts a reasonably well-educated labor force, and it is increasingly open to the global market, including international exporters and investors. Egypt's fiscal and monetary reforms since 1991 have created a stable currency and have allowed it to accumulate reserves equal to one-and-one-half years' worth of imports (*Country Commercial Guide—Egypt*, 1996).

In the 1980s, Egypt faced the problem of low productivity and poor economic management, compounded by the adverse social effects of excessive population growth, high inflation, and massive urban overcrowding. In 1991, the Egyptian government, to alleviate the pressure, undertook wide-ranging structural reform measures. Egypt's reform efforts—and its participation in the Persian Gulf War—also led to massive debt relief under the Paris Club arrangements. Although the pace of reform has been slower than expected under the IMF programs, substantial progress has been made in improving macroeconomic performance. Budget deficits have been slashed, while foreign reserves in 1997 were at an all-time high (ibid). At the present time, Egypt has been moving toward a more decentralized, market-oriented economy and more private companies. These economic reforms and growing investment opportunities have encouraged increasing foreign investment.

In January 1996, the Egyptian government made a major change in the history of the Egyptian economy to privatize its extensive public holdings by establishing a new cabinet to sell off state-owned factories and other companies to both Egyptian and foreign investors. In 1997, several economic laws were introduced, and some were approved, to facilitate the participation of the private sector and to help American and other foreign firms do business in Egypt. Investors in financially insecure businesses will be required to maintain employment levels in the firms they take over, ensuring that layoffs do not cause opposition to the process. Although the government plans major reforms to business legislation, progress is likely to be slow. In May 1997, the new Investment Incentives and Guarantee Laws were approved. Moreover, the Egyptian government, in its next 20-year economic and social development plan, suggests continued government support to restructure the economy and to create a more favorable climate for private firms.

The Egyptian GAAP

In Egypt, the public accounting tradition is the oldest in the Middle East. Borrowing from the British, it was the first in the region to organize its own national accounting profession and to form its own institute of auditors. Outside of Egypt, there were no local accounting bodies. To practice as a public accounting firm, membership in the British public accounting profession was considered sufficient. At the end of World War II, in what was then Palestine, there were no more than five accountants who had British credentials to practice auditing (Gress 1985). Prior to 1954, Egyptian regulations did not legally require an audit of corporate accounts, yet it was done as part of good business practice.

The early start and good business practices notwithstanding, the changes in the style of government made for some detours in the development of Egyptian accounting practices. In the 1950s, the nationalization of important industries put public accounting in cold storage. As noted by Amer (1969), the British-based system was overtaken by the nationalization of the key sector of economy. According to AlHashim (1977), socialism undermined the profession of public accounting. Briston and El-Ashker (1984) show how the change in government

Table 5-1
The Economies of Selected Middle East Countries

Economic Factors			Economic Indicators				
			Egypt	Israel	Jordan	Kuwait	S. Arabia
GDP	PPP		$267.1B	$96.7B	$20.7B	$46.3B	$206.5B
	R.G.R.		5.2%	1.9%	5.3%	1%	4%
	Pc-PPP		$4,400	$17,500	$4,800	$22,300	$10,300
	Com-pos-ite	Agr.	17%	2%	6%	0%	6%
		Ind.	32%	17%	30%	53%	46%
		Ser.	51%	81%	64%	47%	48%
Inflation Rate	CPI		4.9%	9%	3%	3.2%	0%
Labor Force	Total		17.4M	2.3M	1.15M+ 300,000 FW	1.1M (68% FW)	7M (35% FW)
	Agriculture		40%	2.6%	7.4%	3%	5%
	Services		38%	60.6%	62.2%	90%	70%
	Industry		22%	36.8%	20.4%	7%	25%
	Un. Rate		9.4%	7.7%	15 %	1.8%	NA
Budget	Revenues		$19.2B	$55B	$2.7B	$10.3B	$47.5B
	Exp.		$19.8B	$58B	$2.8B	$14.5B	$52.3B
Exports	Total value		$ 5.1B	$20.7B	$1.53B	$14.7B	$56.7B

	Commodities	Crude oil, Cotton	M&E, chem., agr. products	Fertilizers, agr. products, mfg. goods	Oil, refined products, fertilizers	Petroleum & petroleum products
	Partners	EU, U.S., Japan	EU, U.S., Japan	Iraq, India, S. Arabia, EU, UAE	U.S., Japan, Netherlands, Singapore	Japan, U.S., S. Korea, Singapore, France
Imports	Total value	$15.5B	$28.8B	$ 3.7B	$ 7.7B	$25.4B
	Commodities	Food, M&E, fertilizers	Mil. Eq., oil, cons. goods	Oil, food, M&E, goods	Food, vehicles, clothing	M&E, food, chemicals, vehicles
	Partners	EU, U.S., Japan	EU, U.S., Japan	EU, Iraq, U.S., Japan, Turkey	U.S., UK, Japan, Germany, Italy	U.S., UK, Japan, Germany, Italy, France
Debt	External	$30.5B	$18.7B	$7.3B	$8B	NA
Economic Aid	Recipient	ODA–$1.713B	$1.2B	ODA–$424M	0	Donor $100M–Leb.
Exchange Rates	Currency per U.S.$1	£E3.88	NIS3.534	JD0.709	KD0.3055	SR3.745

GDP = gross domestic product; PPP = purchasing power parity; R.G.R. = real growth rate; Pc-PPP = per capita purchasing power parity; CPI = consumer price index; Un. Rate = unemployment rate; ODA = official development assistance from OECD and OPEC members; FW = foreign work force; M&E = machinery and equipment; Mil. Eq. = military equipment.

Source: www.aol.com/Country Studies, May 1999.

Table 5–2
Accounting Differences as Compared with U.S. GAAP and IAS

Accounting Differences	United States	IAS	Egypt	Israel	Jordan	Kuwait	Saudi Arabia
1. Investments	ST-CA-FMV LT-Cost	ST-CA-LCM LT-Cost revalued amount	ST-CA-LCM LT-Cost	ST-CA-MV LT-LCM	Similar to IAS	ST/LT at Cost	ST-LCM LT-Cost
2. Inventory	FIFO/LIFO/ WA with LCM	FIFO/WA benchmark-LIFO allowed/ LCM	FIFO/ WA-LCM	FIFO& WA-LCM LIFO-not permitted	Follow IAS	FIFO/ WA-LCM	FIFO/ WA-LCM
3. Asset Valuation	CA-NRV/LCM NCA-Cost	CA-NRV/LCM NCA-Cost	CA-LCM NCA-Cost	CA-LCM NCA-MV	Follow IAS	CA-NRV/ LCM NCA-Cost	CA-LCM NCA-Cost
4. Equity Method	20-49% Significant influence but lack control	20-50% ownership, if short-term (cost method)	Used in most cases	25%-50% significant influence/no control	Follow IAS	Compliance with IAS	Cost method is usually used
5. Consolidation	50% or more– significant control–purchase method	More than 50%– pooling or purchase method		If voting control over 50%	Follow IAS	Compliance with IAS	Required but seldom prepared

6. Accounting for Income Taxes	Use liability method	Deferral or liability method	Liability method	Liability method	Follow IAS	Follow IAS	Liability method
7. Foreign Currency Translation	Local currency–functional/CR U.S.$–functional-temporal method	Local currency–functional/CR U.S.$–functional-temporal method	Not covered/ Companies use IAS	Subsidiaries independent/ CR, not independent Temporal	Follow IAS	CR-FE G/L treated in different ways	Not covered/ Companies use IAS
8. Accounting for Inflation	Optional–not required	GPP or CC Not mandatory	Not covered/ not used/ Inflation significant	GPP & CC Required	Follow IAS	Follow IAS	Not covered/ Inflation not significant
9. Provision and Reserves	General contingency reserves not permitted	Legal or constructive obligation	No general contingency/ only if permitted by statutory regulations	RE not appropriated for loss contingencies/ general reserves not permitted	Follow IAS	Compliance with IAS	Material contingencies not disclosed/ General contingencies not practiced
10. Disclosure	All basic financial statements/ Footnotes/ Uncertainties	BS/IS/CF/SH equity	BS/P&L/ Changes in CF/ Footnotes not essential	Basic financial statements/ Footnotes essential	Follow IAS	Compliance with IAS	BS/IS/ changes in OE

BS = balance sheet; CA = current assets; CC = current rate; CF = cash flow statement; CR = current rate; CR = current rate method; FE G/L = foreign exchange rate gains or losses; FMV = fair market value; GPP = general purchasing power; IS = income statement; LCM = lower of cost or market value; LT = long-term; MV = market value; NCA = net current assets; NRV = not realizable value; OE = owners' equity; P&L = profit and loss statement; RE = retained earings; SH = shareholders; ST = short-term; WA = weighted average method.

allowed Egypt to move away from socialism to adopt Western economic ideas and international accounting standards. Wallace (1990) argues that in a span of just 13 years, a developing country such as Egypt experimented with various foreign accounting systems without evolving an accounting system/culture unique to its own environment.

At present, Egypt has only statutory requirements and no specific body or guidance for accounting or auditing standards. It is generally accepted that foreign companies or joint ventures may prepare financial statements using historical cost principles. Accounting practices and principles follow internationally accepted accounting standards. Egypt does not have an organization that promulgates accounting standards, similar to the FASB in the United States, however, the Egyptian Society of Accountants has now begun to review international accounting and auditing standards and to use them to issue opinions that form the basis for Egyptian accounting standards.

Overall, the Egyptian GAAP has two different sets: the first is required from public-sector firms owned by the Egyptian government, and it is a uniform accounting system applicable to all industries. The second, discussed below, is applicable to private and foreign companies operating in Egypt. The Egyptian GAAP differs from the U.S. GAAP in the following ways:

1. The law and regulations do not address accounting principles. The law permits any GAAP, provided that such a principle is sound and the resulting financial statements are accurate.
2. Egypt does not have an organization that promulgates the GAAP. Accordingly, it recognizes pronouncements of the American Institute of Certified Public Accountants (AICPA), the FASB, and the IASC.
3. The Egyptian Society of Accountants and Auditors is reviewing standards issued by various international bodies with the end goal of promulgating Egyptian standards.

American joint ventures, such as Amoco-Egypt, keep three sets of books. One set is in U.S. dollars, based on the U.S. GAAP. It presents the financial position and results of operations of the American joint venture as reported to and consolidated with other operations of the parent American company. Another set is in U.S. dollars, based on a cost recovery basis. The third set is prepared for tax purposes for the Egyptian government (Abdallah 1999).

For auditing reasons, accounting records must be kept in Egypt. A general journal of all accounting entries and an inventory ledger must be maintained in Arabic. Books of account are generally maintained in Egyptian pounds, however, oil and gas companies and those operating in the free zones are allowed to maintain one set of their records in U.S. dollars and another set in Egyptian pounds. The Companies Law requires that the auditor be independent with respect to the entity being audited.

In general, the Egyptian GAAP can be described briefly by the following (Price Waterhouse 1995): (1) Financial statements should be prepared using historical cost concepts; (2) Book and tax accounts are generally the same; (3) Relations with parent and related party transactions must be disclosed; and (4) Accounting principles and practices follow internationally accepted standards.

Israel

Overview

The origin of the public accounting system in Israel goes back to the end of World War I when the British, with the help of Arabs seeking independence from the Ottoman Empire, managed to capture Palestine. During the British mandate on Palestine, many laws were enacted, for example, the Companies Ordinance, the Cooperative Societies Ordinance, and the Income Tax Ordinance. These acts helped give birth to the contemporary public accounting and auditing system in what is now Israel. The profession has changed substantially since its origin. Even though the profession originally had British antecedents, given the economic and sociopolitical ties between the United States and Israel, it has moved closer to an American accounting system. The trend seems to be toward accepting and recognizing the accounting principles, the forms of financial reporting, and the standards of auditing (Kesselman and Kesselman 1992).

The growth of larger businesses, the rise of a corporate form of ownership, the development of a capital market, the expansion of Israel's economy, and the need to encourage certain industries have led to the enactment of a wide range of laws dealing with taxes, land appreciation, and the encouragement of industry and capital investment. These laws have contributed to the growth in the public accounting profession in Israel. In contrast to others in its geographical region, Israel's accounting profession is much more developed. A significant number of stocks for the Israeli firms are traded in American and European stock exchanges.

The Israeli GAAP

The following bodies regulate and promote the accountancy profession in Israel:

1. The Auditors' Council, constituted under the Public Auditors' Law.
2. The Institute of Certified Public Accountants (ICPA) in Israel.

The Auditors' Council, a statutory body administered by the Ministry of Justice, is responsible for the implementation of the Auditors' Law. It consists of 13 members, six of whom represent the profession of auditing and six who represent various governmental agencies. The Attorney General or a chosen representative serves as the 13th member and chair of the council.

The Auditors' Council performs the following three functions:

1. Granting licenses to practice to those who have passed a qualifying examination given by the Council and who have acquired practical experience, including articled employment in a firm of certified public accountants or another approved place of training.

2. Proposing ethical and professional standards to the Ministry of Justice, which has the authority to introduce such standards with the approval of the Law Committee of the Knesset.

3. Acting as a disciplinary tribunal for the maintenance of ethical and professional standards. The Council is vested with the power to cancel, or suspend for specific periods, licenses to practice as auditors.

The ICPA is the other organization that directs the public accounting and auditing profession as the central body of accountants in Israel. The functions performed by the ICPA include representing qualified accountants, safeguarding the maintenance of ethical and professional standards and conduct, promoting the independence of its members, and providing guidelines and pronouncements on professional matters. While membership in the ICPA is voluntary, the majority of accountants in Israel are members. The ICPA's pronouncements on auditing and accounting are binding, and its views on related subjects are solicited by the government, the Knesset, and various public bodies. The Minister of Justice is required to consult the ICPA before making regulations regarding the auditors' mode of performance and matters involving professional conduct. The ICPA is an associate member of the IFAC.

The auditing standards prescribed by the ICPA and incorporated in the Auditors Regulations—1973 are substantially the same as those of the American Institute of Certified Public Accountants, although the ICPA has not yet addressed all of the U.S. standards. The standard auditors' report issued by the ICPA assumes that there has been consistency in the application of accounting principles, that the auditor has concurred with any changes in accounting principles, and that these facts have been reported in the financial statements.

With respect to Israeli auditing, an annual statutory audit is required for all companies. Income tax regulations require keeping books of accounts. Auditors review the report of quarterly financial statements issued by quoted companies, companies in which the public has an interest, and all banks and insurance companies.

The basic requirements for preparing financial statements and presenting them to the shareholders' general meeting are prescribed by the Companies Ordinance and the Securities Law. The directors of the company are responsible for the preparation of financial statements. The balance sheet is to be signed on behalf of the board of directors. The directors' reports are included with the financial statements and deal with information regarding the state of a company's affairs and dividend recommendations. The only financial statements required by the Companies Ordinance are a balance sheet and a statement of income. However, the Securities Law and the Securities (Preparation of Financial Statements) Regulations prescribe that companies offering their securities for sale to the public must prepare and publish full financial statements, including a consolidated balance sheet and a statement of income, a statement of cash flows, changes in shareholders' equity, and comprehensive notes to the financial statements. The Securities Law also requires publication of separate financial statements of the parent company.

Given the high rate of inflation in Israel, through a pronouncement, the ICPA in Israel requires certain large, publicly quoted companies to present financial statements adjusted for inflation.

Companies whose securities are traded on the Tel Aviv Stock Exchange, as well as other public companies, are required to submit immediate reports on certain events as prescribed by the regulations. They must file quarterly condensed financial reports (reviewed by the auditors) and annual audited financial statements. The annual audited financial statements of investments that were accounted for by the equity method and not consolidated must be included with the parent company's annual audited financial statements.

Companies also are required to keep proper accounting records under the Companies Ordinance and tax regulations. A number of Israeli companies prepare, and many also publish, their financial statements in U.S. dollars.

The annual financial statements of companies that are not obligated to report under the ICPA rules for inflationary accounting generally include the basic financial statements and notes, normally in Hebrew and in local currency. Many companies prepare translations into the English language and into foreign currency. They include, like their American counterparts, a balance sheet (statement of financial position), a statement of income (profit and loss) and retained earnings, a statement of changes in shareholders' equity, and a statement of cash flow. In addition to the four statements, also provided are notes to financial statements (significant accounting policies, special disclosures, clarifying footnotes, and information on the effect of changes in the purchasing power, or inflation, of local currency on the financial statements).

International accounting standards (IAS) have been adopted by the ICPA and apply in cases where there are no specific pronouncements by the ICPA and no other current practices in Israel. The opinions issued by the ICPA and the accounting principles adopted in Israel generally fall within the framework of IASC standards. They supplement the requirements of the Companies Ordinance, the Securities Authority, and the Tel Aviv Stock Exchange regarding the form and contents of financial statements. In circumstances where a binding accounting principle on a particular subject has yet to be issued, the Securities Authority is empowered to promulgate an accounting principle applicable to publicly quoted companies. However, a new accounting standards board (modeled on the U.S. Financial Accounting Standards Board) has been proposed as a joint venture of the ICPA and the Israel Securities Authority.

To overcome the distorting effect of inflation on financial reporting, the ICPA has issued a series of opinions prescribing various adjustments to companies' financial results. Prior to 1985, companies were required to include figures that were inflation adjusted in their financial statements as supplemental information only.

Fundamental accounting principles followed in the preparation of historical corporate financial statements, including the following: a going concern assumption; an accrual concept for income and expenses; an inclusion of only realized profits at the balance sheet date and provisions for all losses that arise, including those after the balance sheet date; consistency in the application of accounting principles; and the inclusion of assets and liabilities on a cost basis. Companies must prepare their statutory audited financial statements annually. There is no specific date to which accounts must be drawn; however, December 31 (the end of the tax year) is the most common. Generally, the year-end dates of a subsidiary or an affiliate (investee companies) are the same as those of the parent or holding companies, although there are exceptions to this rule.

A large number of differences exist between book and tax treatment of items of income and expenses, especially due to the accounting methods and taxation laws applicable to inflationary conditions. Companies generally prepare their accounts on the bases acceptable to the tax authorities. Tax adjustments not recorded in the books are generally not recognized, other than those required by the income tax laws and regulations.

Jordan

Overview

Jordan is a small Arab country with inadequate supplies of water and other natural resources such as oil and coal. It is located in southwestern Asia, bounded on the north by Syria, on the east by Iraq and Saudi Arabia, on the south by Saudi Arabia and the Gulf of Aqaba, and on the west by Israel. In mid-1989, the Jordanian government began debt-rescheduling negotiations and agreed to implement an IMF-supported program designed to gradually reduce the budget deficit and implement badly needed structural reforms. The Persian Gulf crisis that began in August 1990, however, aggravated Jordan's already serious economic problems, forcing the government to shelve the IMF program, to stop most debt payments, and to suspend rescheduling negotiations. The economy rebounded in 1992, largely due to the influx of capital repatriated by workers returning from the Gulf, but recovery was uneven in 1994–1997. The government is implementing the reform program adopted in 1992, and it continues to secure rescheduling and write-offs of its heavy foreign debt. Debt, poverty, and unemployment remain Jordan's largest ongoing problems (America Online 1999).

Financial reports are affected by the social, political, and economic variables and changes that have occurred in Jordan. In the past five decades, these variables have resulted in laws and regulations that have had a prominent effect on the development of financial reporting (Jahmani, Al-Omari, and Salimi 1996).

No private professional organization is in charge of issuing accounting and auditing standards. A certified public accountant (CPA) may apply the basic accounting knowledge learned during the academic education, in addition to meeting the tax laws and company regulations. As a result, the financial information reported is not comparable across companies and industries (Al-Rai and Dahmash 1998: 180).

The Jordanian GAAP

The first formal recognition of public accountancy as a profession in Jordan was in 1961, when the Jordanian board of accountancy was established by the government. The two major responsibilities of the board are to grant licenses to practice accounting in the public accounting firms and to have the power for disciplinary actions in any illegal practices. Until 1990, the accounting profession applied the GAAP, whether based on U.S. or U.K. GAAP (Al-Rai and Dahmash 1998).

The 1989 Companies Law requires companies to present their balance sheets and profit and loss statements, audited by an independent certified public accountant, within three months of the end of the fiscal year, with footnotes explaining the significant categories of revenues and expenses. It also requires firms to prepare financial statements according to "conventional accounting principles" (Jahmani, Al-Omari, and Salimi 1996: 6–10).

In 1988, as a result of the devaluation of the Jordanian currency (the dinar), there was an urgency to report any foreign exchange losses or gains resulting from foreign currency transactions or translations, which created a need for the establishment of consistent accounting standards in Jordan. On March 13, 1989, the Jordanian Association of Certified Public Accountants decided to adopt the IASs and International Auditing Standards for financial statements issued after 1990. However, no law was passed that could mandate the use of IASs. They are applicable only to the extent that they do not conflict with the law (Jahmani, Al-Omari, and Salimi 1996: 13–14).

Kuwait

Overview

Kuwait is a small, relatively open economy with proven crude oil reserves of about 10% of world reserves. It is located between Iraq and Saudi Arabia on the northeast coast of the Persian Gulf, with an area of 6,800 square miles. Before 1938, the economy was based on pearl diving and activities related to Kuwait's role as a seafaring nation. In 1938, its economy began to change with the discovery of oil, and soon after World War II Kuwait became a major oil exporter. Its huge petroleum reserves are estimated to last another 200 years. Kuwait's oil reserves made its per capita income one of the highest in the world and helped it to start rapidly improving its infrastructure.

The accounting profession in Kuwait began its tangible growth in the early 1950s. Driven by need, the Kuwaiti government passed legislation that required public firms to report audited financial statements. However, there was no stipulation in those early regulations regarding which accounting standards were to be followed. The stock market crash of 1982 had much to do with a lack of accounting, accountability, and professionally credible auditing. Unlike Saudi Arabia, Kuwait does not have accounting standards of its own. Compliance with the standards promulgated by the IASC is mandatory for shareholding and limited liability companies for accounting periods starting on or after January 1, 1991.

The Kuwaiti Association of Accountants and Auditors is the only local professional body of accounting. Law No. 5 of 1981, in setting legal rules governing the auditing profession, requires that registered auditors be natural persons and of Kuwaiti nationality. To practice accounting, members have to pass an exam similar to the CPA exam in the United States. The Kuwaiti Association is a member of the IFAC, which is responsible for issuing International Auditing Guidelines.

The Kuwaiti GAAP

In Kuwait, all business firms are required to keep adequate financial records and books, but they do not have to be maintained in the Arabic language. All books and records of foreign companies operating in Kuwait are subject to the provisions of the Tax Decree of the official Ministerial order. The books and records that should be maintained include a general journal, inventory sheets, a general ledger, an expenses analysis journal, and a stock record.

Law No. 6 of 1962—Practice of Audit of Accounts, amended by Law No. 5 of 1981, was the first law enacted by the Kuwaiti government to regulate the accounting profession. It covers the rights and obligations of auditors and requires that auditors complete their work according to generally acceptable auditing and accounting standards, to be specified by the technical committee (Shuaib 1985: 95–96).

Starting from January 1, 1991, shareholding and limited liability companies are required to use the IAS promulgated by the IASC. Three of the IAS have had a significant impact on accounting and financial reporting in Kuwait, including:

1. IAS No. 24, "Related Party Transactions," which changed the reporting of related party transactions and the quantification of such transactions.
2. IAS No. 27, "Consolidated Financial Statements and Accounting for Investments in Subsidiaries," introduced for the first time in Kuwait to the large family trading groups.
3. IAS No. 30, "Disclosures in Financial Statements of Banks and Similar Financial Institutions," which improved significantly the disclosures of Kuwaiti banks' financial statements.

Audited balance sheet and income statements of both public shareholding and limited liability companies must receive an annual audit. The auditor must be independent and registered with the Ministry of Commerce and Industry. Audited financial statements must be submitted to the Ministry of Commerce and Industry within 10 days of the annual general meeting. In general, the financial statements of Kuwaiti firms also are required to follow international accounting standards.

Saudi Arabia

Overview

This is a well-to-do oil-based economy with strong governmental controls over major economic activities. About 35% of the GDP comes from the private sector. Economic (as well as political) ties with the United States are especially strong. The petroleum sector accounts for roughly 75% of budget revenues, 35% of the GDP, and 90% of export earnings. Saudi Arabia has the largest reserves of petroleum in the world (26% of the proven total), ranks as the largest exporter of petroleum, and plays a leading role in OPEC. In the 1990s, the government intended to bring its budget, which has been in deficit since 1983, back into balance and to encourage private economic activity. Roughly 4 million foreign workers play an important role in the Saudi economy, for example, in the oil and service sectors. Helped by production above its OPEC quota, Saudi Arabia continued to bring its finances closer into balance in 1997, recording a $1.6 billion budget deficit and a $200 million current account surplus. In 1998, the country looked to its policies of maintaining moderate fiscal reforms, restraining public spending, and encouraging non-oil exports. Shortages of water and rapid population growth will constrain governmental efforts to increase self-sufficiency in agricultural products.

During the early oil boom years, as usual, Saudi Arabia allowed the government expenditure to increase, and has since been trying the difficult process of fiscal consolidation. Two decades ago, the Saudi economy was relatively closed to foreign investors. As the government seeks membership in the World Trade Organization (WTO), Saudi Arabia's Supreme Economic Council approved, in February 2000, draft laws on foreign investment and approved the General Investment Authority to provide the mechanism for attracting foreign investors (Mungai 2000: 66).

As the world price of crude oil has jumped up to more than $30 a barrel, at the time of this writing, for the first time since the 1991 Persian Gulf War, Saudi Arabia was believed to be seeking to drop the current price of crude oil at the meeting with Venezuela and non-OPEC producer Mexico. It is expected that oil prices will stabilize soon, if Saudi Arabia and Venezuela, as OPEC heavyweights, would be interested in trying to calm the crude oil market (Kilborn, Nichols, and Cook 2000: 24).

At this time, if the United States and CEOs of major oil MNCs wish to ease the uncertainty of supply of crude oil, as a vital commodity to their economies, should begin by learning to understand and treat petroleum producing and exporting countries as equals, and work with them to accept their cultures instead of dictating how they should behave (Dow 2000: A22).

The Saudi accounting profession is controlled by the Ministry of Commerce (MOC). The MOC, the official agency of the profession, is responsible for issuing public accountant certificates and exercising a disciplinary role. The Saudi accounting profession was given a formal standing by a Royal Decree in August 1974. The decree was titled *Nazam Al Muhasibean*, which translates as "Rules and Regulations for Public Accountants." This was followed by the formation of the High Commission of Public Accountants, composed of representatives from the Ministry of Commerce, the General Public Accounting Office, and academia and the accounting profession.

In 1986, the MOC approved the financial accounting objectives and concepts as a conceptual framework and basis for financial accounting standards. In the same year, it issued two publications: (1) Accounting Objectives and Concepts, which present the Saudi Arabian Standards of General Presentation and Disclosure in the financial statements; and (2) Auditing Standards, which emphasize the professional qualification of auditors, including the discussion of independence, due care, and documentation of auditors' working papers. Both the Accounting Objectives and Auditing Standards may be considered the source of guidelines for the accounting profession and the private sector. The new concepts and standards are similar to the accounting principles issued by the American Institute of Certified Public Accountants (AICPA), however, compliance with the new concepts and standards is not currently enforced by an independent governmental agency or a private organization.

The Saudi Accounting Association (SAA), through its special technical committee comprising Saudi and non-Saudi accountants, and in coordination with the Ministry of Commerce, is in the process of formulating new accounting standards in the Kingdom.

The Saudi GAAP

Saudi Arabia is in the early stage of developing its accounting standards. The Standard of General Presentation and Disclosure (SGAAP), issued by the Ministry of Commerce on May 11, 1990, is the only formal, generally accepted set of accounting principles in Saudi Arabia. The SGAAP issued to date pertains to the requirements of general presentation and disclosure in the financial statements of profit-oriented entities and consolidated financial statements, provides pro-forma examples of presentation, and determines the treatment of accounting changes and contingent gains or losses. The SGAAP requires financial statements to include a profit-and-loss statement, a statement of appropriation of profits, a balance sheet, and an auditor's report. The statement of source and uses of funds is included but not mandatory. No specific presentation format is imposed, except for banks. A joint venture, with its auditor, can establish its own format.

There are, at present, no Saudi standards dealing with important issues such as research and development costs, reporting financial statements by segment, business combinations, and related party transactions. In general, the SGAAP asks for much more detailed disclosures than other Middle East countries, even though additional details are not mandatory. The following accounting issues are unique to the SGAAP:

1. Assets such as property, plant, and equipment cannot be revalued to avoid abuses resulting from artificial increases in their values.

2. Limited liability firms, other than banks, are not allowed to lend their shareholders any money.

3. If the limited liability firm has accumulated losses of more than 75% of its capital, the members, at their meeting, must decide whether it should continue to exist with the partners' commitment to pay its debt or be resolved.

4. That portion of allocated income tax to shareholders, other than citizens of Saudi Arabia and the Gulf Countries Council, and *zakat* (taxes) are either deducted from dividends paid, recorded as a receivable from the shareholders if no dividends are paid, or deducted from their respective shares of reserves in the statement of retained earnings. Since *zakat* are determined on individuals' shares of corporate or partnership profits and assets, it is unusual to record them as a corporate expense.

CPA certificates are given to public accountants only if they have an approved degree in accounting and sufficient practical experience in accounting or auditing. Saudi public accounting titles are usually granted only to Saudi nationals. All large international accounting firms are associated with local accountants and operate under a Saudi name.

COMPARISON OF MIDDLE EAST COUNTRIES' GAAP WITH U.S. GAAP AND IAS

This section includes key accounting differences and similarities of the selected five Middle East countries as compared to the U.S. GAAP and IAS. Certain accounting principles will be used for comparison between Middle East countries, U.S. GAAP, and IAS, as seen in Table 5–2, including investments, inventory, asset valuation, equity method, consolidation, deferred taxes, foreign currency translations, inflation, provisions and reserves, and disclosures. For Jordan and Kuwait, GAAP are in very early stages and allow foreign firms and joint ventures to use IAS. Therefore, in our analysis that follows, the concentration is mainly on U.S. GAAP, IAS, Egypt, Israel, and Saudi Arabia. Kuwaiti and Jordanian GAAP are only covered for issues in which they either differ from IAS or use concepts different from the Middle East countries.

Investments

In U.S. GAAP, SFAS 115 requires that investments that do not confer significant influence on the operation of financial decisions of the investee consist of all debt securities, and generally that all small (less than 20%) investments in equity securities be segregated into held to maturity securities, trading securities, and available-for-sale securities. The first category should be reported at an amortized cost and may be classified as current or non-current assets. Any unrealized gains and losses are excluded from earnings (unless decline is other than temporary). The trading securities should be reported at fair market value and grouped with current assets on the balance sheet. Any unrealized holding gains and losses are recorded on the income statement. The available-for-sale securities should be reported at fair market value and grouped with current assets on the balance sheet.

Internationally, three IAS address several related issues of accounting for investments: IAS No. 25, IAS No. 28, and IAS No. 31. IAS No. 25 covers the general topic of investment in the debt and equity securities of other business entities, for those situations where the investor does not have significant influence over the investee. In this case, investments may be treated using different methods, depending on whether the investments are short or long term. Short-term investments should be carried at market value or lower of cost or market value (LCM) and long-term investments should be carried at a cost revalued amount, applied on a portfolio basis (Epstein and Mirza 1999: 295). IAS No. 28, which addresses investments in associates, is covered under the equity method. IAS No. 31 concerns the accounting by an investor for interest in a joint venture arrangement, which is outside the scope of this book.

In Egypt, short-term investments held as current assets, such as marketable securities, are valued at lower of cost or market value. Long-term investments held as long-term assets are valued at cost. Only unrealized holding losses are recognized on the income statement.

In Israel, trading portfolios of marketable securities, held as a current asset, are stated at market value, and gains and losses are recorded in the income statement. Marketable securities, such as bonds and shares, which are long-term investments are stated at the lower of cost or market value. Short-term investments held for a period of less than 12 months and for trading purposes continue to be stated at market values. All revaluation differences are to be treated as revenue items, except where they represent the reversal of unrealized losses that were previously charged directly to reserves (Price Waterhouse 1995: 105).

In Kuwait, the dominant basis for valuing investments is the cost basis, applied in varying ways. For quoted securities, the lower of cost or market value; for unquoted securities, at cost, and if the cost exceeds the market value, a provision is established. In some companies, investments in domestic securities are valued at their cost, which is less than their market value on the stock market (Hassan, 1985).

In Saudi Arabia, current assets are segregated into main groups in the statement of financial position, according to their nature. For significant items of each group, segregation should be made between the monetary and non-monetary items in the statement of financial position or related notes. Financial statements are prepared using the historical cost basis. Some current assets, such as marketable securities, are carried at the lower of cost or market value. Any value above the cost, such as current value or market value, is seldom used.

Inventory

In U.S. GAAP Accounting Research Bulletin (ARB) No. 43, Chapter 4, allows the use of first in, first out (FIFO), last in, first out (LIFO), and weighted average cost-flow assumptions for estimating inventory cost. The inventory accounting method chosen by management depends on the nature of the industry, certain tax considerations, and a variety of other factors. The basis of accounting for inventories in U.S. GAAP is historical cost including the costs incurred to bring a good to salable condition. However, a firm can depart from using the historical cost basis in reporting inventory when the "market value" of the ending inventory falls below its "cost" (as determined under one of the cost-flow methods), or the LCM (ARB No. 43, Chapter 4, Par. 8).

Internationally, in IAS No. 2, "Valuation and Presentation of Inventories in the Context of the Historical Cost System," the FIFO and weighted average cost methods are defined as benchmark treatments. The LIFO method is an allowable alternative method. Lower of cost or net realizable value is used.

In Egypt, inventories are normally valued at the lower of cost or market value under the Egyptian GAAP. Cost may be determined under any one of the three following methods: actual, average, or FIFO.

Under Israeli GAAP, the inventories are valued at the lower of cost or market value. The costing method should be based on either FIFO or weighted average. The LIFO inventory system bases of inventory valuations, while acceptable in the United States, are not used in Israel, due to their unacceptability for taxation computation.

In Kuwait, inventories are disaggregated into finished goods, goods in transit, work in progress, and raw materials. Three bases for inventory valuation are in use: the FIFO method, the weighted average cost, and a more specific method that clearly defines the term *cost*, but relies on the lower of cost and another basis (such as market value) (Hassan 1985).

Under Saudi GAAP, financial statements are to be prepared using the historical cost principle. Increases or decreases resulting from changes in the general purchasing power of the Saudi riyal are not reflected in the financial statements. Current assets, such as inventory, are sometimes carried at the lower of cost or market value. Costs include both direct and indirect charges. Permissible methods of determining flow of inventory include the FIFO and average cost. The

LIFO method is not acceptable for both religious (*zakat*) and secular tax filing purposes and is therefore rarely used in practice. *Zakat* is a form of religiously required obligation on wealth that Muslims are supposed to pay on monetary and other assets.

Asset Valuation

Assets are defined as the probable future economic benefits obtained or controlled by a particular entity as a result of past transactions or events, or "the company's resources that, in turn, can be deployed to generate a profit for the company" (Haskins, Ferris, Sack, and Allen 1993: 141).

In the United States, assets are generally recorded at their original cost, since this is the most objective basis. However, there are many different kinds of assets, including current and goodwill, investments, and property, plant, and equipment. Current assets are valued at net realizable value (such as accounts receivable).

Internationally, IAS No. 16 requires that an initial measurement of an item of property, plant, or equipment be at cost. That requirement is consistent with U.S. GAAP and practice. The original standard permitted either historical cost or revalued amounts as the basis for reporting property, plant, and equipment; this remains in the revised standard, but historical cost is now designated as the benchmark treatment, with revalued amounts being relegated to the allowed alternative category (Epstein and Mirza 1999: 13).

Assets under the Egyptian GAAP are valued at either the lower of cost or market value or at cost. Marketable securities classified as current assets are stated at the LCM. The ones classified as non-current assets are valued at cost. Inventories are valued at the LCM. Cost may be determined using actual, average, FIFO, or LIFO bases. Real property is carried at historical cost. Plant and machinery are stated at historical cost, less depreciation. Depreciation methods include straight-line, declining-balance, and unit-of-production methods.

In Israel, current assets, such as inventories, are stated at the lower of cost or market value, using the FIFO or weighted-average methods. LIFO is not permitted, because it is not relevant in inflationary economies and is not accepted for tax purposes. Long-term (fixed) assets are normally recorded at cost, however, many companies have adopted the practice of revaluation of assets so their real values could be stated on nominal values due to the inflationary conditions in Israel. Long-term investments, such as marketable securities, are stated at the lower of cost or market value. Short-term investments held as inventory and for trading purposes are valued at market value. All revaluation differences are to be treated in the income statement.

In Kuwait, the fixed assets are being valued at the actual cost paid to acquire them. Property, plant, and equipment are measured at cost and depreciated over their useful lives.

In Saudi Arabia, appraisal, market, or current value methods, which are above cost to the reporting entity, are seldom used. Property, plant, and equipment are generally accounted for at cost under Saudi GAAP. Assets cannot be revalued. The restriction is intended to prevent abuses that result from artificial increases in the value of property, plant, and equipment. There are no requirements for the adoption of current cost accounting.

Equity Method of Accounting

This is a method to value intercorporate equity investments by adjusting the investor's cost basis for the percentage of ownership in the investee's earnings (or losses) and for any dividends paid by the investee; it has been also referred to as the one-line consolidation.

In U.S. GAAP, when an investor's ownership (20%–49%) of an investee's voting stock is of such a size that the investor is able to influence the way the investee conducts its business, the investor is required to adopt the equity method of accounting. Under this method, the investor records its initial investment at the cost paid to acquire the stock. Then, on an ongoing basis, the investor adds to its income its pro rata share of the investee's income (Accounting Principles Board [APB] No. 18).

The equity method generally is not a substitute for consolidation; it is used when the investor has significant influence on the operations of the investee, but lacks control. This significant influence is assumed when the investor owns between 20% and 50% of the investee's voting common stock. Any ownership percentage over 50% presumably gives the investor actual control, making full consolidation of financial statements a must. IAS No. 28 emphasizes that the equity method should be used by the investor for all investments in associates, unless the investment is acquired and held exclusively with a view to its disposal in the near future, or if it operates under severe, long-term restrictions that would preclude making distributions to investors. In the latter cases, accounting using the cost method is preferred (Epstein and Mirza 1999: 321).

In Egypt, purchase or pooling methods of accounting for acquisitions is allowed, depending on the circumstances. In practice, most Egyptian companies use the equity method of accounting.

In Israel, the equity method of accounting is applied to investments where there is significant influence with a holding of more than 25% of voting rights. Voting rights of 25% or less will not be considered as granting significant influence, unless otherwise clearly demonstrated. The threshold for applying the equity method is 10% of the equity capital (Somekh Chaikin 1995: 104).

In Kuwait, the purchase method is used for acquisition. Any resulting goodwill is either recorded as an asset or is amortized. The pooling of interests method may only be used if a combination qualifies as a uniting of interests.

In Saudi Arabia, the cost method is generally used to account for investments in the voting stock of other companies. The standard of general presentation and disclosure does not define the requirements of using the equity method, nor the percentage of voting rights to be considered as granting significant influence over the investee's decisions.

Consolidation

Consolidated financial statements are prepared to reflect the operations and financial positions of a parent company that owns from 51% to 100% and is presumed to have control over its wholly or majority-owned subsidiaries.

In U.S. GAAP, when the investor owns enough of an investee's voting stock (50% or more) to be in a position to control the investee, rather than simply have a significant influence on it, the investor must include all of the investee's assets and liabilities and revenue and expenses in its financial statements as though it owned those assets and liabilities and incurred those revenues and expenses directly. The financial statements of the two parties should be consolidated. However, recently, the U.S. FASB decided that the pooling of interests method should be eliminated. Instead, all business combinations would be accounted for by the purchase method, or acquisition accounting.

Internationally, when the acquired business entity is merged into the acquiring business entity, or when both entities are consolidated into a new business entity, all assets and liabilities are recorded directly on the books of the surviving or new business entity. Depending on whether the conditions stated by IAS No. 22, "Accounting for Business Combinations," are met, the transaction will be treated as either a pooling of interest or purchase method. Either is allowed. Goodwill may be amortized on a systematic basis over its useful life, not exceeding 20 years from the initial recognition.

In Egypt, groups of companies may either be consolidated or accounted for on an equity basis for statutory purposes. In practice, most groups use equity accounting.

In Israel, consolidated techniques are normally applied to investments in subsidiaries that are more than 50% controlled. Business combinations are accounted for by the purchase method, unless specific conditions are met for the implementation of the pooling of interest method. Pooling is seldom applied in Israel. Unconsolidated companies and subsidiaries in which the reporting company exercises significant influence are accounted for under the equity method in the company's consolidated financial statements.

Israeli GAAP requires the amortization of goodwill for up to 10 years, but under certain conditions, exceptions are permitted for up to 20 years. U.S. GAAP permits the amortization of goodwill for up to 40 years. In Israel, proportional consolidation is required for mutual holdings of a joint-venture nature. Conditions indicating control for consolidation, other than over 50% voting rights, may be applied.

In Kuwait, consolidated financial statements and accounting for investments in subsidiaries define subsidiary ownership on the basis of control, require consolidated financial statements from all groups, except wholly owned, foreign, and domestic subsidiaries, and provide guidelines for line-by-line consolidation and disclsoure in a parent company's separate financial statements of its inventory in a subsidiary.

Kuwait companies use the following policies regarding the basis of consolidation of accounts:

1. Holding shares or securities of less than 20% of the company's shares—considered a "commercial investment";
2. Associated companies that hold 20% to 50% of the company's shares;
3. Subsidiaries holding more than 50% of its shares.

Holdings, commercial or in associated companies, are valued on the basis of the net assets of these companies and the proportion of holdings. For commercial investments, the resulting difference between valuation and cost is considered unrealized gains or losses, except for a continuous decline in value, which should be considered a realized loss. In associated companies, they are regarded as realized gains or losses (Hassan 1985).

Under Saudi GAAP, consolidated financial statements are required to comply with the standard of general presentation and disclosure issued by the Ministry of Commerce. However, consolidated financial statements are seldom prepared. The cost method is generally used to account for investments in the voting stock of other companies.

The Saudi standard defines the requirements of disclosing minority rights, reciprocal ownership of shares and differences in the financial periods of the holding company, and the subsidiary or subsidiaries. However, the standard does not define the requirements of preparing consolidated financial statements, or the circumstances under which these statements should be prepared. It also does not address the circumstances necessary for the preparation of consolidated financial statements. In general, business entities follow either U.S., U.K., or international accounting standards for accounting purposes.

Accounting for Income Taxes

Deferred income taxes are the portion of a company's income tax expense not currently payable, postponed because of differences in the accounting policies adopted for financial statement purposes versus those policies used for tax reporting purposes. In general, the objective of accounting for income taxes is to recognize the amount of taxes payable or refundable for the current year.

In U.S. GAAP, SFAS 109, "Accounting for Income Taxes," requires an asset and liability (balance sheet) approach to recognizing and measuring deferred taxes. According to SFAS 109, financial income tax expense is charged to income tax expense. Income tax expense equals the taxes actually owed (a current tax liability) for the current period, plus or minus the change during the current period in amounts payable in the future and in future tax benefits. By using this procedure, any possible income tax statement or balance sheet distortion that may result from differences in the timing of revenue recognition or expense deductibility and asset or liability valuation between GAAP and the Internal Revenue Code is avoided. The income tax expense reported in the entity's income statement reflects the amount of taxes related to transactions recognized in the financial statements prepared under GAAP for the specific period. The deferred tax asset or liability (the difference between income tax expense and income tax payable) reported in the entity's balance sheet clearly reflects the amount of temporary differences that results from differences in timing of revenue recognition or expense deductibility between GAAP and the Internal Revenue Code.

The IASC issued IAS No. 12, "Accounting for Taxes on Income," revised in September 1996, for financial reporting periods beginning on or after January 1, 1998. IAS No. 12 allows full or partial provision of deferred tax on timing differences between the accounting and tax basis of revenues and expenses. It also allows the deferred or liability method. Deferred tax assets should only be carried forward when there is a reasonable expectation of realization. Also contained in IAS No. 12 are the following:

- Accrue deferred tax liability for nearly all taxable temporary differences;
- Accrue deferred tax asset for nearly all deductible temporary differences if it is probable that a tax benefit will be realized;
- Accrue unused tax losses and tax credits if it is probable that they will be realized;
- Use tax rates expected at settlement;
- Non-deductible goodwill—no deferred tax;
- Unremitted earnings of subsidiaries, associates, and joint ventures, which do not accrue tax;
- Capital gains—accrue tax at an expected rate; and
- Government grants or other assets or liabilities whose initial recognition differs from initial tax base are not "grossed up."

In Egypt, deferred tax accounting is not practiced due to differences between book and tax income. Accounting income is determined based on financial statements prepared according to the Egyptian GAAP. Accounting income is adjusted for certain items that are not deductible for tax purposes to figure out the taxable income. These accounting and tax differences are minimized by companies that try to not include non-taxable items.

In Israel, income tax provisions are affected by after-balance sheet changes in tax rates. The liability method is the one most commonly used for deferred taxes. The rules for recognition of a deferred tax asset on loss carryforwards under FAS 109 in the United States are more liberal than in Israel. Recently, the Israel Securities Authority has taken a more liberal attitude.

In Saudi Arabia, income taxes are accounted for as a deduction from income for the year. Income tax returns must be supported by the original books of account and by supplementary records showing how taxable income was determined. The provision for income taxes is based on taxable income. Deferred taxes are not provided for permanent differences between accounting and taxable income. These permanent differences primarily relate to valuation allowances and contingency reserves not deductible for tax purposes.

Foreign Currency Translation

Foreign currency translation is the process of expressing in the reporting currency of the enterprise amounts that are denominated or measured in a different currency.

In U.S. GAAP, SFAS No. 52, "Foreign Currency Translation," states that the foreign subsidiary's accounts should be determined using U.S. GAAP and initially reported in terms of its functional currency. The foreign subsidiary's financial statements thus prepared arc then translated into U.S. dollars using the current rate method. The subsidiary's income statement is converted into U.S. dollars using the average exchange rate for the period, and its balance sheet is converted at the exchange rate existing on the date of translation (at the end of the fiscal year). However, if the foreign subsidiary's operations and financing decisions are mainly made by the parent company, then SFAS No. 8 should be applied, and a temporal method should be used.

The international GAAP dealing with the the translation of foreign currency financial statements and foreign currency translations is covered in IAS No. 21 (revised in 1993), "The Effects of Changes in Foreign Exchange Rates." Under IAS No. 21, the classification accorded to a foreign operation determines the methodology used in translating its financial statements. If the foreign operation is integral to the operation of the reporting entity, the financial statement of the foreign operation should be translated as follows:

1. Foreign currency monetary items should be reported using the closing rate.
2. Foreign currency non-monetary items, when carried at historical costs, should be reported using the exchange rate at the date of the transaction.
3. Foreign currency non-monetary items carried at fair values should be reported using exchange rates that existed when the fair values were determined.
4. All income and expense items should be translated using the average exchange rate.
5. Exchange differences should be recognized as an income or expense during the period in which they arise.

However, under IAS No. 21, if the foreign operation is *not* integral to the operation of the reporting entity, the financial statement of the foreign operation should be translated at the current rate method.

The Egyptian GAAP does not cover the foreign exchange gains or losses, nor the statement in which these gains or losses should be presented (income statement or balance sheet). Companies Law No. 159 permits the use of any generally accepted accounting principle, provided that such a principle is sound and the resulting financial statements are an accurate portrayal of the financial position and results of operations of the company.

In Israel, foreign subsidiaries, presented on a consolidated or an equity basis, must translate foreign currencies to local currencies. The foreign currency translation method to be used depends on whether the foreign subsidiaries' operations are independent or an extension of the Israeli parent's operations. If they are autonomous operations, the restate-translate method should be used. In this case, the financial statements of foreign subsidiaries must be adjusted for inflation in the country of operation and then translated into Israeli currency. All translation gains or losses should be reflected in capital reserves. However, if the foreign subsidiaries' operations are extensions of the parent operation, the translate-restate method should be used, that is, the foreign subsidiaries' financial statements should be translated to the Israeli currency first, and then adjusted for Israeli inflation. Any translation gains or losses should be reflected in the income statement.

In Kuwait, companies translate assets and liabilities at the year-end rates of foreign exchange. In practice, foreign exchange translation gains or losses are treated in different ways (Hassan 1985: 79–80), including:

1. The establishment of a special provision for translation losses, presented on the balance sheet in the owner's equity section, whereas unrealized profits on translation appear on a separate account on the balance sheet;
2. Losses are charged directly to the profit and loss account;
3. Realized or unrealized losses on translation, as in No. 2; and
4. If losses on translation are small, they should be treated as in No. 2.

The Saudi GAAP does not specify any requirements for the foreign currency translation of foreign subsidiaries' financial statements. However, in practice, the Saudi MNCs use IAS No. 21.

Accounting for Inflation

Inflation is measured by a general price index, for example, the Consumer Price Index. Balance sheet valuations are converted, and the purchasing power gain or loss is determined by the difference between the converted and the unconverted amounts.

In U.S. GAAP, at the present time, corporations are not required to present inflation-adjusted data with their basic financial statements. Requirements under

SFAS No. 33 in the past were based on very high inflation rates, but they became optional when inflation rates fell to much more acceptable levels.

The IASC issued IAS No. 15, "Information Reflecting the Effect of Changing Prices," however, this standard is not mandatory. Under IAS No. 15, entities should disclose the following information on a general purchasing power or current cost basis:

• depreciation adjustment
• cost of sales adjustment
• monetary items adjustment
• the overall effect of the above, and any other adjustments

Egyptian GAAP does not address the issue of accounting for inflation. In the 1990s, the inflation rate in Egypt was between 10% and 40%. The Egyptian government launched several comprehensive economic reform programs in the first half of the 1990s to free interest and exchange rates, however, the exchange rates in Egypt have been under governmental control since 1996. For most Egyptian companies, the effect of inflation is not reflected in their financial statements.

In Israel, the ICPA tried to overcome the distorting effect of inflation on financial reporting and disclosure. It issued Opinion No. 36 in 1985, which required that the inflation-adjusted financial statements form the primary financial statements of most large Israeli companies. Under Opinion No. 26, balance sheet items are divided into monetary and non-monetary items. The non-monetary items are adjusted on the basis of the changes in the Consumer Price Index (CPI). In general, Israel has a detailed system of accounting for inflation.

In Saudi Arabia, financial statements are prepared using the historical cost principle. Since the changes in the exchange rates between the Saudi riyal and major international currencies—including the U.S. dollar—are not significant, any increases or decreases in the general purchasing power of the riyal are not reflected in the financial statements. Moreover, the Saudi GAAP does not address inflation in its standards.

Provisions and Reserves

In U.S. GAAP, the term *reserve* is the most confusing and troublesome in accounting. It is defined as an appropriation of retained earnings, it always has a credit balance, and it is never an asset (Kieso and Weygandt 1998: 940). The accounting profession recommends that use of the word "reserve" be confined to appropriations of retained earnings, if it is to be used at all. In some European countries, such as France and Germany, regulations exist that state that a defined percentage of earnings be appropriated to a legal reserve account, until that account (shown in stockholders' equity) equals the defined amount (10% of share capital in France, and 10% of the par value of share capital in Germany). However, in the United States and many other countries, including France and Germany, general contingency reserves are not permitted (Epstein and Mirza 1999: 6).

In September 1998, the IASC issued IAS No. 37, "Provisions, Contingent Liabilities, and Contingent Assets," effective for annual financial statements covering periods beginning on or after July 1, 1999. IAS No. 37 requires that:

1. Provisions should be recognized in the balance sheet when, and only when, an enterprise has a present legal or constructive obligation as a result of a past event; it is probable that an outflow of resources embodying economic benefits will be required to settle the obligation, and a reliable estimate can be made of the amount of the obligation.
2. Provisions should be measured in the balance sheet at the best estimate of the expenditure required to settle the present obligation at the balance sheet date.
3. A provision should be used only for expenditures for which the provision was originally recognized and should be reversed if an outflow of resources is no longer probable.

In Egypt, reserves for general contingencies, such as strikes, business recession, and losses from catastrophes not ordinarily insured, are not allowed. Reserves of profits are allowed, only to the extent permitted by statutory regulations. Contingency provisions, such as loss, are accrued as a charge to income if information is available prior to the issuance of financial statements, assuming that at least one of the following two criteria has been met: (1) it is probable that an asset had been impaired or (2) a liability had been incurred at the date of the financial statements. Material contingencies that are not recorded must be disclosed, at least in the footnotes of the financial statements.

In Israel, retained earnings are not usually appropriated for loss contingencies. Loss contingencies, unlike other appropriations for other purposes, are shown as liabilities or asset valuation allowances. Reserves for general contingencies not related to current operations are not found in practice. Material contingencies that are not recorded must be disclosed. Reserves for losses are not normally allowed for tax deductions until the amount of the loss is paid or the asset is written off. Provisions for doubtful debts are based on the calculated amounts determined by management. The specific identification method is the one most widely used. It is based on the aging of accounts receivable and on management's expertise with customers. The liabilities for employees' severance indemnities under the law are frequently funded with approved severance pay funds, and only the net amounts are shown on balance sheets.

While the Saudi GAAP allows appropriations for other purposes, loss contingencies are generally shown as liabilities or asset valuation allowances. Reserves for general contingencies not related to current operations are not normally found in practice. Estimated losses for specific contingencies, however, should be accrued as a charge to income if certain conditions are met.

In Saudi Arabia, material contingencies that are not recorded should be disclosed. Reserves for losses are generally not deductible for tax purposes until the amount of the loss is paid or the asset is written off. The legal reserve, which is a part of retained earnings, has always been stated separately in the balance sheet under the Saudi GAAP. It is not available for distribution until the company or the bank is liquidated. It can, however, be used to reduce or absorb net annual losses.

Disclosure

In U.S. GAAP, the SEC, in its Accounting Series Release (ASR) No. 166 called for alertness to situations where conditions of major uncertainties may not have been adequately conveyed to readers. In these cases, registrants must consider the need for the specified disclosure of uncertainties and, in extreme cases, deviations from the conventional reporting model.

IAS No. 1 defines the overall considerations for financial statements, including: fair presentation, accounting policies, going concern, accrual basis of accounting, consistency of presentation, materiality and aggregation, offsetting, and comparative information. It also prescribes the minimum structure and content, including certain information required on the face of financial statements:

- balance sheet (current/non-current distinction not required)
- income statement (operating/non-operating separation required)
- cash flow statement
- statement showing changes in equity (various formats allowed)

In Egypt, financial statements include a balance sheet, a statement of profit and loss, and a statement of changes in cash flow. A specific format of the income statement is not mandatory; however, law 159 includes a suggested example that should be followed, and any departure from it should be disclosed. Moreover, the footnotes to the financial statements, under the Egyptian GAAP, are an essential part of the financial statement and should include:

1. Organization, relationship with parent company;
2. Significant accounting policies;
3. Analysis of components of property, plant, and equipment, and inventories;
4. Major commitments, such as extraordinary plant expansion, letters of credit, long-term leases, and purchase obligations;
5. Significant subsequent events;

6. Major contingencies, such as pending lawsuits, guarantees of debts of others, and so on; and

7. Material related-party transactions.

Under the Egyptian GAAP, foreign investors must disclose the details of transactions with related parties. Also, financial statements of subsidiaries owned by two or more companies must disclose their relationship with the parent company.

In Israel, notes to the basic financial statements are an integral part of each statement. The footnotes to the financial statements, under the Israeli GAAPs, include:

1. Significant accounting policies used in preparing the financial statements;

2. Principles of consolidation;

3. Inflation-adjusted financial statements and principles of adjustment;

4. Inventory valuation methods;

5. Goodwill policy;

6. Exchange rates and linkage differences; and

7. Allowances for doubtful accounts receivable.

The SGAAP requires that the accounting policies adopted by an entity be disclosed either as a separate note to the financial statements or as a separate summary to be referred to in the financial statements. It also requires that any change in the accounting policies, if there is any, should be disclosed by: (1) describing the change; (2) justifying the change; and (3) disclosing the effect of the change on the current accounting period. Under the SGAAP, the complete set of financial statements includes: statement of financial position, statement of income, and statement of changes in owners' equity. Current liabilities should include amounts payable that will be settled within one year from the date of the statement of financial position, or within the normal operating cycle, whichever is longer. Liabilities for which contractual arrangements have been made for their settlement from other than current assets should be removed from current liabilities. Current liabilities should be segregated into main groups under separate headings, according to their nature.

COMPARATIVE ANALYSIS OF ACCOUNTING DIFFERENCES AND SIMILARITIES

After discussing the 10 accounting issues for the selected Middle East countries, as compared to the U.S. GAAP and IAS, it is helpful to make a comparative analysis of differences and similarities across the countries. Table 5–2 summarizes these:

1. Accounting treatment for investments: Egypt, Jordan, Kuwait, and Saudi Arabia are following IAS, and Israel is using the market value for short-term investments.

2. Inventory valuation: all four Arab countries follow the IAS; Israel does not permit the use of the LIFO because of the effect of inflation. IAS permit the use of the LIFO as an alternative.

3. Asset valuation: U.S. GAAP and IAS are similar, and all selected Middle East countries use the same method.

4. Equity method: Under both U.S. GAAP and IAS, the equity method should be used if the percentage of ownership is between 20% and 50%, and if there is a significant influence on management decisions, but no control. All selected Middle East countries follow the same pattern as the U.S. GAAP and IAS, except Saudi Arabia, which uses the cost method for financial reporting.

5. Consolidation: In all selected countries, financial statements are consolidated if the voting controls 50% or more of subsidiaries. Recently, the FASB decided to use only the purchase method for consolidated financial statements. IAS still provide an option between the purchase and pooling of interest methods.

6. Accounting for income taxes: All selected Middle East countries are using the liability method, the same as the U.S. GAAP and IAS.

7. Foreign currency translation: Israel, Jordan, and Kuwait are consistent with the U.S. GAAP and IAS. The GAAP of both Egypt and Saudi Arabia does not cover the foreign currency translation, however, foreign firms and joint ventures are allowed to use IAS.

8. Accounting for inflation: under U.S. GAAP, this is not required, because the inflation rate is not significant (around 5% for the past 10 years). Under the IAS, it is not mandatory to account for inflation unless the country has a hyperinflationary economy. Among the selected Middle East countries, Israel has the highest inflation rate. The Israeli GAAP requires the use of both general purchasing power (GPP) and current cost accounting. Egypt has the second highest inflation rate (about 20% annually). The Egyptian GAAP does not cover the accounting for inflation topic. Both Jordan and Kuwait follow the IAS. In Saudi Arabia, the inflation rate is not significant, therefore, SGAAP does not cover it.

9. Provision and reserves: All selected countries do not allow the use of general contingency reserves, however, in Egypt, these may be used if permitted by the Egyptian statutory regulations. In Saudi Arabia, no general or material contingencies are disclosed in practice.

10. Disclosure: All countries in the study require the disclosure of all basic financial statements. The only difference lies between Egypt and Israel in the footnotes of the financial statements. The Israeli GAAP considers the footnotes an essential part of financial disclosure, to be included with the basic financial statements. Egypt does not consider the footnotes essential, and it may be acceptable to present financial statements without any footnotes.

SUMMARY AND CONCLUSIONS

This chapter presents the accounting systems and practices of the five selected Middle East countries. First, the accounting systems and practices of each of the five selected countries are discussed. In Egypt, foreign companies or joint ventures may prepare financial statements using the historical cost principle. Accounting practices and principles for foreign and joint-venture companies usually follow internationally accepted accounting standards in most accounting issues. Egypt does not have an organization that promulgates accounting standards, similar to the FASB in the United States, however, the Egyptian Society of Accountants has now begun to review international accounting and auditing standards and to use them to issue opinions that form the basis of Egyptian accounting standards.

In Israel, the only financial statements required by the Companies Ordinance are a balance sheet and a statement of income. However, the Securities Law and the Securities Regulations prescribe that companies offering their securities for sale to the public must prepare and publish full financial statements, including a consolidated balance sheet and a statement of income, a statement of cash flow, changes in shareholder equity, and comprehensive notes to the financial statements. International accounting standards (IAS) have been adopted by the ICPA and apply in cases where there are no specific pronouncements by the ICPA and no other current practices in Israel. The opinions issued by the ICPA and the accounting principles adopted in Israel generally fall within the framework of the IASC standards. In those circumstances where a binding accounting principle on a particular subject has yet to be issued, the Securities Authority is empowered to promulgate an accounting principle applicable to publicly quoted companies.

In Jordan, the Companies Law requires firms to present their balance sheet and profit and loss statement, audited by an independent certified public accountant, with footnotes explaining the significant categories of revenues and expenses. It also requires firms to prepare financial statements according to "conventional accounting principles." The Jordanian Association of Certified Public Accountants decided to adopt the IAS and International Auditing Standards for financial statements issued after 1990. However, no law was passed to mandate the use of IAS; they are applicable only to the extent that they do not conflict with the law.

In Kuwait, all business firms are required to keep adequate financial records and books. All books and records of foreign companies operating in Kuwait are subject to the provisions of the Tax Decree of the official Ministerial order. Beginning January 1, 1991, shareholding and limited liability companies must use the IAS promulgated by the IASC. Audited balance sheet and income statements of both public shareholding and limited liability companies are required for an annual audit. The auditor must be independent and registered with the

Ministry of Commerce and Industry. In general, the financial statements of Kuwaiti firms also are required to follow IAS.

Saudi Arabia is in the early stage of developing its accounting standards. The only formal, generally accepted accounting principle of Saudi Arabia is the Standard of General Presentation and Disclosure (Saudi GAAP), issued by the Ministry of Commerce. The Saudi GAAP issued to date pertains to the requirements of general presentation and disclosure in the financial statements of profit-oriented entities and consolidated financial statements, provides pro-forma examples of presentation, and determines the treatment of accounting changes and contingent gains or losses. The Saudi GAAP requires that financial statements include a profit-and-loss statement, a statement of appropriation of profits, a balance sheet, and an auditor's report. No specific presentation format is imposed, except for banks. A joint venture, with its auditor, can establish its own format.

Second, key accounting similarities and differences are analyzed and compared to U.S. GAAP and IASC; these include investments, inventory, asset valuation, equity method, consolidation, deferred taxes, foreign currency translation, inflation, provisions and reserves, and disclosures. Table 5–2 summarized the accounting differences and similarities of selected Middle East countries, as compared to U.S. GAAP and IAS.

It may be concluded that the selected Middle East countries are following the U.S. GAAP and IAS for seven out of 10 accounting issues. The only difference is that Israel is using the fair market value of accounting for short-term investments. Accounting for inflation, as one of the other three accounting issues, is treated differently by the selected Middle East countries. The Egyptian GAAP covers it but does not require it, even though the average inflation rate was 20% a year from the period 1995–1999. The Saudi Arabian GAAP does not cover the inflation issue, however, the inflation rate in Saudi Arabia is not significant. Israel, with the highest inflation rate in the Middle East, mandates the use of both general price level adjustments and current cost accounting. Of the remaining two accounting issues, equity accounting and consolidation, Saudi Arabia is the only country using the cost method for consolidated financial statements.

As can be seen from the previous analysis, the adoption of IAS by Middle East countries is likely to have a strong impact on the financial reporting practices that are followed by listed business entities in the Middle East, particularly since IAS 1, "Presentation of Financial Statements," clearly rules out any "soft" application of IAS. Companies preparing financial statements under IAS now have to ensure not only that their accounting policies comply with them, but also that they present the financial information in the form and with all of the disclosures mandated by IAS (Khanna 1999).

In the absence of both a local or a regional body of GAAP and a private regional professional organization, it is important for Middle East stock markets to adopt IAS as the financial reporting and disclosure framework for all companies listed or seeking a listing on the stock market. The acceptability of IAS is reinforced by the fact that local banks may accept financial statements prepared under IAS, and the Big Five accounting firms operating in the Middle East have been encouraging their clients, with considerable success, to prepare their financial statements under IAS.

Investors and creditors must be protected and encouraged to participate in the local stock exchange market. The Arab stock market has to formulate a comprehensive, well-structured, and strictly enforceable regulatory mechanism, which results in accountability and effective standards of responsibility. One of the pillars of any such regulatory mechanism has to be a proper financial reporting framework. This requires the adoption of comprehensive and relevant GAAP to ensure uniformity, consistency, and comparability in accounting and the financial information disclosed in companies' financial statements. This will make it easier for investors when making decisions based on comparisons and benchmarking between the performance of one business entity against others in the same industry in the same location. The long-overdue move to establish stock exchange markets in Arab countries needs to be backed by IAS.

REFERENCES

Abdallah, Wagdy. "Accounting Standards in Saudi Arabia and International Accounting Standards." *International Review of Accounting* 2 (1997), 27–41.

———. "American Joint Ventures in the Middle East: The Case of Amoco-Egypt—Managerial, Financial, and Tax Implications." *Middle East Business Review* 3(1) (1999), 49–64.

Accounting Principles Board (APB), No. 18.

Accounting Research Bulletin No. 43. "Inventory Pricing" (ch. 4).

AlHashim, Dhia D. "Social Accounting in Egypt." *The International Journal of Accounting Education and Research* 12 (Spring 1977), 127–142.

Al-Juraid & Company. *Accounting Objectives and Concepts in the Kingdom of Saudi Arabia—Standard of General Presentation and Disclosure.* Jedda, Saudi Arabia: Deloite Ross Tohmatsu International, May 1990.

Al-Rai, Ziad K. and Naim Dahmash. "The Effects of Applying International Accounting and Auditing Standards to the Accounting Profession in Jordan." *Advances in International Accounting* (Supplement 1, 1998), 179–193.

Amer, Metwalli B. "Impact of Public Ownership on the U.A.R. Accounting Profession." *The International Journal of Accounting Education and Research* 4 (Spring 1969), 49–61.

America Online. Country Studies, May 1999.

Briston, Richard J. and Ahmed A. El-Ashker. "The Egyptian Accounting System: A Case Study in Western Influence." *The International Journal of Accounting Education and Research* (Spring 1984), 129–155.

Crossborder Monitor. "Middle East and North Africa Outlook." New York, January 15, 1997.

Country Commercial Guide—Egypt. Cairo: Dar-El-Tiboa El-Kawmeya, 1996.

Dow, Ronald. "Foreign Policy Failure Produced Rise in Heating Oil." *Boston Globe*, February 25, 2000, A22.

Egyptian Investment Law No. 230 of 1989.

Epstein, Barry J. and Abbas Ali Mirza. *IAS 99—Interpretation and Application of International Accounting Standards.* New York: John Wiley & Sons, 1999.

Ernst & Young. *Doing Business in Kuwait.* New York: Ernst & Young International, 1993.

———. *Doing Business in Saudi Arabia.* New York: Ernst & Young International, 1993.

Financial Accounting Standards Board (FASB). "Original Pronouncements." Norwalk, Conn.: FASB.

Gress, Edward J. "Public Accounting in Selected Middle East Countries: A Historical Perspective." In V. K. Zimmerman (ed.), *The Recent Accounting and Economic Developments in the Middle East.* Urbana-Campaign: University of Illinois, Center for International Education and Research in Accounting, 1985, 167–175.

Haskins, Mark E., Kenneth R. Ferris, Robert J. Sack, and Brandt R. Allen. *Financial Accounting & Reporting.* Burr Ridge, Ill.: Richard D. Irwin, 1993.

Hassan, Naim. "International Accounting Standards: Desirable as a Short-Term Solution in the Case of the Arab Gulf States?" In V. K. Zimmerman (ed.), *The Recent Accounting and Economic Developments in the Middle East.* Urbana-Champaign: University of Illinois, Center for International Education and Research in Accounting, 1985, 69–100.

International Accounting Standards Committee (IASC). *International Accounting Standards.* London: IASC, 1999.

Jahmani, Yousef, Ahmad Al-Omari, and Anwar Y. Salimi. "The Development of Financial Reporting in Jordan." Working Paper presented at the IABD, 1996.

Kesselman and Kesselman. *Guide to Investment in Israel.* Tel Aviv: John Wiley, 1992.

Khanna, Nitin. "A Commercial Hub for the Middle East?" *Accountancy* 123 (February 1999), 78–79.

Kieso, Donald E. and Jerry J. Weygandt. *Intermediate Accounting,* 9th ed. New York: John Wiley & Sons, 1998.

Kilborn, Robert, Judy Nichols, and Stephanie Cook. "U.S.A." *Christian Science Monitor,* February 18, 2000, 24.

Mungai, David. "Middle East and Africa." *World Trade* 13 (February 2000), 66–68.

Price Waterhouse. *Doing Business in Egypt.* New York: Price Waterhouse World Firm Services, 1995.

Shuaib, A. "Auditing Standards in Kuwait." In *Comparative International Auditing Standards.* Sarasota, Fla.: American Accounting Association, 1985, 95–102.

Somekh Chaikin. *Doing Business in Israel.* New York: Price Waterhouse World Firm Services BV, 1995.

Wallace, R.S.O. "Survival Strategies of a Global Organization: The Case of the International Accounting Standards Committee." *Accounting Horizon* (June 1990), 1–22.

Chapter 6

International Accounting Standards and Their Impact on Accounting Practices and Principles of Selected Middle East Countries

Comparability of financial reports of companies investing or operating in the Middle East is essential for global trade, finance, and investment. Full comparability may be achieved either by standardization, uniformity, or harmonization of accounting principles. Standardization of accounting is the process of establishing the rules that specify how to prepare financial statements or Generally Accepted Accounting Principles (GAAP) that determine the type of information that financial statements should contain and how that information should be prepared (Mueller, Gernon, and Meek 1997: 38) Under uniformity, accounting rules and practices are identical for all business units in the same industry.

Harmonization of accounting principles is the process of "increasing the compatibility of accounting practices by setting limits on how much they can vary" (Choi, Frost, and Meek 1999: 248). In other words, harmonization of accounting principles means that the differences among nations should be kept at a minimum. It may be acceptable to have alternative accounting principles in different countries, as long as they are in "harmony" with each other and reconciliation of the differences is acceptable (Iqbal, Melcher, and Elmallah 1997: 35).

This chapter addresses the need for the internationalization of accounting standards in general, and the role of the International Accounting Standards Committee (IASC) and its effect on accounting principles and practices in the Middle East. The efforts of various constituents involved in the development of international and auditing standards, including the FASB, SEC, IOSCO, IFAC, and other professional organizations, are discussed. This chapter also covers the relevance of International Accounting Standards (IAS) in Arab countries and Israel, and if new regional standards are needed, how they can be developed and enforced in the countries in the region.

THE NEED FOR INTERNATIONAL ACCOUNTING STANDARDS

There has been a growing recognition of the urgent need for enforcing a core set of internationally uniform recognized standards to ensure that the information upon which investors, creditors, and other users base their investing and financing decisions is comprehensive, reliable, consistent, and internationally comparable.

MNCs prepare financial reports for shareholders, creditors, potential investors, and other users that can vary widely from one country to another, sometimes even within the same country. Without harmonized accounting standards, accounting reports can lack comparability. Management may incur unnecessarily higher costs in preparing different financial reports for different countries. Moreover, investors or businessmen may have difficulty assessing a company's financial performance due to a lack of comparable financial statements. Thus a single, uniform set of high-quality, globally applied and enforced accounting standards is essential for both domestic and cross-border investment and financing decisions.

Competition among the international capital markets may be negatively affected, and MNCs may have to bear higher costs of capital because of the difficulties involved in financial analysis. The credibility of accounting suffers, and accounting reports will significantly lose credibility if a MNC reports different profit numbers in different countries under different GAAPs for exact business transactions.

There is now a need for a set of high-quality international accounting standards that will have a significant impact on the flow of capital between markets and the pricing of capital within markets. The important issue is not whether we should have a set of high-quality international standards, but when and how this might materialize.

THE ROLE OF THE INTERNATIONAL ACCOUNTING STANDARDS COMMITTEE (IASC)

The International Accounting Standards Committee (IASC) is an independent, private organization working to achieve uniformity in accounting principles used by business entities and other organizations for financial reporting around the world. The IASC was formed in 1973 through an agreement made by professional accounting organizations from Australia, Canada, France, Germany, Japan, Mexico, the Netherlands, the United Kingdom and Ireland, and the United States. Since 1983, the IASC's members have included all of the professional accountancy bodies that are members of the International Federation of Accountants (IFAC).

At present, 143 professional accounting organizations in 104 countries are members (including five associate or affiliate members and four affiliate members). Many other organizations are now involved in the work of the IASC. These organizations represent over 2,000,000 accountants worldwide. International Accounting Standards (IAS) are used in several countries around the world, either directly or as the basis for developing national accounting standards. IAS also are used in many countries not represented within the IASC's membership. Overall, there are two main stated goals of the IASC (IASC 1999):

1. To formulate and publish in the public interest international accounting standards to be observed in the presentation of financial statements and to promote their worldwide acceptance and observance; and

2. To work generally for the improvement and harmonization of regulations, accounting standards, and procedures relating to the presentation of financial statements.

In general, the IASC prepares IAS in accordance with due process. Due process ensures that IAS are of high quality and require appropriate accounting practices in particular economic circumstances. Due process also ensures, through consultation with the Consultative Group, the IASC's member bodies, standard-setting bodies, and other interested groups and individuals on a worldwide basis, that IAS are acceptable and valuable to the users and preparers of financial statements.

Setting International Accounting Standards

The development of an internationally acceptable set of high-quality accounting standards depends on the establishment of an internationally acceptable accounting standard-setting body. To date, the IASC has held itself out as the international standard-setting body because of its broadly based membership and its two stated goals. The most important question is: Is the IASC becoming the global accounting standard-setting body? First, it is important to look at the process of making up the accounting standards by the IASC, its strucure, and the quality of IAS. Second, the issue of the recognition and acceptance of IAS by national standard-setting bodies will be addressed. Finally, the role of the FASB, SEC, IOSCO, and the Group of Four (G4) in establishing high-quality international accounting standards will be explored.

For each standard, a steering committee of the IASC has the responsibility of making recommendations to the board. The committee normally publishes a draft statement of principles or another discussion document that sets out the various possible requirements for each standard. Subsequently, the board publishes an exposure draft for public comment, and it then examines the arguments put forth in the comment process before deciding on the final form of the standard. With a vote of two-thirds of board members, an exposure draft can be issued, and with a vote of three-quarters of board members, the final standard is approved. The six steps of the IASC procedure, or due process, to develop International Accounting Standards, are discussed below (IASC 1999).

1. The IASC board sets up a steering committee that includes representatives from the accountancy bodies in at least three other countries, and representatives from other organizations who are represented on the board or the Consultative Group or who are experts in a specific topic or issue.

2. The steering committee identifies and reviews all of the accounting issues associated with the main topic. It considers the application of the IASC's framework for the preparation and presentation of financial statements to those accounting issues and also studies national and regional accounting requirements and practice. After identifying the issues involved, the committee submits to the IASC board a point outline of the detailed scope of the topic.

3. After receiving comments from the board on the point outline, the steering committee prepares and publishes a draft statement of principles (DSOP). The purpose is to propose for comment the underlying accounting principles that will form the basis for preparing the exposure draft. Comments are invited from all interested groups.

4. The steering committee reviews the comments on the DSOP and agrees on a final statement of principles. The statement of principles is submitted to the board for approval and is then used as the basis for preparing an exposure draft of proposed IAS.

5. The steering committee prepares the exposure draft for approval by the board. After revision, and with the approval of at least two-thirds of the board, the exposure draft is published. Comments are invited from all interested groups during this period.

6. The steering committee reviews all of the comments and prepares a draft of IAS for review by the board. After revision, and with the approval of at least three-quarters of the board, the standard is published.

The IASC has completed and submitted its core standards to the IOSCO for endorsement. Some believe that, "For the first time, IASC can say that it has a comprehensive set of standards covering all the major areas of importance to general business" (ICMA 1999). It is not clear whether the core set of standards is of high quality or if the IOSCO will endorse the standards or not for cross-border financial reporting. In many countries, acceptance of IAS for domestic reporting purposes by national authorities will be a function of their acceptability for cross-border purposes. The current body of standards now comprising IAS is much improved over those in place prior to the commencement of the improvement program. However, is it of sufficiently high quality to be acceptable to the IOSCO? Who will be the key players in deciding on this issue? (McGregor 1999: 160).

IAS have gained greater acceptance, and the IASC has shown leadership in many projects covering areas where new standards need to be developed. However, the international accounting standard-setting environment is on the edge of major reform. At present, the IASC considers major structural reform with the recent publication by its strategy working party of the discussion paper "Shaping IASC for the Future." The FASB has indicated its intention to help in the establishment of a high-quality international accounting standard-setting body.

Currently, no single set of high-quality international accounting standards that could be acceptable for both domestic and cross-border financial reporting exists, due to the lack of acceptance of IAS in most capital markets, and the adoption of U.S. GAAP by MNCs in order to raise capital in the U.S. market. It is believed that the truly international standard setter is the FASB. Moreover, the FASB has played a world leadership role in the development of accounting standards for many years, and the standards published by other standard-setting bodies, including the IASC, have often been based on the FASB's (McGregor 1999: 163).

The Structure of the IASC

The IASC consists of five bodies. Its responsibilities are described as follows (IASC 1999):

1. The IASC board makes decisions on accounting principles and publishes them in the form of International Accounting Standards.
2. The Consultative Group advises the board on technical issues in IASC projects, on the IASC's work program, and on strategic matters.
3. The Advisory Council reviews the board's strategy and plans to ensure that the needs of the IASC's constituencies are being met; it prepares an annual report on the board's effectiveness; it promotes participation in and acceptance of the work of the IASC by the accountancy profession, the business community, the users of financial statements, and other interested parties; it seeks and obtains funding for the IASC's work in a way that does not impair the IASC's independence; and and it reviews the IASC's budget and financial statements.
4. The Standing Interpretations Committee considers accounting issues that are likely to receive divergent or unacceptable treatment in the absence of authoritative guidance and develops, for board approval, interpretations of IAS.
5. A strategy working party was formed in January 1997 to consider the strategy of the IASC for the period following completion of the work program in 1998. The group addresses matters such as the IASC structure, operating procedures, relationships with national standard setters, the IASC's involvement in training and education, and funding.

In 1998, the IASC's strategy working party (SWP) presented a proposal for a three-tier system encompassing a standards development body (the Standards Development Committee, comprised mostly of "representatives" of national standard-setting bodies), a standards approval body (the IASC board), and an oversight body (the trustees). The rationale of these proposals was primarily to provide a mechanism for achieving a greater level of involvement of national standard-setting bodies. In December 1999, by a unanimous vote, the IASC approved the proposed structure for an organization that, very soon, will become the world's setter of accounting standards. The proposed restructuring of the

IASC will create an organization that is independent and objective in setting acceptable standards for all major international stock markets worldwide (Cheney 2000: 14).

In recent years, this issue has created tensions between the IASC and national standard setters, especially the Group of Four (G4)—Australia, Canada, New Zealand, the United Kingdom, and the United States, as the IASC has assumed the role of standard setter rather than merely "standard harmonizer." This lack of representation on the IASC board constitutes a barrier to coalition of accounting standards, in the sense of national and international standards converging with one another. It is believed that the reform proposals are an acknowledgment that the continued exclusion of the major national standard-setting bodies from direct participation in the IASC standard-setting process has created a climate of competition, not cooperation (McGregor 1999: 159–168).

The problem with this proposal is the failure of the body to be responsible for the development of standards (the Standards Development Committee) with the power to issue standards without first obtaining the approval of another body (the restructured IASC board). Under the proposed structure, decisions of the body with acknowledged expertise to develop high-quality accounting standards can be overridden by a body that may comprise individuals with little or no experience in standard setting and/or inadequate knowledge of the matters which are the subject of particular standards. It is highly unlikely that national standard-setting bodies will be prepared to devote the considerable resources necessary to make this initiative a success if this critical aspect of the proposal remains in place, as evidenced by the FASB's vision of an acceptable international accounting system. The FASB makes its objections to the proposal crystal clear by stating that under its vision

The decision-making body has full authority to set standards. That is, it is independent from other decision-making bodies, it has the power to innovate, and its decisions are not subject to approval of another body that could veto decisions based on self-interested objectives. (FASB 1998: 26)

The AICPA believes that the standard-setting board should be comprised of "highly skilled, experienced individuals with varied backgrounds, including financial statement users, preparers, public accountants, academics, national standard setters, and regulators" (AICPA, July 1999: 11). In the meantime, the SEC's acceptance or rejection of the core standards already developed by the IASC becomes critical to the success of a universal set of international accounting standards.

The Quality of International Accounting Standards

World capital markets are demanding high-quality international accounting standards, MNCs and politicians are encouraging their development, and all capital market regulators and standard setters are actively pursuing their development. It may be believed that we are almost there with the completion by the IASC of its core set of standards. The IASC has been vigorously pursuing the goal of developing a set of high-quality international accounting standards with the support of several organizations, including governments, capital market participants, regulators, and standard setters around the world. In their view, all that is left is the endorsement by the IOSCO. However, it is not an easy decision for the IOSCO, and it is more likely that the chance that the IAS will be endorsed by both the IOSCO and the SEC is a remote one. This issue is explained below.

While the IASC may fail to gain support from some countries for reasons more to do with sectional interests than high-quality financial reporting, the fundamental reason the support will not be forthcoming is that the IAS will be perceived to be of inadequate quality. The criteria by which the IOSCO will assess the IAS have not been made known. However, it can be assumed that the criteria specified by the SEC will be indicative. The SEC has said that for the standards to gain acceptance, they must:

1. include a core set of accounting pronouncements that constitutes a comprehensive, generally accepted basis of accounting;
2. be of high quality and result in comparability and transparency and provide for full disclosure; and
3. be rigorously interpreted and applied (Sutton 1999).

It is more likely that the SEC will be influenced significantly by the views of the FASB. In fact, the SEC has made it known that it will be looking to the FASB for advice. Moreover, the FASB (1998: 5), in its vision paper, states that

A reasonably complete set of unbiased accounting standards that require relevant, reliable information that is decision useful for outside investors, creditors, and others who make similar decisions would constitute a high-quality set of accounting standards.

The paper notes that each of those standards should:

1. be consistent with the guidance provided by an underlying conceptual framework;
2. avoid or minimize alternative accounting procedures;
3. be unambiguous and comprehensible; and
4. be capable of rigorous interpretation and application.

In concluding this section, it has been a common conclusion of most academicians and practitioners that developing a single set of high-quality accounting standards that may be appropriate for both domestic and cross-border financial reporting will not be achievable under the IASC's existing structure, as its strategy working party has implicitly acknowledged.

Recognition and Support for the IASC

The IASC has adopted a work plan to produce a comprehensive core set of high-quality standards, aimed at a more general acceptance of IAS for cross-border listings. This work plan has been reviewed by the technical committee of the IOSCO. In July 1995, the committee said that successful completion of the work plan would allow it to recommend endorsement of IAS for cross-border capital raising and listing purposes in all global markets. In March 1996, because of the strong demand for early completion of its work program, and recognizing that a delay would cause inconvenience and cost to international companies, the IASC decided to adopt fast-track procedures for completing its program of core standards.

Several MNCs and international financial institutions prepare their financial reports in accordance with IAS. Moreover, many companies in many countries, including the Middle East, endorse IAS as their own, either without amendment or with minor additions or deletions. The appendix at the end of this chapter presents the companies and other organizations of the Middle East that are using IAS. Many stock exchanges accept IAS for cross-border listing purposes. The IASC works closely with the national standard-setting bodies, securities regulatory agencies, and stock exchanges in individual countries that accept IAS for cross-border listing purposes, intergovernmental organizations (such as the European Commission, the OECD, and the UN), and development agencies such as the World Bank.

The AICPA organization considers the IASC an independent standard-setting body unaffiliated with any professional organization, country, or national standard setter. The AICPA supports the IASC for its efforts to improve its structure, and it agrees with the IASC that its primary objective should be to develop high-quality accounting standards that provide transparency and comparability of information useful to investors and lenders in making economic decisions (AICPA, June 1999: 12).

The IOSCO expects the IASC to provide mutually acceptable IAS for use in multinational securities offerings and other international offerings. Currently a number of stock market exchanges require foreign issuers to present financial statements in accordance with IAS. Consequently, hundreds of MNCs disclose the fact that their financial statements conform with IAS.

In 1993, the IOSCO agreed on a list of core standards for use in financial statements of MNCs involved in cross-border offerings and listings. IAS that already deal with most of the core standards exist. The IOSCO has already endorsed IAS 7, Cash Flow Statements, and it has indicated to the IASC that 14 of the existing IAS do not require additional improvement if the other core standards are successfully completed.

In 1995, the IOSCO's technical committee agreed that successful completion of the board's current work plan would mean that IAS comprise a comprehensive core set of standards. Completion of comprehensive core standards that are acceptable to the technical committee allows it to recommend the endorsement of IAS for cross-border capital raising and listing purposes in all international markets.

On April 30, 1999, the IOSCO technical committee submitted a letter of comment to the IASC in response to the IASC strategy working party report, *Shaping IASC for the Future*. An excerpt follows:

The Technical Committee represents some of the world's largest and most developed markets. Both the Technical Committee and the IASC agree that there is a compelling need for high quality, comprehensive international accounting standards oriented to the needs of investors. A shared goal of both bodies is that financial statements prepared in accordance with such standards can be used in cross-border offerings and listings as an alternative to national accounting standards. (IASC 1999)

For the IOSCO, the endorsement by the SEC is very important. To develop a set of "truly international standards" for cross-border financial reporting, it is essential to facilitate access to the liquid and low-cost U.S. capital market. Of course, access is possible now, but in some non-U.S. MNCs' executives' minds, it is too costly to comply with the U.S. GAAP. The SEC thus faces a significant dilemma—it must either satisfy itself about whether IAS are of equal quality to the U.S. GAAP or, if they are not, it must either withhold its endorsement or endorse a set of standards that will not provide the same quality of information to U.S. capital market participants as domestic standards. The FASB and the New York Stock Exchange (NYSE), the major players in the U.S. capital market, have a vested interest in the outcome of the SEC's decision-making process.

The NYSE aggressively seeks the business of issuers from around the world. From its perspective, the U.S. GAAP represents a significant barrier to new listings and the benefits perceived to flow therefrom. "Because IAS could provide entree to NYSE listings for U.S. GAAP–shy companies, they have had the support of the NYSE and sympathetic politicians for some time" (McGregor 1999: 162).

INTERNATIONAL ORGANIZATIONS AND THEIR ROLE IN THE GLOBALIZATION OF ACCOUNTING STANDARDS

International Federation of Accountants (IFAC)

The International Federation of Accountants (IFAC) is a worldwide organization of national professional accounting organizations. It was established in 1977 with much wider responsibilities than the IASC, including the development and promulgation of International Standards on Auditing (ISA) and a code of ethics, education guidelines, studies and statements for the public sector and assistance to those accountants in business. Insofar as accounting standards are concerned, the IFAC's role is to assist in their promulgation and encourage their development.

The IFAC's member bodies—143 independent professional bodies in 103 separate countries—have undertaken to use their best endeavors to ensure that the IFAC's standards and guidelines are introduced within their own countries. Membership in the IFAC automatically includes membership in the IASC. There are several standing technical committees of the IFAC, including: international auditing practices, education, forum on ethics, financial and management accounting, public sector, and information technology.

As far as auditing standards are concerned, the IFAC's work has in the past concentrated on the verification of financial statements, but it is now beginning to work on other areas where the opinion of the independent auditor can add value and credibility to the information provided by directors and management. Therefore, we may anticipate standards and guidance in areas such as prospective financial information, key performance indicators, corporate governance, and matters that may not primarily be financial in nature. In brief, the auditing profession has recognized the growing needs of an increasing range of stakeholders for more extensive, detailed assurance services beyond the traditional audit (Harding 1999).

The IFAC has a vested interest in the IASC's working party's proposals and will be a key player in the restructuring process. The professional accounting bodies in Australia, Germany, Malaysia, New Zealand, the United Kingdom, and the United States have all had primary responsibility for the development of accounting standards or guidelines in their respective countries. The transfer of power to a government or an independent private-sector body in those countries was not necessarily welcomed by the professional accounting bodies, and the loss of influence and public profile was regretted. The recent successful public profiling of the IASC and the influence it has had on the development of accounting standards in individual countries has indirectly restored to these accounting bodies a degree of influence over the development of their national standards. In addition, in other countries, such as Canada, where the professional accounting bodies have retained the primary responsibility for setting national accounting standards, the bodies may be concerned that a restructured, independent IASC may be a catalyst for an independent review of the structure of national standard-setting arrangements (McGregor 1999).

Financial Accounting Standards Board (FASB)

The FASB is straightforward in the standard-setting process. It has supporters such as the Securities and Exchange Commission (SEC), whose chairman stated that while international harmonization is desirable for the United States, its standards are accepted throughout the world, and its quality is unmatched. All of the FASB's meetings are open to the public. The FASB has to maintain the high-quality financial reporting by SEC registrants, which are the most significant contributions to the efficiency of the U.S. capital market. It will have in mind the likely reaction of domestic issuers to a SEC decision to allow foreign registrants to apply "lower quality" standards. It will also have in mind the relative positioning of national and international standard-setting bodies. Endorsement by the IOSCO and the SEC will significantly increase the chances of the IASC becoming the global standard-setting body (McGregor 1999: 162).

The FASB, in its vision paper, makes the clear statement that,

Worldwide acceptance of internationally recognized standards and a global standard-setting process is impossible without U.S. acceptance and participation. As the largest capital market, the United States is the primary target in the drive for internationally recognized standards. U.S. support is necessary to the legitimacy of any set of international standards, and the United States has much to contribute to ensuring [that] those standards are of high quality. (FASB 1998: 1)

The FASB must be a major player in the redesign of the international accounting standard-setting model. It is the world's most powerful standard-setting body and presides over the world's largest capital market. It has unmatched expertise in standard setting and the most rigorous, comprehensive set of accounting standards in existence.

The FASB's vision paper is significant in signaling its intention to participate in the establishment of an acceptable international accounting standard-setting arrangement. The FASB has the experience and qualification of having a set of high-quality international accounting standards to facilitate the flow of capital between countries and to optimize the allocation of countries' scarce resources. However, never before has it been so explicit about its willingness to support an international accounting standard-setting system, or about how such a system should be structured.

It is believed that the FASB does not support a three-tier system. Rather, the standard-setting board (the Standards Development Committee, under the IASC model) should be independent and not have its decisions subject to a veto by another body. As noted above, this feature of the working party's proposals is critical in gaining the support of those likely to lose power under the proposed new arrangements. To a large extent, the FASB vision mirrors the models prevailing in the United States and the United Kingdom—models that have proven to be very successful.

The European Union

In 1957, the Treaty of Rome established the European Union (EU) with the goal of harmonizing the legal and economic systems of it members. Unlike the IASC, the European Commission, which is the governing body of the EU, has full authority for its accounting directives throughout the member countries.

The EU attaches great importance to the harmonization of international accounting standards as a contribution to its objective of fair and effective competition. IAS are important to even-handed competition among the capital markets of Europe, as well as to all markets for goods and services. While the EU has in the past thrown its weight behind the IASC to facilitate access by European companies to Third World country capital markets, it has, to date, withheld carte blanche to use IAS, since Europe has been concerned about safeguarding its negotiating power in the IASC. Recently, the EU has been concentrating its efforts in the accounting area to assist in the integration of Europe's capital markets post-European currency unit (McGregor 1999: 164).

Although it is expected that IAS will continue to play a key role in the regulation of financial reporting by European companies, it is clear that the IASC has been warned that continued EU support is based on continued European influence over the IASC, as reflected in renewed support for a European Accounting Standards Board (EASB). Ostensibly the establishment of such a board would improve the capacity of EU members to participate in the IASC's due process and facilitate the consistent application of IAS across member states. However, politically, the formation of a EASB would be a clear message to the IASC to remember that, despite its efforts to gain U.S. support, its major support base is still in Europe (McGregor 1999: 165).

ARE IAS RELEVANT FOR MIDDLE EAST COUNTRIES?

This question has several dimensions. Are Middle East countries (including Arab countries and Israel) similar to each other in their cultural, economic, political, legal, and educational environmental variables? Do Arab countries have different cultural, political, legal, and educational environmental factors than Israel? If so, will IAS be relevant for Israeli and/or Arab needs? If not, do Middle East countries need a different, harmonized accounting system more relevant to their environment? Are the differences between Israel, Arab countries and other countries currently using IAS so large as to not justify the use of IAS for their financial reporting systems? Is the U.S. GAAP more relevant to Arab countries than IAS?

Accounting systems and reporting practices usually arise from the need to inform the interested groups in the society in which they are developed. Therefore, in every society of every Middle East country, accounting systems and practices are expected to be a function of the environmental factors that influence business practices in that society. Financial reports also are expected to reflect the outcome of those Middle East environmental factors.

An accounting "standard" is a model, an example, or a criterion that outlines how certain accounting items or transactions on financial statements or reports should be measured and presented, and what information should be disclosed for the interested users. The three accounting standards applicable to our analysis include:

1. the local standards, established by the national standard-setting body;
2. the U.S. standards, as set by the FASB; and
3. the International Accounting Standards, established by the IASC.

If every country in the Middle East decides on using one standard versus another, it will result in the creation of different financial statements, depending on the circumstances. MNCs such as IBM or Johnson & Johnson, who wish to acquire one of the major factories in Egypt or start a joint venture in Kuwait, may need to become familiar with all local accounting standards. The dilemma of different standards raises even more questions. Which accounting standard should they use to present their financial statements for review? Which accounting standard should be adopted by MNCs and world capital markets? The answers to these questions create challenges for the IASC and national standard-setting organizations in the Middle East and around the world. The outcome and the standards agreed upon affect global financing and investing in the integrating world economy. The decision also affects the viability and procedures of Middle East standard-setting groups in every country (Sturge 1998).

To make national accounting standards harmonize with IAS means that the differences between IAS and national standards should be kept to a minimum. Harmonization has many advantages, including the comparability of international financial information. Another advantage of harmonization is that Egyptian companies' financial statements may become comparable to those of British, Japanese, or Singaporean companies, which will help alleviate the current misunderstanding about the reliability of non-U.S. MNCs' financial statements. And still another advantage is the reduction of the cost of consolidating divergent financial statements.

However, harmonization might entail imposing Western accounting principles on Middle East countries whose business and accounting practices are less developed than the West (Hamid, Graig, and Clarke 1993: 132). It also ignores the fact that accounting is considered a socio-technical activity, in any country, including human, non-human, financial, and non-financial resources or techniques, as well as interaction between the two. Moreover, Hamid et al. (1993) suggested that cultural inputs, such as religion, should not be ignored, because they are confounding elements in harmonizing IAS.

In the Middle East, local accounting standards were originally developed when the world market was not as global as it is today. Those standards in individual Middle East countries were based on their unique social, legal, and educational environmental variables, with little regard for standards in other countries. Moreover, the increasing integration of the global economy has created the need for international standards. Financial professionals at all levels are finding it increasingly more challenging to analyze statements that are produced with a wide variety of standards. At present, many countries have participated in the work of the IASC and support its goals.

In Egypt, no private professional accounting organization exists to promulgate its general accounting standards. The Central Accounting Organization, a branch of the government, sets the accounting principles for state-owned business firms. The Egyptian Society of Accountants and Auditors is a member of the IASC and the IFAC. Foreign companies investing or operating in Egypt are allowed to use IAS; however, Egyptian companies do refer to the use of IAS. The Egyptian American Bank is the only one listed on the IASC's list of companies referring to their use of IAS.

In Kuwait, the Kuwait Association of Accountants and Auditors is the local professional body of accountants, with approximately 530 members. The association is a member of the IFAC, which is responsible for issuing International Standards on Auditing. KSCs–Kuwaiti shareholding joint stock companies and KSC(c)s–Closed shareholding companies must comply with the standards promulgated by the IASC.

In Saudi Arabia, the Ministry of Commerce and the Saudi Organization of Certified Public Accountants (SOCPA) control the accounting profession. The SOCPA introduced a professional qualification for Saudi nationals, similar to the U.S. certified public accountant designation. In circumstances not covered by a specific SOCPA standard, Saudi companies should look for guidance to U.S. GAAP, modified as appropriate to Saudi circumstances. The development of the accounting profession is proceeding at an accelerated pace since the formation of the SOCPA. The Professional Partnerships Law encourages further growth of the accounting profession by permitting national practitioners to affiliate with large international accounting firms (Ernst & Young International 1999).

Similarities and Differences between Middle East Countries

An understanding of how Middle East cultural values affect cross-national accounting diversity can be useful in efforts to reduce that diversity and to enhance the comparability of accounting information worldwide.

In Chapter 3, we discussed the effect of cultural values, including religion, on accounting systems and practices of developing countries in general and on the Middle East in particular, using the Hofstede–Gray theory. It has been found that there are difficulties in harmonizing IAS because of the significant effect of different culture values on the achievability of uniform IAS (Hofstede 1980, 1987, 1991; Gray 1988; Perera 1989; Nobes 1983, 1984; Violet 1983; Belkaoui and Picur 1991; Fechner and Kilgore 1994; Baydoun and Willett 1995; Doupnik and Salter 1995). Moreover, as international comparisons of accounting practices have revealed differences, research has identified that cultural and religious variables have a considerable effect on a country's accounting system and practices (Hamid, Graig and Clarke 1993; Baydoun and Willett 1995).

If we take a closer look at the Arab countries, it may be true that accounting systems and practices in certain Arab countries have been significantly influenced by several Islamic cultural values, with religion being the most significant. It may not be acceptable by those countries to use IAS as a substitute for their national accounting standards. If the national cultural values of Islamic society shape and reinforce both accounting systems and practices, it is suggested that it will be a rational decision to harmonize the accounting standards of those countries as one subgroup of the international community. However, it is not known at present whether it will be costly for the IASC to develop regional international accounting standards. With additional investigation of the cultural values and accounting systems and practices of Middle East countries, it may be possible to come up with a reasonable solution.

There are conflicting groups of culture in the Middle East: Arabs and Israelis. The Arab countries have many things in common, although they may perceive themselves from time to time as having different political and economic aims. The three main common characteristics of the Arabs are concentrated in their cultural values; these are basic values, basic religious attitudes, and basic self-perceptions (Nydell 1996). Notwithstanding that some of them are very rich, they are all developing countries attempting to build a modern business infra-structure within limited social and physical resources. However, Arab countries represent the largest, most diverse, and most politically influential Muslim ethnic group in the world (Bethany World Prayer Center 1997). The historical link between Arabs and the Islamic religion is still very strong.

Arab cultures are more heavily influenced than are Americans by institutions such as family, religion, and government, which interact to shape the value systems of individuals and groups. These cultural differences have been directly linked to differences in managerial practices and accounting systems and practices that have been evidenced in these two cultures (Yasin, Green, and Zimmerer 1992: 77).

A good illustration of how Middle East countries' financial reporting works is to take a look at the stock market in both Arab countries and Israel. In Arab countries, stock markets may be inefficient in terms of valuation, especially compared to those of the United States and Europe. Investors and financial institutions must pay more attention to countries with better growth prospects (Egypt and Tunisia, for example) and to firms whose shares are currently un-dervalued but have a market niche that would help support their profitability and growth.

Azzam (1999) concluded that by emerging market standards, Arab stock markets are small, representing almost 9% of the total market capitalization of the 38 emerging markets in Asia, Latin America, Africa, and Eastern Europe. At the end of 1998, the total capitalization of the 12 Arab stock markets stood at $157.8 billion, with the Saudi stock market, the largest in the region, accounting for 27% of the total. Morever, in the six GCC states—Bahrain, Kuwait, Oman, Qatar, Saudi Arabia, and the United Arab Emirates—most banks produce two sets of audited statements—one set for the central bank, the other for share-holders and third parties (Tokunaga, Blakeway-Phillips, and Aitken 1989).

Some believe that accounting systems and practices in the Arab countries may be becoming increasingly diverse, with more and more companies following U.S.-style accounting practices. Kantor, Roberts and Salter (1995) have concluded that the evidence from their study tends to contradict this assertion. Instead, it has been found that the accounting practices in the three Arab countries examined are remarkably similar. They also found out that, in general, differences in financial reporting practices are driven by differences in financing patterns. And it is expected that the Arab countries, in the near future, will move more toward adopting the accounting practices commonly followed in the United States as the typical pattern of financing corporation changes.

When we compare the accounting practices and education of Arab countries to American and European countries, we expect to see a difference. Thus Egypt, Saudi Arabia, and the United Arab Emirates should all differ from Western countries such as the United Kingdom, France, or the United States. In the latter countries, there is more emphasis on strict financial accounting and auditing, whereas in the former countries, the emphasis is on information needed for economic planning at the macro level. Another difference is the relative emphasis on income measurement. In developed countries, income determination is one of the most important tools, because the majority of businesses are privately owned. This is not the case in Arab countries, because government ownership is far more dominant than private ownership (Kantor et al. 1995).

Also, Kantor et al. (1995), in their study, examined 100 financial reporting practices and found that only three were significantly different across the three selected Arab countries. Given the nature of these economies, these differences are relatively minor. In contrast to this finding, substantial differences emerge between this group and the Western countries. Of the 100 issues examined, only 30 did not differ between the Arab countries and at least one of the three Western countries (see Table 6–1).

Moreover, Kantor et al. (1995) considered three Western countries individually, and they found that the least differences emerged between the Arab group and France, with only 21 of the 100 issues resulting in significant differences. This is in marked contrast to the position of either the United Kingdom, where 46 of the items resulted in significant differences, or the United States, where significant differences emerged for 59 items. The reasons for these findings may lie in the very different cultures of the societies and in the perceived role of financial reports and accounts. It is particularly noticeable that differences across the Arab countries and the United Kingdom and the United States emerge with regard to both measurement and disclosure issues (Kantor et al. 1995).

It also is important to point out that differences in measurement issues are due to requirements in the United Kingdom and the United States concerning areas of accounting that are relatively sophisticated, where national accounting standard setters are relatively new in these countries. To some extent, these differences stem from variations in corporate financing patterns, with companies in the Arab countries tending to rely far more on government financing or funds from a relatively small local elite. However, these institutional differences are likely to be reinforced by cultural differences that also encourage the relative secrecy found in the Arab countries. Still, cultural differences between the Arab countries and the United States will remain. Therefore, it is probable that even if these countries succeed in energizing their emerging stock markets and continue to privatize more and more industries, many fundamental differences between financial reporting practices in the Arab countries and the United States will remain (Kantor et al. 1995).

In general, IAS are of great use to Arab countries or other countries that do not have their own national standard-setting body or the financial and non-financial resources for the full process of preparing appropriate accounting standards to meet their needs. The preparation of accounting standards involves considerable cost and, quite apart from the advantages of uniformity, it would not be economic for each country to have a separate process and separate set of standards. Some Middle East companies use IAS for their financial statements to list their securities on the stock markets. The names of these companies are included in the appendix at the end of this chapter.

However, if Arab or Islamic countries are looking ahead to having one regional standard setter and one set of international financial reporting standards, the following four principles are essential in achieving this ultimate goal:

1. All Arab countries involved in global financial reporting must have a common mission or objective of financial accounting and reporting.
2. Arab countries must have a process for developing financial reporting standards that is accepted and trusted by all constituents, one that ensures that the mission of the standard setter is fulfilled.
3. Arab countries should develop standards that achieve high quality.
4. One regional standard-setting body should be formed and must have the power to enforce accounting standards for all national companies in the region.

Under the threat of further financial crises on an even worse scale, and with world recession widely predicted, Arab governments, intergovernmental agencies, and global financial institutions now have a real fear that the crisis in Asia will be repeated elsewhere, and on an even greater scale. Facing this threat, Arab countries may have been forced to look for ways of securing greater economic stability for the future. And, at last, after several years of largely unproductive debate, there is a growing trend to enforce a core set of internationally recognized standards to ensure that the information upon which investors and other stakeholders base their decisions is transparent, comprehensive, reliable, consistent, and internationally comparable (Harding 1999: 17). The accounting profession in Arab countries has to participate in the development of regional, high-quality accounting standards and cooperate with accounting firms serving the business community in implementing those standards.

Table 6–1
Financial Reporting Practices That Were Not Significantly Different between Selected Arab and Western Countries

Broad Concepts	• Revenue is recognized when its realization is reasonably assured.
	• Costs of sales and expenses are appropriately matched against sales and revenues.
	• Disclose departures from historical cost convention.
Accounting Policies	• Disclose any accounting principle or method chosen from two or more alternatives.
	• Disclose the effect of any change in the accounting principles and methods used from period to period.
	• Disclose the effect of changes in general price level in the financial statements or notes to the accounts.
	• Disclose the effect of changes in prices of inventory and/or fixed assets in the financial statements or notes to the accounts.
	• Disclose comparative figures for the prior year in the financial statements.
Fixed Assets and Depreciation	• Disclose basis on which fixed assets are stated.
	• Fixed assets are stated at cost of acquisition or construction, less accumulated depreciation.
	• Costs of construction of fixed assets consist of the direct costs of labor and materials, plus an appropriate portion of overhead.
	• Depreciation is provided for by the declining method or another method having a similar effect, such as the sum-of-years digits.
	• Disclose depreciation method.
	• Disclose depreciation charges.
	• Disclose amount of accumulated depreciation.
Inventories	• Disclose basis on which inventories are stated.
	• Inventories are stated at the lower of cost or market.
	• Market value of inventories is interpreted as net realizable value defined as estimated selling price, less any reasonably predictable costs of completion and disposal.
	• Disclose method of determining the cost of inventories (i.e., LIFO, FIFO, etc.).

140

Investments	• Disclose basis on which investments are stated. • Investments in marketable securities classified as current assets are stated at the lower of cost or market value. • Investments in marketable securities classified as long-term assets are stated at the lower of cost or market value.
Liabilities	• Disclose current position of long-term debt classified as current liability. • Shareholders' equity. • Disclose rights and preferences to dividends and principal. • Amounts for future losses or other nonspecific contingencies are appropriated to reserves. • Reserves for specific or general purposes are set up by charges to (or reduction of) net income.
Other Items	• Intangible assets other than goodwill are amortized over the period to be benefited.
Income Statement	• Disclose sales and other revenues. • All gains and losses are included in net income.
Foreign Currencies	• The closing exchange rate is used in translating all assets and liabilities, except in hyperinflationary economies.

Source: Kantor et al. 1995: 31–45.

Israel's Accounting and IAS

Israel is located in the Middle East, and it is not an Arab country. People have different cultural values in Israel, and they behave, live, and make their business decisions differently than Arabs. The Arab–Israeli conflict is nearly coming to an end. The Middle East is now open for business. Business, not politics, will drive the Middle East peace process.

On September 28, 1995, in Washington, D.C., Israel and the Palestine Liberation Organization (PLO) signed the interim agreement on the West Bank and Gaza Strip, which marked a significant breakthrough in the Middle East peace process as well as in the regions' economic and business prospects. The agreement provides Palestinian autonomy in the Gaza Strip and West Bank town of Jericho.

The final steps of negotiations between Israel and the Palestinian Authority were supposed to be underway by February 2000; however, disagreement on the implementations and the results are major barriers to achieving the stated goal, which is permanent resolution of all outstanding issues between the state of Israel and the Palestinian Authority. The Israeli and Palestinian negotiators remain far apart on major issues such as Jewish settlements, borders, security, water, Palestinian refugees, and Jerusalem.

Israel has witnessed a growth in foreign investment over the past two years. The signing of the Oslo Accords between Israel and the PLO, the peace treaty with Jordan, and increased diplomatic ties throughout Africa, Asia, and the Middle East have instilled international investor confidence in Israel. As the peace process develops, the Israeli corporate sector can expect to benefit from a peace dividend.

With respect to accounting standards, Peter Agars noted that "new" countries, meaning those in which the profession had relatively recent roots, such as Australia and Israel, were much more flexible and ready to adopt new standards than were "old" countries—such as the United Kingdom and Holland—where the accounting profession has been long established (Landau 1992).

The origin of the public accounting system in Israel goes back to the end of World War I, when the British, with the help of Arabs seeking independence from the Ottoman Empire, managed to capture Palestine. During the period of the British mandate on Palestine, a number of laws were enacted, such as the Companies Ordinance, the Cooperative Societies Ordinance, and the Income Tax Ordinance. These acts helped give birth to the contemporary public accounting and auditing systems in what is now Israel. The profession has changed substantially since its origin. Even though the profession originally had British antecedents, given the economic and sociopolitical ties between the United States and Israel, it has moved closer to the American accounting system. The trend seems to be toward accepting and recognizing the accounting principles, the forms of financial reporting, and the standards of auditing (Kesselman and Kesselman 1992).

The growth of larger businesses, the rise of a corporate form of ownership, the development of a capital market, the expansion of Israel's economy, and the need to encourage certain industries have all led to the enactment of a wide range of laws dealing with taxes, land appreciation, encouragement of industry, and capital investment. These laws have contributed to the growth in the public accounting profession in Israel. In contrast to the others in its geographical region, Israel's accounting profession is much more developed. A significant number of stocks for the Israeli firms are traded in American and European stock exchanges.

The Tel Aviv Stock Exchange (TASE) was founded in 1953, replacing the Tel Aviv Securities Clearing House, which began operations in 1935. Thirteen banks and 14 brokerage firms make up the exchange's 27 members. In the stock market, floor trading is conducted by member firms and by some mutual fund and portfolio managers who participate as associate members. As of January 1995, 350 large- and medium-sized companies were traded on the main list. Another 287 small-capitalization companies traded on the parallel list (*Global Investor* 1995).

International Accounting Standards published by the IASC have been adopted by the ICPA and apply in cases where there are no specific pronouncements by the ICPA and no other current practices in Israel. The opinions issued by the ICPA and the accounting principles adopted in Israel generally fall within the framework of IASC standards. They supplement the requirements of the Companies Ordinance, the Securities Authority, and the TASE regarding the form and contents of financial statements. In circumstances where a binding accounting principle on a particular subject has yet to be issued, the Securities Authority is empowered to promulgate an accounting principle applicable to publicly quoted companies. However, a new accounting standards board (modeled after the U.S. Financial Accounting Standards Board) has been proposed as a joint venture of the ICPA and the Israel Securities Authority.

Financial statements prepared in conformity with Israeli generally accepted accounting principles comply with IAS in all material respects.

The Israeli Institute of Certified Public Accountants, a member of the IASC, has indicated that standards published by the IASC apply if no specific pronouncements or generally accepted accounting principles in Israel relate to the particular item. For such items, U.S. Generally Accepted Accounting Principles also are considered (Ernst & Young International 1999).

SUMMARY AND CONCLUSIONS

This chapter addresses the need for the internationalization of accounting standards for the Middle East, the role of the IASC, and its effect on accounting principles and practices in the Middle East. It discusses and emphasizes the importance of understanding the efforts of various constituents who are involved in the development of international and auditing standards, including the IFAC,

FASB, EU, SEC, IOSCO, and other professional organizations. This chapter also covers the relevance of IAS in Arab countries and Israel, and if new regional standards are needed, how they can be developed and enforced in the countries in the region.

There has been a growing recognition of the urgent need for enforcing a set of high-quality international accounting standards: (1) to provide investors, creditors, and other users with relevant, comprehensive, reliable, consistent, and internationally comparable information for their investing and financing decisions; and (2) to help the correct flow of capital between markets and the pricing of capital within markets. However, this depends on the establishment of an internationally acceptable accounting standard-setting body. To date, the IASC has been the predominant international standard-setting body because of its broadly based membership and its two stated goals.

The IASC has been vigorously pursuing the goal of developing IAS with the support of several organizations, including the IOSCO, SEC, capital market participants, regulators, and standard setters around the world. However, the IASC has not been endorsed for its core standards by the IOSCO. It is not an easy decision for the IOSCO, and it is more likely that both the SEC and the FASB will have a significant impact on this issue.

If every country in the Middle East has the choice to decide on using local standards, U.S. standards, or IAS, this will result in the creation of different financial statements, depending on the circumstances. Local accounting standards in the Middle East were originally developed when the world market was not as global as it is today. The standards in individual Middle East countries were based on their unique social, legal, and educational environmental variables, with little regard for the standards in other countries.

If the national cultural values of Islamic society shape and reinforce both accounting systems and practices, it may be a rational decision to harmonize the accounting standards of those countries as one subgroup of the international community. However, it might be costly for the IASC to develop regional international accounting standards.

Kantor et al. (1995) have found that differences across the Arab countries and the United Kingdom and the United States emerge with regard to both measurement and disclosure issues, due to variations in corporate financing patterns with companies in the Arab countries, which tend to rely far more on governmental financing or funds from a relatively small local elite. However, these institutional differences tend to be reinforced by cultural ones that also encourage the relative secrecy found in the Arab countries. Kantor et al. (ibid.) added that even if the Arab countries succeed in energizing their emerging stock markets and continue to privatize more and more industries, many fundamental cultural differences between financial reporting practices in the Arab countries and the United States will remain.

It is advisable that if Arab countries are looking ahead to adopt one regional standard setter and one set of international financial reporting standards, the following four principles are essential in achieving this ultimate goal:

1. Arab countries involved in global financial reporting must have a common objective of financial accounting and reporting.

2. Arab countries must have a process for developing financial reporting standards that is accepted and trusted by all constituents, one that ensures that the mission of the standard setter is fulfilled.

3. Arab countries should develop standards that achieve high quality.

4. One regional standard-setting body should be formed and must have the power to enforce accounting standards for all national companies in the region.

In Israel, IAS have been adopted by the ICPA (Israeli Certified Public Accountants) and apply in cases where there are no specific pronouncements by the ICPA and no other current practices in Israel. The opinions issued by the ICPA and the accounting principles adopted in Israel generally fall within the framework of IASC standards. Therefore, financial statements of Israeli or other companies are more likely to be prepared according to IAS, and, consequently, they will be comparable.

In conclusion, under the threat of further financial crises on an even worse scale, and with world recession widely predicted, Arab governments, intergovernmental agencies, and global financial institutions now have a real fear that the crisis in Asia will be repeated elsewhere and on an even greater scale. Facing this threat, Arab countries may have been forced to look for ways to secure greater economic stability for the future. Now it is more important than ever for Arab countries to enforce a core set of internationally recognized accounting standards to ensure that the information upon which investors and other stakeholders base their decisions is transparent, comprehensive, reliable, consistent, and internationally comparable. Currently Arab countries have no choice but to follow IAS until they have their own regional accounting standards. Moreover, the accounting profession in Arab countries has to participate in the development of regional, high-quality accounting standards and to cooperate with accounting firms serving the business community in the area implementing those standards.

APPENDIX: COMPANIES AND OTHER ORGANIZATIONS IN THE MIDDLE EAST USING IAS

BAHRAIN

1. Arab Banking Corporation
2. Arab Insurance Group (BSC)
3. Bahrain Middle East Bank
4. Bahrain Telecommunication Co. (Batelco)
5. Bank of Bahrain and Kuwait
6. Gulf International Bank
7. Investcorp Group
8. Tampella
9. Trust International Insurance Co.

EGYPT

10. Egyptian American Bank

JORDAN

11. Cairo Amman Bank

KUWAIT

12. Aijal Real Estate Co.
13. Al Ahleia Insurance Co.

14. Al Ahli Bank of Kuwait
15. Al-Hasibat Electronic Co.
16. Altamdeen Real Estate Co.
17. Bank of Kuwait and the Middle East
18. Bobain Petrochemicals
19. Burgan Bank
20. Commercial Bank of Kuwait
21. Commercial Facilities Co.
22. Contracting and Marine Services Co.
23. Education Services Co.
24. Gulf Cable and Electrical Industries Co.
25. Gulf Insurance Co.
26. Independent Petroleum Group
27. International Murabaha
28. Kuwait Cement Co.
29. Kuwait Finance House
30. Kuwait Financial Centre
31. Kuwait Food Company
32. Kuwait Foundry Co.
33. Kuwait Hotels Co.
34. Kuwait Insurance Co.
35. Kuwait International Investment Co.
36. Kuwait Investment Co.
37. Kuwait Investment Projects Co.
38. Kuwait Metal Pipe Co.
39. Kuwait National Cinema Co.
40. Kuwait Pearl Real Estate Co.
41. Kuwait Portland Co.
42. Kuwait Real Estate Bank
43. Kuwait Real Estate Co.
44. Kuwait Shipbuilding & Repairyard Co.
45. Kuwait United Poultry Co.
46. Livestock Trading and Transport Co.
47. National Bank of Kuwait
48. National Cleaning Co.
49. National Industries
50. National Investments Co.
51. National Real Estate Co.
52. Public Warehousing Co.
53. Salhia Real Estate Co.
54. Shuaiba Paper Products Co.
55. Stores and Refrigerating Industries Co.
56. Sultan Centre

57. The Gulf Bank
58. United Industry Co.
59. United Realty Co.
60. Warba Insurance Co.

OMAN

61. Areej Vegetable Oils & Derivatives Ltd.
62. Naseejoman
63. National Bank of Oman
64. National Commercial Bank
65. National Mineral Water Co.
66. Oman Arab Bank
67. Oman International Bank
68. Oman Refreshment Company

QATAR

69. Qatar National Navigation and Transport Company Ltd.

SAUDI ARABIA

70. The National Commercial Bank
71. United Saudi Bank

UNITED ARAB EMIRATES

72. Abu Dhabi Islamic Bank
73. Abu Dhabi National Hotels
74. Al Ain Ahlia Insurance Co.
75. Al Dhafra Insurance Co.
76. Commercial Bank of Dubai
77. Emirates Bank International
78. Emirates Industrial Bank
79. Emirates Insurance Co.
80. Emirates Merchants Bank Ltd.
81. Invest Bank
82. MashreqBank
83. National Bank of Fujairah
84. National Bank of Ras Al-Khaimah
85. National Bank of Umm Al-Quaiwain
86. National Marine Dredging Co.
87. Union National Bank
88. United Arab Bank

Source: www.IASC.org.U.K., November 15, 1999. Israel's companies were not included on the list of the IASC.

REFERENCES

AICPA. "AICPA Supports International Standards." *The Practical Accountant* 32 (June 1999), 12.

———. "AICPA Hops on FASB Bandwagon for International Standards Setting Reform." *The CPA Journal* 69 (July 1999), 11.

Azzam, Henry T. "Arab Stock Markets: Country-by-Country Analysis and Review." *Middle East Executive Reports* 32 (April 1999), 9–17.

Baydoun, Nabil and Roger Willett. "Cultural Relevance of Western Accounting Systems to Developing Countries." *Abacus* 31, no. 1 (1995), 67–91.

Belkaoui, Ahmed Riahi and Ronald D. Picur. "Cultural Determinism and the Perception of Accounting Concepts." *The International Journal of Accounting* 26 (1991), 118–130.

Bethany World Prayer Center. "The Unreached Peoples Prayer Profiles—The Diaspora Arabs." www.bethany.com, 1997.

Cheney, Glen. "IASC Accepts Proposal for Worldwide Standard Setting." *Accounting Today* 14 (January 24–February 6, 2000), 14–17.

Choi, Frederick D. S., Carol Ann Frost, and Gary K. Meek. *International Accounting*, 3rd ed. Upper Saddle River, N.J.: Prentice Hall, 1999.

Doupnik, Timothy S. and Stephen B. Salter. "External Environment, Culture, and Accounting Practice: A Preliminary Test of a General Model of International Accounting Development." *The International Journal of Accounting* 30 (1995), 189–207.

Ernst & Young International. www.doingbusinessin.com/SaudiArabia, November 1999.

Fechner, Harry H. E. and Alan Kilgore. "The Influence of Cultural Factors on Accounting Practice." *International Journal of Accounting* 29 (1994), 265–277.

Financial Accounting Standards Board (FASB). *International Accounting Standard Setting: A Vision for the Future.* Norwalk, Conn.: FASB, 1998.

Global Investor. "Israel." 1995, 81.

Gray, S. J. "Toward a Theory of Cultural Influence on the Development of Accounting Systems Internationally." *Abacus* (March 1988), 1–15.

Hamid, Shaari, Russell Graig, and Frank Clarke. "Religion: A Confounding Cultural Element in the International Harmonization of Accounting?" *Abacus* 29, no. 2 (1993), 131–147.

Harding, Frank. "Corporate Credibility—Why a Harmonised Global Accountancy Framework Matters." *Accountancy Ireland* (April 1999), 16–17.

Hofstede, Geert. *Culture Consequences.* Beverly Hills, Calif.: Sage Publications, 1980.

———. *Accounting and Culture.* Barry E. Cushing (ed.). Sarasota, Fla.: American Accounting Association, 1987.

———. *Cultures and Organizations—Software of the Mind.* London: McGraw-Hill, 1991.

IASC Web site. http://www.iasc.org.uk, November 16, 1999.

ICMA. "IASC Celebrates an Historic Year." *Management Accounting* (May 1999), 12.

Iqbal, M. Zafar, Trini U. Melcher, and Amin A. Elmallah. *International Accounting: A Global Perspective.* Cincinnati, Ohio: South-Western College Publishing, 1997.

Kantor, Jeffrey, Clare B. Roberts, and Stephen B. Salter. "Financial Reporting Practices in Selected Arab Countries: An Empirical Study of Egypt, Saudi Arabia, and the

United Arab Emirates." *International Studies of Management & Organization* 25 (Fall 1995), 31–45.

Kesselman and Kesselman. *Guide to Investment in Israel.* Tel Aviv: Price Waterhouse, 1992.

Landau, Philip. "Special Report: An Inside Look at the 5th Jerusalem Conference on Accountancy." *Journal of Accountancy* (January 1992), 22–24.

McGregor, Warren. "An Insider's View of the Current State and Future Direction of International Accounting Standard Setting." *Accounting Horizons* (June 1999), 159–168.

Mueller, Gerhard G., Helen Gernon, and Gary K. Meek. *Accounting—An International Perspective.* Chicago: Richard D. Irwin, 1997.

Nobes, C. W. "A Judgmental International Classification of Financial Reporting Practices." *Journal of Business Finance and Accounting* (Spring 1983), 1–19.

———. *International Classification of Financial Reporting.* London: Croom Helm, 1984.

Nydell, Margaret K. *Understanding Arabs: A Guide for Westerners.* Yarmouth, Maine: Intercultural Press, 1996.

Perera, M.H.B. "Toward a Framework to Analyze the Impact of Culture on Accounting." *The International Journal of Accounting* 24 (1989), 43–44.

Sturge, Derrick. "Who Sets the Standard?" *CMA Management* (March 1998), 3–4.

Sutton, M. H. "International Harmonization of Accounting Standards: Perspectives from the Securities and Exchange Commission." Speech delivered to the American Accounting Association 1997 Annual Meeting, Dallas, TX. In Warren McGregor, "An Insider's View of the Current State and Future Direction of International Accounting Standard Setting," *Accounting Horizons* (June 1999), 159–168.

Tokunaga, Tadaaki, Matthew Blakeway-Phillips, and Robert Aitken. "Accountancy Bank Audit: Abreast of the Trend." *The Banker* (October 1989), 18–22.

Violet, W. J. "The Development of International Accounting Standards: An Anthropological Perspective." *International Journal of Accounting Education and Research* (Spring 1983), 1–12.

Yasin, Mahmoud M., Ronald F. Green, and Tom Zimmerer. "Executive Courage Across Cultures: An Organizational Perspective." *International Journal of Commerce and Management* 1 (1992), 75–87.

Chapter 7

Performance Measurement and Evaluation of Foreign Subsidiary Managers in the Middle East

INTRODUCTION

A MNC has a distinctly different and more complicated mode of operation than a domestic company. One of the main reasons for international operations in the Middle East is to take advantage of existing economic differences among countries, including differences in taxation, capital markets, product costs, and product-selling markets. If the only objective of MNCs is to maximize profits, their products should be manufactured in the least-cost production countries (such as Egypt and Jordan) and sold in the best-market countries (such as Saudi Arabia or European countries).

MNCs usually invest in Middle East countries to improve their competitive position in the Middle East in accordance with their long-range strategy, to meet tariff and quota restrictions in selling their products, and to secure otherwise unobtainable raw materials. Another important reason, as stated above, is to take advantage of economic differences. To achieve these objectives, management must have a global attitude so that it will be as concerned and involved with each of its Middle East and other foreign operations around the world as it is with U.S. operations and will attempt to rationalize and manage its operations in a global manner rather a domestic one, within the constraints of the Middle East social, economic, political, legal, and educational conditions.

However, MNCs may have relatively little influence and no direct control over Middle East environmental factors. Therefore, a MNC needs a separate set of measurements for the planning, control, and evaluation of its managers' performance, one that is substantially different from the set utilized by domestic business units.

Traditionally, performance evaluation systems have been used to compare the actual performance of Middle East subsidiaries with expected performance, to facilitate the measurement of subsidiaries in meeting some predetermined set of criteria to help top management in making resource allocation decisions so that corporate resources are directed to subsidiaries where expected returns are the highest, and to motivate decision makers to achieve their goals and overall corporate objectives.

In this chapter, the traditional performance evaluation measures used by American MNCs in managing their Middle East and foreign subsidiary managers will be examined first. A suggested performance evaluation system for Middle East countries will then be presented. The proposed system estimates foreign subsidiary managers' relative performance after considering the effects of non-controllable Middle East environmental factors on the measured performance of Middle East subsidiaries. Last, the suggested environmental model will be applied to a Middle East subsidiary of an American MNC to illustrate how MNCs can implement it in practice.

Traditional Performance Evaluation Measures of Middle East Subsidiary Managers

Historically, many management accounting techniques were oriented toward measuring earnings. Recently, these traditional techniques have been criticized because they were too narrow in focus and did not reflect the realities of Middle East markets of MNCs. The feeling is that an array of objectives should be considered in the management accounting evaluation process. In addition, many other factors affect the value of currently used techniques of performance evaluation. Among these are:

1. The organizational structure and environmental factors that interact in a complicated Middle East market might make profit measures misleading as the prime criteria for the evaluation of subsidiary performance.

2. The use of a company-wide rate of return on investment (ROI) criterion not only might neglect important aspects of Middle East subsidiary operations but also could fail to consider the real objectives for which the subsidiary was established.

3. The selection of an investment base for use of ROI can yield results, which either encourages desirable or undesirable action by subsidiary managers.

4. Because MNCs conduct business in many countries, each using a different currency, management must decide the extent to which Middle East subsidiary managers should be held responsible for foreign exchange losses.

Recently, however, it has been felt that a broader range of objectives should be considered. International accountability measures now in use include ROI, operating budget comparisons, and residual income.

Abdallah and Keller (1985: 344) surveyed American MNCs and discovered that internal accountability measures have not been developed to the extent required for the proper evaluation and control of MNC managers and subsidiaries. Most American MNCs use the same basic techniques to evaluate Middle East manager performance as they do to evaluate Middle East subsidiary performance. Moreover, the same performance evaluation techniques are used domestically as well as internationally, without regard for the social, political, and economic complexities facing MNCs in Middle East countries.

A commonly used measure of performance is the ROI. Most MNCs require their Middle East subsidiaries to use the same budgeting and financial planning techniques as domestic subsidiaries. These MNCs use the profit center concept or the investment center concept to measure ROI as the main performance measure (Mauriel 1969: 37). In some cases, profit compared to budgeted profit is the principal measure of profitability with ROI the secondary measure (Bursk et al. 1971: 43).

Other measures used to evaluate the managerial performance of MNCs are profit, budgeted sales compared to actual sales, cash flow potential from a foreign subsidiary to a U.S. parent company, return on investment, budgeted ROI compared to actual ROI, and residual income (Morsicato and Radebaugh 1979: 85).

A more appropriate performance evaluation system is needed to estimate Middle East subsidiary managers' relative performance after considering the effects of Middle East non-controllable environmental factors.

How Do MNCs Evaluate Their Middle East Subsidiary Managers' Performance?

Almost without exception, American MNCs use more than one criterion to measure the results of their international activities. However, they tend to place more emphasis on one over the other, using the remainder for supplementary purposes (Persen and Lessig 1978: 64). The traditional performance measures used in American MNCs to evaluate the performance of Middle East subsidiaries and their managers are discussed in the paragraphs that follow.

Rate of Return on Investment

ROI is expressed as a fraction. Its numerator is the profit earned by a Middle East subsidiary; its denominator is the investment in the subsidiary. ROI is a generally accepted measure of the long-run profitability of a business entity. It is assumed to have the following advantages (Bursk et al. 1971: 17–18):

1. It is a single, comprehensive figure influenced by everything that has affected the financial conditions of a Middle East subsidiary.
2. It measures how well the Middle East subsidiary manager uses the assets of the MNC to generate profits.
3. It is a common denominator that can be compared directly among subsidiaries, among subsidiaries and outside companies, or among subsidiaries and alternative investments.

However, many problems face MNCs in using ROI as the company-wide criterion for measuring performance. First, it oversimplifies a very complicated decision-making process and tries to combine three major elements in one single ratio—planning, control, and decision making (Bierman 1978: 410). Using a single rate of return for each Middle East foreign subsidiary is too simple to be used as a base for all trade-offs between investments and profits in a MNC.

Second, with respect to the numerator, the measurement of Middle East subsidiary income for the rate of return calculation is complicated by intercompany transactions. The effect of one subsidiary on the return streams of other subsidiaries needs to be accounted for, however, such assessments are difficult to perform (Choi, Frost, and Meek 1999: 364).

Third, with respect to the denominator, it is difficult to obtain a satisfactory monetary basis for the value of the investment. For example, using the gross book value of the investment base may lead to sub-optimal decisions, because a manager may increase his or her ROI by scrapping perfectly useful assets that do not contribute profits equal to the Middle East subsidiary's goal.

Fourth, Middle East operations are often established for strategic economic motivations for going abroad rather than for profit maximization. However, top management forgets this fact when evaluating the performance of Middle East subsidiary managers. Therefore, using a company-wide performance ROI criterion to evaluate the profitability of Middle East subsidiaries and the performance of their managers is inadequate and misleading as well.

Fifth, the reported results of any Middle East subsidiary are directly affected by many environmental constraints: (1) Social, economic, political-legal, and educational policies and actions of host governments can drastically affect the reported results of a Middle East subsidiary; (2) Foreign exchange controls have a significant effect on both a subsidiary's and a manager's performance (Persen and Lessig 1978: 45); and (3) Since MNCs conduct business in many countries, top management must decide upon the extent to which managers of Middle East subsidiaries are to be held responsible for foreign exchange losses (Robbins and Stobaugh 1973: 35).

Operating Budget Comparisons

Comparisons of actual results with operating budgets have been used widely for performance evaluation of Middle East activities (Persen and Lessig 1978: 45). Variances between budgeted and actual results can be analyzed to evaluate the performance of Middle East subsidiaries and their managers and, finally, corrective actions may be taken.

In a MNC, the same budgetary procedures are often used for both domestic and Middle East operations. The budget has been used for supplementary information on Middle East subsidiary performance, however, a MNC may still select ROI as a key item in the budget (Robbins and Stobaugh 1973: 83).

The Committee on International Accounting of the American Accounting Association (1973: 253) has indicated that when the operating results of foreign

subsidiaries are evaluated on the basis of their conformity with budgeted results, the performance evaluation is often less than satisfactory, because the
budget is prepared only for key factors such as profit and control and not considered for exclusion. In addition, this approach does not distinguish between
foreign subsidiary performance and foreign subsidiary manager performance.
Moreover, Bursk et al. (1971: 126) have indicated that if the profit budget of a
foreign subsidiary does not provide an accurate "rate measure" of short-term
profitability, other non-financial techniques must be used to evaluate the performance.

Other Performance Evaluation Measures

Other measures are used by MNCs for performance evaluation, such as cash
flow potential from the foreign subsidiary to the U.S. subsidiary, residual income, contribution to earnings per share, return on sales, return on investment
(adjusted for inflation), and other ratios (Persen and Lessig 1978: 25–33). These
performance evaluation measures have been well covered in the literature and
need not be considered here.

Performance evaluation measures used in MNCs have often failed to consider
adequately the environmental variables surrounding Middle East operations because of the difficulty of measuring and incorporating those variables into traditional management accounting approaches. As a result, measuring the
performance of Middle East subsidiaries and their managers on the basis of ROI
or any other currently used measure of performance tends to encourage suboptimal decisions because of a lack of goal harmonization between the Middle
East subsidiary and top management.

Abdallah and Keller (1985) surveyed 64 MNCs to determine the financial
measures currently used to evaluate the performance of foreign subsidiaries and
their managers, the use of different performance evaluation systems for domestic
and foreign operations, and the relationship between the firm's environmental
variables and its performance evaluation systems.

The international division officers were asked to indicate the measures their
firms used in the performance evaluation of Middle East and foreign subsidiaries
and their managers and to rate each measure in terms of its importance. Nearly
86% of the sample group used budgeted profits compared to actual profits to
evaluate the performance of foreign subsidiaries. Figure 7–1 compares the four
measures in terms of their importance in the evaluation of foreign subsidiaries'
performance.

As for Middle East and foreign subsidiary managers, 87% of the sample used
the same criterion, budgeted profits compared to actual profits, as the primary
measure of performance, with ROI (67%) as a secondary measure. Figure 7–2
provides a comparison between the ROI, profits, budgeted ROI compared to
actual ROI, and budgeted profits compared to actual profits as a measure of a
foreign subsidiary manager's performance. Moreover, it was found that 82% of

Figure 7–1
Comparing Financial Measures Used to Evaluate Performance of Foreign Subsidiaries

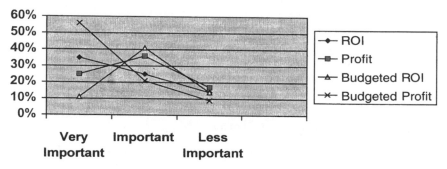

the sample group used the same basic techniques to evaluate a foreign subsidiary manager that they used to evaluate foreign subsidiary performance.

Evaluating the performance of MNC Middle East managers and subsidiaries requires a special concern analysis. The distinction that should be made in performance evaluation relates to who has control over revenues, assets, personnel, and expenses. When measuring Middle East manager performance, the focus of the evaluation technique should be on the factors that the manager can control or has significant influence over. Therefore, there is a need for a new performance evaluation model that will consider the effect of environmental constraints on a manager's internal accountability.

THE MIDDLE EAST ENVIRONMENT AND ITS EFFECT ON PERFORMANCE EVALUATION

In this section of the chapter, the three major groups of Middle East environmental factors are first discussed, including, economic, sociological, and political-legal factors. Then the proposed performance evaluation model that fits the Middle East environment will discussed, analyzed, and applied to a Middle East subsidiary of an American MNC.

ECONOMIC ENVIRONMENTAL FACTORS

MNCs invest in Middle East countries to take advantage of economic differences, as discussed previously. The main strategy of MNCs is to produce in countries where production costs are least and to sell in countries where selling prices are highest.

MNCs may sometimes utilize resources more effectively than domestic enterprises by transferring idle or underutilized resources. They also try to use the

Figure 7–2
Comparing Financial Meausres Used to Evaluate Performance of Foreign Subsidiary Managers

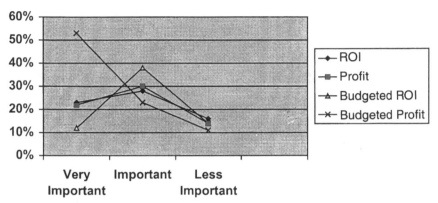

most efficient and profitable technology in extracting, refining, or manufacturing raw materials in Middle East countries.

Inflation, tariff barriers, fluctuating exchange rates, trade barriers and restrictions, balance of payments disequilibrium, and restrictions of foreign trade policies are the most significant economic factors affecting international performance evaluation systems.

Inflation

Inflation is the decline in the general purchasing power of the monetary unit. Wide variations and rapid changes in inflation rates from one country to another are an important factor when MNCs are designing their international performance evaluation systems. In the absence of inflation, performance evaluation systems can be based on traditional domestic measures of performance with confidence in accounting information. However, when prices change, this confidence is weakened. Subsidiary managers also find historical cost accounting data inadequate for many managerial decisions.

Higher inflation rates in a country cause the price of goods transferred to another country where lower inflation rates exist to rise, and subsidiaries in the latter country become less competitive. The subsidiary managers in that country find it more difficult to sell their products in the local market and, consequently, their competitive position is impaired. Generally, relative inflation rates have an impact on the international business of MNCs.

There is a direct relationship between inflation rates and interest rates. When a country has a low interest rate, it also has a low inflation rate, and vice versa. However, a high inflation rate combined with a high interest rate in a country may discourage any new investment by MNCs and, consequently, affect the goods transferred to that country.

Tariffs and Duties

Tariffs and duties are another environmental factor that may affect international business activities in general, especially the performance of Middle East subsidiaries and their managers. A tariff is the tool most commonly used as a form of trade restriction by governments. A tariff is "a tax, or duty, levied on a commodity when it crosses the boundary of a customs area." A customs area usually coincides with national political boundaries (Robock and Simmonds 1983: 138).

Transfer pricing policies, as a tool of international performance evaluation measures, can be used to reduce tariffs imposed on imports into the country or exports outside of the country and, consequently, the cost for a MNC will be less. However, foreign countries may feel that they are losing their revenue because of the manipulations of the transfer pricing policies of MNCs, and they may not accept the transfer price set by the MNC if it is too high.

Any country can use a tariff or a duty as a tool to exercise control over goods transferred out of or into the country. If the tariff is imposed on outgoing goods, it is called an export duty; if it is imposed on incoming goods, it is called an import duty.

Middle East governments impose tariffs on imports and exports for three main reasons: (1) to raise revenue for the government; (2) to control the direction of foreign trade; and (3) to protect domestic production against foreign competition. In Middle East countries, providing a source of revenue for the government is ranked as the most important reason for imposing tariffs. In developed countries such as the United States, tariffs are used to restrict and control the import of goods.

In general, Middle East governments can affect the international trade of specific products through the differences in tariff rates. High tariffs can be imposed on products that a country does not want to import, and low tariffs or zero tariffs may be imposed on essential products that are badly needed for the national economy.

In international business, the effect of tariffs on MNCs' profitability varies, depending on the particular country. For countries that depend on foreign materials or finished goods, import tariffs may be low and, consequently, MNCs may be encouraged to transfer more goods to their foreign subsidiaries domiciled in these countries. On the opposite side are countries whose national products must compete against foreign imports. Governments, under these circumstances, impose high tariffs on imports of certain products to protect their own national products. MNCs may try to overcome these additional costs of paying high tariffs by using low transfer prices on their goods transferred into these countries. Under these circumstances, the performance of Middle East subsidiary managers will not be a reflection or realistic indicator of managers' actions.

Foreign Exchange Rates

The exchange rate of a country is the economic indicator of how strong or weak the economy of a Middle East country is. It provides the link between the national economy and the rest of the world economy. Any economic event, such as bankruptcy of one of the major banks in the country or a large deficit in the balance of payments for the second or third year in a row, has a direct impact on a country's exchange rate. Foreign trade policies, for example, affect the exchange rate directly when the supply or demand for a country's products moves up or down.

The country's budget is considered one of the key factors for MNCs to make their own predictions of the government's intentions regarding tax laws and regulations, foreign exchange control policy, cash movement restriction policy, and any other variables that may affect a country's currency in the short or long run. The budget of a country can show the direction in which the economy may move. It indicates tariff policy, foreign trade policy, tax policy, foreign defense policy, Middle East government spending, and many other budgetary decisions that may have a direct impact on currency markets.

Inflation is one of the key indicators of internal currency depreciation of a country, a fact that may lead to external currency depreciation. There is no perfect direct relationship between inflation and currency devaluation; the relationship is usually indirect and takes time to become evident.

MNCs must take all of the above factors into consideration when designing their international performance measurement systems to ensure that their objectives in the Middle East can be achieved within the appropriate management control systems.

Balance of Payments

Balance of payments summarizes all of the economic transactions between the home country and the rest of the world. These transactions include goods and services, transfer payments, loans, and investments. Inflation and interest rates, national income growth, and changes in money supply have a significant impact on a country's currency and its present and future exchange rates. All of these factors may affect the balance of payments.

The balance of payments shows the net effect of all currency transactions of a country over a given period of time. When the balance of payments shows a deficit over a period of several years, it is an indication of the likely weakening of the value of a country's currency. This will be a threat to the currency's stability, and it is more likely that the currency will be devaluated.

Deficits and surpluses in the balance of payments affect a country's currency in different ways. National income, money supply, prices, employment, interest rates, and foreign exchange rates are among the most important variables usually affected by a deficit or surplus.

MNCs should be aware that when a Middle East country's balance of payments shows deficits for one year after another, the government is probably considering one or more of its tools to correct or reduce its deficit. Therefore, MNCs should be aware of restrictive monetary or fiscal policies, such as currency or trade controls, for currency devaluation or to control inflation (Ball and McCulloch 1985: 281). MNCs may change their international transfer pricing policies and their performance measurement system to alleviate the impact of the new national policy of a country on their cash movements, the value of goods or services transferred into or out of the country, and the foreign exchange risk.

SOCIOLOGICAL ENVIRONMENTAL FACTORS

Sociological environmental factors include cultural and religious mores, attitudes toward growth and stability, and other societal values. These international sociological constraints interact with international political, legal, and economic environmental factors. The emotional feelings, for example, of a country toward foreigners may lead to laws, rules, restrictions, or regulations that significantly affect business firms operating abroad (Farmer and Richman 1980: 167). The feelings and attitudes of people in a given country are reflected in the regulations and rules that that country has established with respect to foreign subsidiary operations.

Some of these variables may have an impact on the financial control systems of MNCs investing in different countries, and each may affect the nature and degree of the success of MNC control systems required in each host country environment. Therefore, MNCs must consider seriously all sociological variables and their impact on Middle East operations when designing their internal evaluation systems. They need to direct their attention toward what events might change the underlying social feelings and attitudes of people, which in turn would lead political groups to alter their current tax and tariff laws, foreign exchange controls, and many other regulations to new and different ones under various national policies. As a result of any change that might occur in the current laws and regulations, MNCs must alter their pricing policies and performance measurement systems to achieve their major objectives.

POLITICAL AND LEGAL ENVIRONMENTAL FACTORS

Political and legal environmental factors include price controls, government instability, changes of political groups or government, timing of election, nature of elections, and confiscation of local operations. All of these variables can create a high degree of risk or uncertainty, can alter the investment climate, and can have a significant effect on MNCs' performance evaluation measures.

It is important that MNCs know how the legal constraints and political actions of a given country directly affect their international transfer pricing policies. Since each country is independent, "It is expected that each will have a somewhat different legal structure than others, and that politics of one country will also have different impacts than those of other countries" (Farmer and Richman 1980: 185).

The allocation of resources is a potential source of conflict. On the one hand, the home office of the MNC wishes to exercise control measures over the utilization of its resources in Middle East countries to ensure that these resources are used efficiently and profitably. On the other hand, the Middle East country seeks to control the resources of MNCs to make sure that they are used in the best national interest. As a result, the government of the host country may interfere by imposing protective measures that prevent a Middle East subsidiary from managing its operations efficiently.

How MNCs Should Evaluate the Performance of Their Middle East Subsidiary Managers

Unfortunately, all Middle East environmental variables are beyond the subsidiary manager's control, so managers should not be held responsible for the effects of these variables on the results of their activities. The challenge for a manager is that he or she may have two choices: (1) to change the environment in the country—including economic, political-legal, social, and educational conditions—as appropriate for his or her system or (2) to change the internal accountability or performance measurement techniques to fit the country's environment.

What can a manger do to change the environment in Egypt, Israel, Jordan, Kuwait, or Saudi Arabia to fit his or her MNC's performance measurement system? Can the manager change the dominant cultural attitude, for example, in Saudi Arabia? Can the manager change the economic system, for example, in Jordan, from communism to capitalism? Can the manager change the political circumstances, for example, in Kuwait, to a highly stable condition? Can the type of formal education and technical training of the manager, for example, in Egypt, be identical to American educational and training programs?

Of course, the correct answer to these questions is no, the subsidiary manager cannot, because all of these variables are far beyond the manager's control. It may be essential to distinguish between the performance of the Middle East subsidiary and the performance of its manager, because they seldom coincide, especially when Middle East environmental conditions are distinctly different from domestic conditions. The manager's performance should be measured and evaluated on the basis of the activities or items that he or she can control, such as direct materials, direct labor costs, and the subsidiary's revenue. All activities

Table 7–1
Data of Four American MNCs and Their Foreign Subsidiaries

Company (assumed)	Industry	Countries
MNCA	Oil and Gas Industry	Bahrain, Egypt, Kuwait, Spain, and Saudi Arabia
MNCB	Steel Industry	Canada, Egypt, Israel, Mexico, and Jordan
MNCC	Chemical Industry	Brazil, Kuwait, France, Saudi Arabia, and United Kingdom
MNCD	Electric and Electronic Industry	Australia, Egypt, South Africa, Singapore, and United Arab Emirates

or items that are not under the manager's control, such as income tax expense or interest rate on loans, should be excluded from the performance measurement report.

The Middle East subsidiary should be measured and evaluated on the basis of all activities and items needed for conducting the business so MNC top management can decide whether the investment should be expanded, reduced, or terminated. All revenue and cost items that cannot be controlled by the Middle East subsidiary manager should be allocated to the Middle East subsidiary.

The Suggested Performance Evaluation Model for Middle East Subsidiaries

To look for the appropriate measures of performance evaluation systems to fit MNCs' operating activities in the Middle East, and the extent to which these measures have been designed to reflect environmental differences from one country to another, the author surveyed 178 MNCs. Fifty-six replies from MNCs' officers were received, for a total response rate of 31.5%.

Table 7–1 presents data for four of the selected samples of American MNCs that participated in the research and the nature of their business activities. Table 7–2 presents financial information on the same four American MNCs included in Table 7–1. It is broken down into total assets, gross revenue, and income after taxes. The ROI is included in the last column, and it is calculated by dividing income after taxes by the total assets of each foreign subsidiary.

For example, in the MNCA, the Saudi Arabian subsidiary realized the highest ROI (29%), which measures the profitability of a foreign subsidiary, among the five foreign subsidiaries, and the Spanish subsidiary realized the lowest ROI (9%).

Table 7–2
Financial Information of Foreign Subsidiaries (in millions of dollars)

Company	Country	Total Assets	Gross Revenue	Income after Taxes	Actual ROI
MNCA	Bahrain	$100	$94	$19.00	19.0%
	Egypt	$74	$88	$8.88	12.0%
	Kuwait	$140	$132	$22.40	16.0%
	Spain	$55	$60	$4.95	9.0%
	Saudi Arabia	$200	$220	$58.00	29.0%
MNCB	Canada	$60	$105	$10.00	16.7%
	Egypt	$28	$32	$5.09	18.0%
	Israel	$29	$22	$9.86	34.0%
	Mexico	$65	$74	$9.10	14.0%
	Jordan	$90	$110	$5.04	5.6%
MNCC	Brazil	$66	$80	$7.59	11.5%
	Kuwait	$98	$117	$22.54	23.0%
	France	$125	$140	$13.75	11.0%
	Saudi Arabia	$240	$222	$48.00	20.0%
	U.K.	$190	$206	$36.48	11.8%
MNCD	Australia	$112	$140	$33.60	30.0%
	Egypt	$99	$109	$16.83	17.0%
	South Africa	$110	$99	$9.90	9.0%
	Singapore	$198	$250	$53.46	27.0%
	U.A.E.	$180	$175	$34.56	19.2%

Let us evaluate the performance of Middle East subsidiary mangers using the financial information presented in Table 7–2, assuming that the performance evaluation measure is the ROI. In MNCA, it would be concluded that the manager of the Saudi Arabian subsidiary did the best job in managing his subsidiary (with a ROI of 29%), compared to the other four managers, while the manager of the Spanish subsidiary of the same MNC did the worst job (with a ROI of 9%).

For MNCB, the Israeli subsidiary achieved the highest ROI, 34%. The subsidiary in Jordan came in with the lowest ROI, 5.6%, although its gross revenues are the highest of all of the five foreign subsidiaries of MNCB. This comparison may be incorrect, however, because not all managers are working under the same environmental conditions. For example, Spain does not have the same social, political, economic, legal, or educational conditions as Saudi Arabia, and Jordan does not have the same environmental conditions as Israel.

How Should the Performance of Middle East Subsidiary Managers Be Measured?

If you were the manager of an Egyptian or a South African subsidiary and worked for an electric and electronic MNC such as MNCD, would you be evaluated on the basis of a ROI of 17% or 9%, respectively, compared to a manager in Australia who realized a ROI of 30%? Would you challenge the environmental conditions in Egypt or South Africa? Would the Australian subsidiary manager be promoted and rewarded on the basis of almost twice your ROI? Were the social, economic, or political conditions in Egypt or South Africa considered when evaluating the managers' performance?

Briefly, the performance evaluation systems now used by MNCs do not respond to these Middle East environmental challenges and changes. Rather, the performance measure such as ROI, or any other measure, includes the effect of these environmental variables, even though they are not and cannot be controlled by subsidiary managers. To consider the effect of one variable, management must examine all other Middle East environmental variables and their interactions as they affect the performance of Middle East subsidiaries.

For example, economic power has always been used for political stability, and social attitude or movement may cause governmental intervention. To implement a control system that is adequate and appropriate for MNC operations, Middle East environmental variables should be measured in a manner that helps the MNC rate how well the Middle East manager has done his or her job on the basis of controllable factors only. It seems appropriate, therefore, for American and non-American MNCs to adopt a more relevant performance evaluation system that will estimate the relative managerial contributions among Middle East and foreign subsidiary managers, after considering the effects of non-controllable Middle East environmental factors for a particular period of time (Abdallah 1984).

How Does the Performance Evaluation System Work in the Middle East?

The measured performance of a Middle East subsidiary can be described as the sum of:

1. the effect of the levels of Middle East non-controllable environmental factors, under which the subsidiary is operated;
2. the effect of the Middle East subsidiary manager's actions after considering the effects of non-controllable environmental factors; and
3. other factors not explained by this model.

The objective of this model is to estimate the relative managerial performance of Middle East managers after considering the effects of Middle East non-controllable environmental factors. Table 7–3 lists the 16 Middle East non-controllable environmental factors for an American or a non-American subsidiary. To show how the Middle East subsidiary manager's actual contribution can be measured, let us look at MNCA's oil and gas subsidiary, operating in Egypt (see Table 7–2). The statistical tool for analyzing the data is step-wise multiple regression and correlation.

In order to measure, or assign a value to, the non-controllable environmental factors, each international division officer was asked to rate the level of each of the 16 environmental variables in terms of their effect on subsidiary performance in particular countries. These factors were measured by using rank order measures. Each factor was rated separately on a scale from 0 to 100; 0 means that there was no effect of the factor on the overall subsidiary performance, and 100 means that the impact of the factor was very important.

The environmental model of the Middle East subsidiary can be computed as follows: When Y is the total measured performance of the Middle East subsidiary as ROI, M_s is the managerial contribution of the Middle East subsidiary manager, and X is a Middle East environmental factor (see Table 7–3):

$$Y = .7227* - [0.0089** X_{10} - 0.0175X_{14} - 0.0046X_{16}] + M_s***$$

When the levels of non-controllable Middle East environmental variables are $X_{10} = 35$, $X_{14} = 90$, and $X_{16} = 85$, and Y (ROI) = 12% (see Table 7–2). Then,

$$.12 = .7227 - [0.0089 (35) - 0.0175 (90) - 0.0046 (85)] + M_s***$$

$$.12 = .7227 + [0.3115 - 1.575 + .391] + M_s$$

$$.12 = .7227 [-0.8725] + M_s$$

$$M_s = .12 - [.7227 - 0.8725] = .12 - [-0.1498]$$

$$M_s = .12 + .1498 = 0.2698 \text{ or } 26.98\%.$$

* This number represents the regression constant; it indicates ROI when the non-controllable Middle East environmental factors are equal to zero.
**These are the regression coefficients that express the relationship between the non-controllable Middle East environmental factors and the measured performance of the Middle East subsidiary.
***This is the managerial contribution by the Egyptian subsidiary manager.

As one can see, the Middle East environmental factors—the extent and degree of technical training and the skills of persons obtaining such training and the qualification of trainers (X_{10}), the dominant social attitude toward authority, power, and accountability of supervisors and managers (X_{14}), and the social attitude and values toward wealth and material gain (X_{16})—had significantly affected the measured performance (in terms of ROI) of the Egyptian subsidiary

Table 7–3
The Middle East Environmental Variables

The Environmental Groups	The Non-Controllable Environmental Variables
Economic Variables	X_1 The general economic framework, including the overall economic organization of the country
	X_2 The organization and operation of the central banking system, including controls over commercial banks and the money supply
	X_3 Economic stability, including the vulnerability of the country to economic fluctuations
	X_4 Capital markets and their honesty, effectiveness, and efficiency
Political-Legal Variables	X_5 The effectiveness and efficiency of the legal system
	X_6 The effect of the defense policy on business
	X_7 The effect of the foreign policy on business
	X_8 The degree of political stability and its effect on business (political risk)
Educational Variables	X_9 The quality of formal education and how it fits the needs of the country
	X_{10} The extent and degree of technical training and the skills of persons obtaining such training, and the qualifications of trainers
	X_{11} Management training programs to improve the skills and abilities of managers
	X_{12} The percentage of the total population and those employed in the industry with a post–high school education
Social Variables	X_{13} The dominant social attitude toward domestic and foreign business managers
	X_{14} The dominant social attitude toward authority, power, and accountability of supervisors and managers
	X_{15} The dominant cultural attitude toward teamwork and collective achievement and productivity
	X_{16} The social attitude and values toward wealth and material gain

of the American MNCA oil and gas company operating in Egypt. As a result, the managerial contribution of the Egyptian subsidiary manager is 0.2698, or 26.98%.

Since managers in Middle East countries operate under different environmental conditions, they face various economic, social, political, legal, and educational issues or problems. In setting Middle East subsidiaries' goals, these differences should be taken into consideration by top management. In our example of the Egyptian subsidiary, insomuch as all variations in the performance of the foreign subsidiaries related to the oil and gas industry and the Middle East countries, the average foreign subsidiary manager achieves zero as a result of his or her managerial contribution. The better-than-average foreign subsidiary manager achieves a positive rating for his or her managerial contribution, and the below-average manager achieves a negative rating for his or her managerial contribution.

With respect to the Egyptian subsidiary, the measured performance (in terms of ROI) was 12%, and after extracting the effect of non-controllable Middle East or Egyptian environmental factors (0.1498, or 14.98%), the managerial contribution attributable to the Egyptian subsidiary manager's actions became 0.2698 (or 26.98). Thus an appropriate target ROI for a subsidiary in the Egyptian environment and oil and gas industry should be at least 0.1490. The current manager's contribution was .2698.

Because the estimated managerial contribution of a foreign subsidiary does not depend on the level of non-controllable Egyptian environmental factors, it can be comparable among managers of different foreign subsidiaries of the same company, or MNCA, in our example.

From the viewpoint of MNCA's top management, both managerial contribution and non-controllable environmental factors are important, because top management can, in the long run, control both of these components of the measured performance. Because the measured performance of the foreign subsidiary depends primarily on a particular location within the same industry, top management should devote more attention to location selection in investment decision making, especially in the Middle East.

Using actual data on the level of Middle East environmental factors rather than opinions would help make the model much more realistic. Because MNCs have their own resources—financial and human—there will be no difficulty applying this model.

The adoption of such a performance evaluation system requires no major adjustments of a traditional management accounting system to evaluate the performance of Middle East subsidiary managers. The only added factors are the actual levels of non-controllable Middle East environmental factors, under which the Egyptian or any other Middle East subsidiary operates. Those Middle East environmental factors can be identified, assessed, and incorporated into the present system as a basis for making the MNC performance evaluation system objective, operational, and practical.

SUMMARY AND CONCLUSIONS

This chapter introduced, discussed, and analyzed the performance evaluation problem of MNCs in evaluating their Middle East subsidiaries and managers. First, traditional performance evaluation measures were discussed. For most MNCs, the objective and practical way in which to treat the effects of environmental factors on foreign operations has not been reached. A Middle East subsidiary manager's performance should not reflect how well the manager has done without regard to Middle East environmental variables, but how well the manager has performed his or her job within those environmental factors.

Traditional management accounting techniques are inadequate to appropriately solve these problems, and MNCs are unable to achieve satisfactory and desired levels of performance evaluation. Management accounting techniques have not adequately considered the distinct characteristics of the environment within which MNCs operate and manage their businesses.

Second, a suggested performance evaluation system for Middle East countries was presented. The proposed system estimates foreign subsidiary managers' relative performance after considering the effects of non-controllable Middle East environmental factors on the measured performance of Middle East subsidiaries. Third, the suggested environmental model will be applied to a Middle East subsidiary of an American MNC to illustrate how MNCs can implement it in practice. Some guidelines on the effect of the important issues in managerial, financial reporting, and taxation of American joint ventures in the Middle Eastern countries can be illustrated to top management using the suggested model. Countries' rules, regulations, facts, and experiences that uniquely affect management and financial reporting of American–Middle East joint ventures also were discussed.

There are many implications of this proposed model for performance evaluation for Middle East subsidiary managers and for decision making in allocating the limited resources (human and financial) of MNCs. One possible implication is that new advanced management accounting techniques should be developed and used to facilitate the measurement and evaluation of the performance of Middle East subsidiary managers of MNCs. Certainly the proposed Middle East environmental model is useful for MNCs when designing a system of performance evaluation for subsidiary managers. The proposed system incorporates the distinction of each Middle East environmental factor into its design. This new system will surely lead to improved systems, improved planning, and an improved decision-making process and outcome.

REFERENCES

Abdallah, Wagdy M. *Internal Accountability: An International Emphasis*. Ann Arbor, Mich.: UMI Research Press, 1984.

———. "Change the Environment or Change the System." *Management Accounting* (October 1986), 33–37.

Abdallah, Wagdy M. and Donald Keller. "Measuring the Multinational's Performance." *Management Accounting* (October 1985), 26–30.

Ball, Donald A. and Wendell H. McCulloch, Jr. *International Business*, 2nd ed. Plano, Tex.: Business Publications, 1985.

Bierman, Harold. "ROI as a Measure of Managerial Performance." In Don DeCosta et al. (eds.), *Accounting for Managerial Decision-Making*, 2nd ed. Santa Barbara, Calif.: Wiley/Hamilton, 1978.

Bursk, Edward C. et al. *Financial Control of Multinational Operations*. New York: Financial Executive Research Foundation, 1971.

Choi, Frederick D.S., Carol Ann Frost, and Gary K. Meek. *International Accounting*, 3rd ed. Upper Saddle River, N.J.: Prentice Hall, 1999.

Farmer, Richard N. and Barry M. Richman. *International Business*, 3rd ed. Bloomington, Ind.: Cedarwood Press, 1980.

Mauriel, J. J. "Evaluating and Control of Overseas Operations." *Management Accounting* (May 1969), 35–39.

Morsicato, Helen G. and Lee H. Radebaugh. "Internal Performance Evaluation of Multinational Enterprise Operations." *The International Journal of Accounting* 15 (Fall 1979), 77–94.

Persen, William and Van Lessig. *Evaluating the Financial Performance of Overseas Operations*. New York: Financial Executive Research Foundation, 1978.

Robbins, Sidney M. and Robert B. Stobaugh. "The Best Measuring Stick for Foreign Subsidiaries." *Harvard Business Review* 51 (January–February 1973), 4–9.

Robock, Stefan H. and Kenneth Simmonds. *International Business and Multinational Enterprises*, 3rd ed. Homewood, Ill.: Richard D. Irwin, 1993.

Part III

Tax Systems in the Middle East and Transfer Pricing Strategies

Chapter 8

Tax Systems of Selected
Middle East Countries

INTRODUCTION

In the United States and most industrial countries, sales taxes, individual income taxes, corporate taxes, and other types of taxes are considered part of daily life. Potential investors, including MNCs, need (1) to decide where their investments will bring the highest return on invested capital after tax with the lowest political and business risk, (2) to determine the most favorable country for a particular investment, and (3) to look at regional opportunities for cost savings and improvements in efficiency in their tax affairs (Ernst & Young International 1999). Comparative tax rates and regulations of the United States and of foreign countries are important input factors to help make successful investing decisions.

American citizens who have been transferred to work in Middle East countries remain subject to U.S. taxation. As a result, their U.S. employers need to consider taxes in structuring an expatriate assignment policy in these no-tax or low-tax countries of the Middle East. Generally, citizens of the United States working abroad are subject to host-country income taxes and U.S. income taxes on both base salary and the various over-base allowances employers typically pay for living expenses and as incentives. Employers should structure compensation packages that result in tax neutrality and provide relevant assistance for expatriates in preparing their tax returns (Robins and Bishko 1991).

Obviously it is necessary to look at each country separately when an investment is contemplated. Tax planning opportunities should be reviewed in the region as a whole, in conjunction with tax planning in each individual country (Bartlett 1997). To meet future needs, every MNC or businessperson has to set his or her tax strategy on the bases of several factors for overseas investment. One of the most important factors is to understand local tax regulations and authorities, therefore, tax planning and strategies are just as important in the Middle East as in other countries.

Another important factor that requires particular attention when planning an investment in the Middle East is technology transfer, including know-how, software development and sales, management fees, licensing, and royalties. In some countries, license fees and royalties are taxed at the maximum rates, with no deductions allowed. Software sales in the Middle East are often licensed, and the entire sale could be subject to tax. It is sometimes possible to have an agreement for technical assistance performed totally outside of a particular country. If the agreement is worded carefully and does not call for a local presence, it is not taxable and it may be claimed as a tax-deductible expense in the country from which payments are made. Provisions are often disallowed as an expense (Bartlett 1997). No Middle East country allows losses to be carried back, however, there are varying periods for which these losses can be carried forward. In Saudi Arabia, operating losses may not be carried forward at all (ibid.).

The Middle East region is considered one of the most strategic and attractive areas in the world to do business. MNCs can be very successful in investing their capital and managing their businesses in the Middle East, however, appropriate tax planning should be done in advance including the following five major steps:

1. Get access to all up-to-date tax information in the region and in the selected country.
2. Start your tax planning as soon as your project is initiated.
3. Involve your local partner(s) in your tax planning.
4. Minimize your tax burden by
   a. choosing the most appropriate investment tools, such as joint ventures or wholly owned subsidiaries;
   b. structuring contracts in the most convenient and appropriate manners;
   c. taking advantage of all tax holidays and other incentives available; and
   d. coordinating the tax burden in the Middle East with your home country to take advantage of any tax treaty provisions and other tax credit opportunities.
5. Design your pricing policy, including transfer pricing strategies, after considering all tax and custom issues.

GENERAL CHARACTERISTICS OF MIDDLE EAST TAXATION

Tax systems in the Middle East countries are not coded to the same extent as those in industrialized countries. In general, the political regimes in the Middle East are well aware that taxation without representation can lead to such politically unsettling events. For this very reason, "no representation without taxation" is the chorus of choice in these countries (Gordon 1999). With regional trends in establishing taxation policies, governments have to balance the need for non-oil revenues with the encouragement of new foreign investment. Several Arab countries have recently reformed their tax systems, and the common theme is a reduction in the maximum corporate tax rate to levels common in industrial countries.

The ability to successfully impose and collect taxes includes a great deal of institutional sophistication. Most Arab countries lack this sophistication and strenuously avoid using direct taxation as a means of revenue. Efficient institutions offer states a great deal of credibility, and Arabs throughout the region remain cynical about their governments' ability to effectively run the affairs of the country (Gordon 1999).

It often comes as a surprise to foreign businesspeople that not only are corporate taxes imposed on business profits in many Middle East countries, the rates also are sometimes quite high compared to Western countries, as seen in Table 8–1. Taxes on salaries and wages exist in all Middle East countries except the Gulf Cooperation Council (GCC) countries. However, in several GCC countries, a tax is imposed on the income of foreign individuals from business activities and professions. All countries impose customs duties, and a few have sales and other miscellaneous taxes (Bartlett 1997).

The countries where significant developments have recently taken place are Egypt and Jordan. Direct taxation in most Arab countries is extremely low and nonexistent in most of the Gulf states. Political reasons are the reason. In Saudi Arabia, the only direct withholding tax on personal income is the 2.5% *zakat* (contribution), a tax imposed by Islamic law.

Another important issue MNCs should consider in their tax planning is that the GCC countries are coordinating many areas of mutual interest. An obvious example with direct business implications includes not only taxation but also customs duty harmonization, centralization of management, training programs, and many other activities. Although this has not yet been completed, it may offer opportunities for regional tax planning. For example, products manufactured in a GCC company can be exported to other GCC countries without customs tariffs if they are regarded as national products (Bartlett 1997).

Most countries offer tax incentives that can be of significant benefit to MNCs investing in the Middle East. The main incentive is the tax holiday. Tax holidays, combined with other incentives, such as subsidized loans to finance local expenditure, customs duty exemptions, and a lack of exchange controls in most countries, help make the Middle East an attractive place to invest, despite the high tax rates that are still imposed in certain countries (ibid.).

Table 8–1
Middle East Taxation at a Glance

Countries	Corp. Tax Rates	Personal Income Tax	Customs Duties	Tax Treaties	Losses Carry Back	Losses Carry Forward	Tax Holiday	Other Taxes (d)	With-holding Taxes
Egypt	40%	20–32%	40–80%	(a)	No	5 years	5–12 years	Yes	32%
Jordan	35%	30%(c)	Up to 200%	(a)	No	6 years	5 years	Yes	10%
Israel	36%	15–50%	20–60%	(a)	No	Unlimited	2–10 years	Yes	15%
Kuwait	55%	Nil	4–25%	(a)	No	Unlimited	10 years	No	No
Palestine	38.5%	48%	(c)	No	No	6 years	3 years	No	5%
Saudi Arabia	45%	Nil	12–20%	France	No	No	5–10 years	No	(b)

The table of footnotes should only be used as a guide.

a. Double tax treaties have been signed with various countries.

b. Withholding taxes are calculated at corporate tax rates on a deemed profit basis between 15–100% on the payments to non-residents.

c. New customs duty regulations will be introduced soon.

d. Other taxes include stamp duties, municipal taxes, and so on.

Source: http://www.eyi.com/mideast/mebbtaxc.htm.

THE TAX SYSTEMS IN SELECTED MIDDLE EAST COUNTRIES

The Tax System in Egypt

General

1. From a corporate perspective, Egypt is a moderate tax jurisdiction.
2. Fiscal authorities do not give binding rulings, but they do issue internal interpretative instructions.
3. Direct and indirect taxation accounts for almost 55% of revenue.
4. Deduction, treaties, and tax credit give double tax relief.
5. Expatriate personnel are exempt from social insurance.
6. Hotel ownership and operating companies are exempt from all taxes for five years from the start of activity (tourism law).
7. Egypt has entered into tax treaties for withholding and double taxes with several counties, including Belgium (January 1, 1998), Bulgaria, Indonesia, Lebanon, Malaysia, Pakistan, Poland, Qatar, the Russian Federation, Singapore, South Africa, Turkey, and the Ukraine. It also has initialed double tax treaties with Jordan, Oman, and Yemen. Other tax treaties are underway with Albania, Algeria, Bahrain, Kazakhstan, Malawi, Malta, Mauritania, North Korea, and South Africa.

Taxable Income

The taxable corporate income is the total revenue after deducting all expenses, exempt income, and relief for losses brought forward (allowed for five years only). Certain capital gains are taxed. Tax paid on income from movable capital is deducted in computing taxable income for corporate tax purposes, for Egyptian corporations, for foreign corporations in Egypt, and for joint ventures or branches of foreign corporations in Egypt, subject to corporate tax on total net profits. Such profits are taxable if they are derived from Egyptian operations or from Egypt as well as from abroad, unless the foreign activities are performed through a permanent establishment located abroad.

The principal taxes in Egypt are those levied on different kinds of income, such as corporate income tax, tax on income from movable capital, tax on commercial and industrial profits, tax on profits on noncommercial professions, tax on salaries and related earnings, development duty tax, and general sales tax. Corporate income tax is computed on the basis of taxable profits determined according to the GAAP, modified for tax purposes by certain regulations primarily concerning inventory valuation, depreciation, provisions, and intercompany transactions and expenses. Organization and start-up expenses may be capitalized and amortized over three to five years. Losses not allowed for are carried back, but they may be carried forward for up to five years.

The deductibility of a branch's share of the overhead of the head office is limited to 7% of turnover. The amount of head office expenses to be allowed as a deduction is subject to negotiation, and it is possible to attribute all expenses to the activities of the branch rather than to the head office.

For tax purposes, inventory is usually valued at the lower of cost or market value. Cost is defined as purchase price plus direct and indirect production costs. For accounting purposes, companies may use any acceptable method of inventory valuation, such as the FIFO or weighted-average cost. Provisions for losses or future financial commitments, certain but not accurately quantifiable, are deductible if they are used for stated purposes. Provisions for dubious trading debts are not deductible until the bad debt is written off. All provisions should not exceed 5% of the company's net annual profit.

Depreciation of assets relevant to the nature of the business is allowable. It may be calculated using either the straight line or double declining balance method. The current straight-line depreciation rates set forth in tax authority regulations are building, 2%, furniture, 6%, office and accounting machines, 12–20%, motor vehicles, 20–25%, and plant and machinery, 10–15%. Higher tax rates may be negotiated for identifiable, abnormal wear and tear.

Consolidated tax returns can be prepared if all operations are owned by the same company. Aggregation is not allowed if operations are owned by separate companies, even if they are owned by the same parent company. However, one company can be the owner of more than one operation, and losses from one operation may be offset against profit from another operation if the same company owns all operations.

Another important issue is transfer pricing. The general rule is that intercompany transactions must be carried out at arm's length, as if between unrelated parties. Should the Egyptian tax department consider that transactions between related parties are not recorded at appropriate amounts, these transactions may be revalued or tax deemed on an assessed basis. In other words, for purchases from a head office or foreign affiliates, any difference between the transfer price and the prevailing market price may be justified by showing evidence to the Egyptian tax authorities.

For fiscal years ending after January 19, 1998, corporations must file their tax returns within four months of the end of the accounting year, which is April 30 for calendar-year taxpayers. Extensions of time to file returns are not granted.

Tax Rates

In 1997, the standard tax rate of corporate profits was 40% on the annual taxable net profits of a company. However, exceptions to this rate included the following:

- A 32% tax was imposed on an industrial company's profits realized from an industrial activity or profits acquired through export operations;
- A 32% tax was imposed on certain types of gross income, such as income derived from movable capital, interest from certain government bonds, and commission and brokers' fees. Tax on payments had to be withheld by the payer or beneficiary; and

- A 40.55% tax was levied on profits of oil prospecting and production companies. If annual net profits exceeded E18,000 (approximately $5,000), an additional 2% development duty was imposed on the total annual net profits.

In regard to individuals and partnerships, a unified income tax is applied according to the category of activity. These categories are summarized as follows: salaries are subject to tax rates of 20% on the first E50,000 per year and 32% on the excess. Egypt also imposes stamp duties, inheritance, social security, sales, and entertainment taxes.

However, the corporate tax rates of corporations are summarized below.

Types of Tax	Rate (%)
Corporate Income Tax	40
Capital Gains Tax	40
Branch Tax	40
Withholding Tax	
Dividends	0
Interest	32
Royalties from Patents	32
Net Operating Losses (Years)	
Carry Back	0
Carry Forward	5

Capital Gains

In general, capital gains from the sale of productive assets are taxable unless the proceeds are reinvested within the two subsequent years in assets that result in improved or increased production. Administratively, the tax on the gain is paid in the year of disposal. A credit is claimed in the year of reinvestment. If the sales proceeds of capital assets are used in the same year or during the following two years to buy new capital assets that contribute to increased and improved production, a tax credit calculated on capital gains is granted in the year of sale or in the years following the sale or replacement.

Tax on capital gains is calculated at ordinary corporate tax rates in the same way as ordinary business profits and is not calculated separately. Trading and capital losses realized on sales of other assets are deductible against taxable capital gains.

Dividends, Interest, and Royalties

Dividends or interest derived from shares, debentures, and bonds listed on the Egyptian Stock Exchange are exempt from taxes. Dividends distributed by an Egyptian company are not subject to withholding tax, because they are paid out of corporate profits that are taxed under normal rules. However, dividends received by residents from foreign sources are considered income from movable capital and are subject to a tax rate of 32%. Foreign taxes paid abroad, such as taxes on foreign-source dividends and interest, may be deducted from income from movable capital that is subject to tax. Moreover, tax treaties between Egypt and other countries regulate the credit for taxes paid abroad on income subject to corporate income tax in Egypt.

With respect to interest, interest expense is generally deductible for tax purposes if the borrowed funds were used in the business for bona fide purposes. For interest income, only 10% is included in the calculation of a company's corporate tax. In addition, foreign-source interest is subject to unified movable capital tax. The unified movable capital tax paid reduces the interest income included in ordinary taxable income. In other words, 10% of interest income after deducting unified movable capital tax is subject to corporate tax.

In general, royalties are treated as ordinary income and are taxed at corporate rates or as stipulated in the double taxation treaties. Where royalties are paid to a foreign company with headquarters abroad and no branch in Egypt, corporate income tax is normally withheld by the payer at a 32% rate. The tax is levied on the "gross" amount (without any deductions) or as stipulated in the double taxation treaty with the country of the receiving entity.

Tax Incentives and Tax Holidays

Incentives for foreign investors include tax holidays, customs exemptions, and guarantee against nationalization. Tax holidays of 5, 10, or 20 years are granted on foreign capital invested in Egypt according to Law No. 8 of 1997, which replaced Law No. 230 of 1989. Tax holidays of five years are allowed for projects established under the Investment Law—extended for an additional five years on a project-by-project basis. It grants 10 years of tax holidays for projects in new industrial zones. Exemptions are extended an additional five years as necessitated by public interest.

Companies in free zones are permanently exempt from all taxes. Projects in new industrial zones and certain other areas are exempt from tax for 10 years from the beginning of the first financial year following the commencement date of their activities.

Industrial corporations are exempt from tax for five years from the beginning of the financial year following the commencement date of their activities, if they have 50 employees or more and if they maintain proper accounting books.

The Tax System in Israel

General

1. Since financing Israel's massive public consumption has required heavy taxation, in some years the Israeli citizen has borne the highest tax burden, relative to income, in the world.

2. During the first decade of Israel's establishment, taxes equaled one-eighth of the GNP; in the 1960s, the proportion reached one-quarter; it wavered between one-third and one-half in the 1970s, and it peaked at 52% in 1986; since then, it has fallen again.

3. At no time, however, has taxation covered more than two-thirds of the government budget.

4. In most years, indirect taxes, such as customs duties, purchase tax, value-added taxes (VAT), and the like, accounted for the bulk of tax collections.

5. Direct taxes amounted to less than one-quarter of all tax revenues until the early 1960s, climbed to around one-third in the early 1970s, to nearly one-half at the end of that decade, and reached an all-time high of 57% in 1984.

6. Since then, the weight of direct taxes has decreased. In 1993, it constituted 48% of all tax revenues; total state revenues from taxes and fees were $21.9 billion, representing 39.7% of the GDP.

Taxable Income

Israel uses the classical system of corporate taxation, in which income is taxed at the corporate level and on distribution to shareholders. In general, taxation in Israel is based on the concept that Israel-source income, wherever received, and foreign source income received in Israel are taxable. Resident and non-resident companies are generally subject to Israeli corporate tax on income accrued or received in Israel unless otherwise provided for in tax treaties. Resident companies are also subject to tax on their income from an overseas business that is controlled and managed in Israel and on their worldwide capital gains.

Taxable income is based on financial statements that are prepared according to the GAAP and derived from acceptable accounting books. In principle, expenses are deductible if they are wholly and exclusively incurred in the production of taxable income. Several items may require adjustment for tax purposes, such as R&D expenses, depreciation expenses, and travel expenses.

The Israeli tax law also prescribes a series of inflation adjustments to the taxable income of businesses in Israel. Inventory may be valued at the lower of cost at market (LCM) value. Cost may be determined using one of the following methods: actual, average, or FIFO. LIFO is not allowed for tax purposes. Bad debts are deductible when they become uncollectible. Special rules apply to employee-related provisions, such as severance pay, vacation pay, and sick pay.

Depreciation of fixed assets, used in the production of taxable income, is allowable at prescribed rates. An accelerated depreciation method may be used in many cases. For assets purchased or acquired in 1998, industrial companies may depreciate new assets using the straight-line method at annual depreciation rates of 4% to 16% for buildings and 20% to 40% for equipment. Alternatively, they may depreciate equipment using the declining-balance method at rates between 30% and 50%.

Consolidated tax returns, subject to certain conditions, are permissible for a holding company and its industrial subsidiaries if the subsidiaries are all engaged in the same line of production or a common line of production in which the largest amount has been invested. For tax purposes, a holding company is one that has invested at least 80% of its fixed assets in industrial subsidiaries and controls at least 50% (or two-thirds, in certain cases) of voting rights in those subsidiaries.

Business losses may be offset against gains from any source in the same year. Any net business losses may be carried forward for an unlimited number of years to offset business income.

The Israeli tax authorities recognize intercompany transactions, provided that they are based on normal commercial terms and practices. In general, all transactions between related parties (intracompany transactions) should be at arm's length (the transfer price). A new international reform bill was introduced and became effective January 1, 1999. Under the new tax reform system, tax-assessing officers may adjust transfer pricing transactions for tax purposes to market prices if the assessing officer believes that the transactions were influenced by related-party transactions (such as family connections or control of 25% or more of the issued share capital or voting power), and if such influence resulted in less or more profit than would normally be expected between unrelated parties. The bill also empowers the Tax Commission to issue transfer pricing rules (Jerusalem.newsroom@reuters.com 1999).

Tax Rates

In Israel, the regular company tax rate for profits and real capital gains is 36%. Company tax rates ranging from 0% to 25% are available for approved enterprises or properties and in other cases. However, corporate tax rates are summarized below.

Types of Tax	Rate (%)
Corporate Income Tax	36
Capital Gains Tax	36
Branch Tax	36
Withholding Tax	
Dividends	25
Interest	25
Royalties from Patents	25
Net Operating Losses (Years)	
Carry Back	0
Carry Forward	Unlimited

Capital Gains

A capital gains tax is imposed on the disposal of fixed and intangible assets where the disposal price is in excess of the depreciated cost for tax purposes.

Israeli and foreign companies are generally subject to Israeli tax on their capital gains relating directly or indirectly to assets in Israel, including Israeli securities, unless a tax treaty provides otherwise. Resident companies are also subject to capital gains tax on their capital gains derived abroad. With a proposal, effective on January 1, 1999, Israeli capital gains taxes are also imposed on the disposal of assets satisfying one of the following requirements:

- The asset was located in Israel at the time of disposal;
- The asset was located in Israel for the majority of the period that it was owned; or
- The asset was used primarily in Israel.

Moreover, the proposal includes capital gains taxes imposed on the disposal of shares in foreign companies if 50% or more of a foreign corporation's assets are located in Israel, including shares in Israeli resident companies and rights in such shares.

There are two components of capital gains: real and inflationary. The real gain is taxed at the regular corporate tax rate of 36%. The inflationary component is exempt from tax to the extent that it accrued on or after January 1, 1994, and it is generally taxable at a rate of 10% to the extent that it accrued before that date. Capital gains derived from sales of Israeli real estate or sales of interests in real estate entities are subject to land appreciation tax at rates similar to those applicable to other capital gains.

Capital losses may be used to offset capital gains of the same tax year or in the following seven tax years. In each year, capital losses are first offset against real gains and then offset against inflationary amounts.

Special rules apply to securities traded on the Tel Aviv Stock Exchange and approved foreign stock exchanges. Companies conducting business in Israel are subject to tax at the regular company tax rate on realized gains and certain unrealized gains with respect to such securities. No Israeli tax is imposed on capital gains from securities traded on the Tel Aviv Stock Exchange that are derived by Israeli and foreign residents not conducting business in Israel. Similarly, no Israeli tax is imposed on non-business–related capital gains from securities of Israeli industrial companies and industrial holding companies that are traded on exchanges in designated foreign countries.

Dividends, Interests, and Royalties

Dividends paid out of the profits of approved enterprises are generally subject to a 15% withholding tax. A 25% withholding tax is generally imposed on dividends paid out to other profits (regular profits). However, resident companies are exempt from company tax on dividends paid out of regular profits by other resident companies.

Branches of non-resident companies are subject to a 15% branch tax on their approved enterprise profits after the deduction of the company tax. Generally, the branch tax is payable with the company tax. However, the tax commissioner may allow payment of the branch tax to be deferred until the profits are with-drawn from Israeli business operations. Many of Israel's tax treaties include tax-sparing provisions under which regular taxes, rather than reduced Israeli taxes, may be credited against income tax imposed in the investor's country of residence on dividends or branch income derived from an approved enterprise.

Interest received or accrued is generally included in the normal calculations to ascertain a company's taxable income. However, Israeli tax regulations require that when a loan is made carrying an interest rate less than the rate of increase in the consumer price index (CPI), the difference between the actual interest rate and the rate of increase in the CPI is to be added as imputed income to the taxable income of the company granting the loan and is to be taxed at the standard tax rate without offseting any expenses or losses. Loans granted by financial institutions in the normal course of business are exempt from this rule, which also contains other specific exemptions.

Royalties are part of the normal taxable income of a company. Tax deductions at source are credited against the tax liability of the recipient company in the year of receipt.

Tax Incentives and Tax Holidays

Foreign investment funds dedicated to investing at least US$20 million in Israel-related investments in industry or other specific sectors may be granted a 20% tax rate, or a complete exemption in certain foreign pension funds or similar institutions exempt from tax in their home country.

Under Israel's tax treaties, resident companies that derive or receive income from abroad may qualify for double tax relief in the form of a tax credit or an exemption. Alternatively, a foreign tax credit or a reduced Israeli tax rate (usually up to 25%) may be claimed under Israel's unilateral relief provisions. Moreover, foreign residents who receive little or no relief for Israeli taxes in their home countries may be granted a reduced Israeli tax rate by the Minister of Finance. In practice, the reduced rate is at least 25% and applies to capital gains only.

Approved industrial, commercial, and residential rental properties may qualify for reduced tax rates on rental income (and on gains derived from sales of certain buildings that have a residential element; a building has a residential element if at least 50% of the floor space is rented for residential purposes for a prescribed number of years). The reduced rates are the same as the ones for approved enterprises. A tax holiday and grants may also be available to approved industrial properties, depending on their location.

Preferential tax treatment may be allowed with respect to the following: agriculture, oil, movies, international trading, R&D financing, and nonresidents' bank accounts. Non-tax incentives include financial support for the following: R&D, development of production prototypes, investment in new facilities or products to promote competition with foreign companies (trade exposure fund), exporters, export agents, equipment leasing to approved enterprises, and textile collections.

The Tax System in Jordan

General

Jordan could have become a center for economic dynamism in the Arab world. Instead, it has consistently relied on foreign aid and influence, painting itself as a pivotal piece in the Israeli conflict and peace process. But Jordan is not alone in shirking industrialization and economic diversification. Few of these states recognize the need for restructuring their economies before a crisis hits (Gordon, 1999).

- Income tax is levied on corporate entities and foreign branches, on taxable profits from all sources arising, or deemed to arise, in Jordan.
- The tax rates are flat rates. Rates for resident corporations vary. In 1997, mining, industrial projects, hotels, hospitals, transportation, and construction were taxed at 15%; banking, insurance, and financial services were taxed at 35%; and other companies were taxed at 25%.
- Foreign tax relief is granted in accordance with tax treaties signed with other specific countries.
- Personal taxation is levied on salaries and benefits, including housing and airfares. The rates are calculated using an escalating scale. The maximum rate is 30%, plus a social welfare tax of 10% of the income tax.
- There is a 7% sales tax and certain other minor taxes.
- Jordan has entered into tax treaties that primarily relate to transportation with Austria, Bahrain, Belgium, Canada, Cyprus, Denmark, Egypt, France, Iraq, Italy, Kuwait, Oman, Pakistan, Qatar, Romania, Saudi Arabia, Spain, Syria, Tunisia, Turkey, the United Arab Emirates, the United States, and Yemen.

Taxable Income

According to Jordanian tax law, all income earned in Jordan from trading or other sources is taxable. All business expenses incurred to generate income are allowable, with certain limitations. A specific percentage of entertainment expenses is deductible. Head office charges are limited to 5% of net adjusted income. Provisions are not allowable as tax deductions. Statutory maximum depreciation rates are set for various types of fixed assets. If the rates used for accounting purposes are greater than the specified rates, the excess is not allowed. The tax law allows accelerated depreciation rates, effective from January 1, 1996.

Income tax is levied on corporate entities and foreign branches with respect to taxable profit from all sources arising or deemed to arise in Jordan. Income is deemed to arise in Jordan if one of the following is located there:

• the place of performance of work; or

• the place of delivery of work.

Jordanian tax law does not have a provision for filing consolidated returns or for relieving losses within a group of companies. Taxpayers are allowed to carry forward unabsorbed losses to offset the profits of subsequent periods, up to a maximum of six years. Losses may not be carried back.

Tax Rates

In general, corporate tax rates are summarized below.

Types of Tax	Rate (%)
Corporate Income Tax	35
Capital Gains Tax	
On Share	0
On Depreciable Assets	35
Branch Tax	35
Withholding Tax	
Dividends	10
Interest	10
Royalties from Patents	10
Net Operating Losses (Years)	
Carry Back	0
Carry Forward	6

However, different rates of corporate income tax are levied on different types of businesses, as shown below.

Sector	Rate (%)
Hospital, hotel, industrial, and mining as well as construction and transportation (if the paid-up capital of the company exceeds JD 1 million)	15
Banking, exchange (foreign-exchange dealers), financial, insurance, and inter-mediation (brokerage)	35*
Others	25

*In all cases, the tax levied on any category of bank, financial company, or insurance company must not be less than 25% of its annual reportable incomes (not necessarily equal to annual profits) before any deduction for reserves or distribution, but after taking into consideration any losses carried forward.

Capital Gains

Capital gains on the sale of shares by Jordanian or foreign shareholding companies are not taxable, except for financial institutions subject to special limitations stated in the law. Capital gains on sales of depreciable assets are taxed at the normal corporate income tax rates.

Dividends, Interest, and Royalties

A 10% distribution tax, which is withheld at source, is imposed on payments of cash dividends to residents and non-residents. A resident company is one incorporated in Jordan. Stock dividends and the capitalization of profits are not subject to this tax. Profits transferred abroad by foreign companies operating in Jordan are considered distributed profits and are subject to the 10% distribution tax, which is withheld at source.

Tax Incentives and Tax Holidays

The tax regulations provide incentives to taxpayers who choose to make payments in advance. The following credits can be claimed:

- 6% on payments made in the first month after the fiscal year-end;
- 4% on payments made in the second month after the fiscal year-end; and
- 2% on payments made in the third month after the fiscal year-end.

The Tax System in Kuwait

General

- Foreign companies carrying on a trade or business in Kuwait are liable for tax. Kuwaiti registered companies wholly owned by Kuwaitis and companies incorporated in GCC countries, wholly owned by GCC citizens, are not subject to income tax.

- Kuwaiti income tax is imposed at rates of up to 55% on taxable profits exceeding KD 375,000 ($1.2 million). These rates have remained unchanged since 1970.

- Kuwait has treaties in force for avoidance of double taxation with China, Cyprus, France, Germany, Italy, and Romania. Treaties with several other countries are at various stages of negotiation or ratification.

- No personal income tax is levied in Kuwait either on salaries or on income derived from commercial activities.

- A draft bill is under consideration in parliament, which would allow the collection of *zakat* from Kuwaiti companies.

There are no individual income taxes in Kuwait. The first income tax law appeared in the Kuwait Income Tax Decree No. 3 for 1955, and it was amended by another decree in 1957 to redefine the taxpayer as "any body corporate carrying on trade or business in Kuwait either directly or through an agent and also any body corporate carrying on trade or business in Kuwait as an agent for other."

The initial purpose of the law was to impose an income tax on oil companies operating in Kuwait when no other significant foreign business existed there. Since then, the law has become, in text and practice, a general tool for the taxation of all foreign companies working not only in but also for Kuwait.

Taxable Income

Under Kuwaiti tax law, foreign "bodies corporate" carrying on trade or business in Kuwait or in the areas known as the "Specified Territory" (see below) are subject to tax. Kuwaiti-registered companies wholly owned by Kuwaitis and companies incorporated in GCC countries that are wholly owned by GCC citizens are not subject to income tax. "Body corporate" refers to an association formed and registered under the laws of any country or state and recognized as having a legal existence entirely separate from that of its individual members. Partnerships fall within this definition.

The "Specified Territory" consists of the partitioned neutral zone between Kuwait and Saudi Arabia and the islands of Kubr, Qaru, and Umm Al Maradim and their territorial waters.

Foreign companies carrying on a trade or business in the Specified Territory are subject to tax under Law No. 23 of 1961, in accordance with the following rules:

- The entire taxable profit derived in the Specified Territory under Kuwaiti control and administration is subject to tax.
- 50% of the taxable profit derived in the portion of the offshore partitioned zone under the control and administration of Saudi Arabia is subject to tax.

Amiri Decree No. 3 of 1955 and Law No. 23 of 1961 differ primarily in tax rates.

Foreign companies can operate in Kuwait (or in the Specified Territory, under Kuwaiti administration) either through an agent or as the minority shareholder in a locally registered company. In principle, the method of calculating tax is the same for companies operating through an agent and for minority shareholders. For minority shareholders, tax is levied on the foreign company's share of the profits (whether or not distributed by the Kuwaiti company), plus any amount receivable for interest, royalties, technical services, and management fees.

The Kuwaiti tax law does not cover the transfer-pricing issue in detail. The Kuwaiti tax authorities deem the following profit margins for imported materials:

- materials manufactured by affiliates, 10% to 15% of cost; and
- materials imported from unrelated parties, 5% to 10% of cost.

Regarding the transfer pricing policy, the imputed profit described above is normally subtracted from the cost of materials and equipment claimed in the tax declaration. If the revenue from the materials and equipment supplied is identifiable, the Department of Income Tax normally reduces the cost of such items to show a profit on such materials and equipment in accordance with the percentages described above.

Tax Rates

The tax rates of Kuwaiti corporations in 1999 are described below.

Types of Tax	Rate (%)
Corporate Income Tax	55
Capital Gains Tax	55
Branch Tax	55
Withholding Tax	
Dividends	0
Interest	0
Royalties from Patents	0
Net Operating Losses (Years)	
Carry Back	0
Carry Forward	Unlimited

Details of the corporate tax rates under Amiri Decree No. 3 of 1955 follow:

Taxable Profits		Rate (%)
Exceeding (KD)	Not Exceeding (KD)	
0	5,250	0
5,250	18,750	5
18,750	37,500	10
37,500	56,250	15
56,250	75,000	20
75,000	112,500	25
112,500	150,000	30
150,000	225,000	35
225,000	300,000	40
300,000	375,000	45
375,000	—	55

The tax rates under Law No. 23 of 1961 are:

| Taxable Profits | | Rate (%) |
Exceeding (KD)	Not Exceeding (KD)	
0	500,000	20
500,000	—	57

Kuwaiti income tax is not progressive; consequently, total profit is taxed at the appropriate rate from the above table. If taxable profit is only marginally higher than the previous limit, tax is calculated by adding the actual excess to the amount payable on the previous limit. For example, on KD 38,000 of taxable income derived in Kuwait, the tax is KD 37,500 at 10% = KD 3,750, plus KD 500, giving a total tax of KD 4,250.

Capital Gains

Capital gains on the sale of assets and shares by a foreign shareholder are treated as normal business profits and are subject to tax at the rates stated above. Capital losses incurred on the disposal of capital assets are allowed as deductions from income.

Dividends, Interest, and Royalties

In general, when a foreign company has a minority shareholder interest in a locally registered company, tax is levied on the foreign company's income (whether distributed or not), plus any amounts received for interest, royalties, technical services, or management fees. In other words, dividends are not taxed. Tax is assessed on the share of profits attributable to the foreign shareholder, according to the audited financial statements of a company, adjusted for tax purposes.

Interest is only usually accepted if it is paid directly by the branch to a bank in Kuwait and is reasonable in relation to the activities of the business in Kuwait. Interest incurred outside of Kuwait is usually disallowed.

Tax Incentives and Tax Holidays

To encourage investments in local industrial undertakings, Law No. 65 of 1996 offers the following incentives:

• reduced import duties on equipment and raw materials;
• protective tariffs against competing imported goods;
• low-interest loans from local banks;
• export assistance; and
• preferential treatment on government supply contracts.

The extent to which credits will be granted under Industry Law No. 65 of 1996 remains to be clarified. In addition, Law No. 12 of 1998, which was effective from May 25, 1998, allows foreign companies to hold shares in Kuwaiti leasing and investment companies. It also grants a five-year income tax holiday to foreign companies with respect to their shares of profits in leasing and investment companies. Procedures regarding the holding of shares by foreign companies in Kuwaiti investment companies and the tax holiday will be announced by the government.

The Tax System in Saudi Arabia

General

- Corporate income tax is assessed on profits arising or deemed to arise in Saudi Arabia of foreign partnerships and foreign corporate entities and on profits attributable to foreign shareholders in Saudi corporate entities. However, for income tax, foreigners do not include citizens of GCC countries. Saudi and GCC nationals are subject to *zakat*.

- Taxable income includes all income and profits derived from operations inside of Saudi Arabia or from operations inside and outside of Saudi Arabia at the same time.

- Tax applicable to non-GCC taxpayers is at progressive rates of up to 45% on taxable profits exceeding SR1,000,000 ($270,000) for corporations and up to 30% on taxable profits exceeding SR66,000 for individuals. There is no income tax on the salaries and wages of employees in Saudi Arabia, but there are social security taxes.

- In practice, no company directly engaged in the production of crude oil or gas and petrochemicals is known to have been required to pay income tax under the corporate income tax decrees.

- Taxes are imposed on oil-producing companies at direct, agreed-upon rates with their host government.

- Nationals of GCC countries are treated as Saudis and subject to a religious tax called *zakat*. *Zakat* is paid by the GCC owners of businesses. The rate is 2.5% of capital employed that is not invested in items such as fixed assets and long-term investments, adjusted by the net results for the year.

Taxable Income

Income tax is assessed on profits arising or deemed to arise in Saudi Arabia earned by foreign partnerships and foreign corporate entities and on the share of a foreign shareholder in the profits of a Saudi corporate entity. However, for income tax purposes, foreigners do not include citizens (nationals) of countries that are the members of the GCC. In a company incorporated in a GCC state, the share of profits attributable to interests owned by GCC nationals in that company is subject to *zakat*. The share of profits attributable to interests owned by non-GCC nationals in that company is subject to income tax. Income is deemed to arise in Saudi Arabia if services are performed in Saudi Arabia or performed inside and outside of Saudi Arabia at the same time.

The most acceptable basis to the Department of Zakat and Income Tax (DZIT) for assessing tax liabilities is the audited financial statement, adjusted for tax purposes. In exceptional cases, tax is assessable under the arbitrary basis—no financial statements are presented, and the liability is calculated on a deemed profit at a minimum of 15% of gross revenue. The DZIT may increase this percentage at any time, depending on the nature and circumstances of the contract and its view of profitability of the contract. The DZIT discourages the arbitrary basis, preferring the financial statement method.

Indirect expenses may not be deducted from the revenue of a Saudi business. Similarly, the allocation of costs by a head office to a branch is not allowed. In general, normal business expenses are deductible. The allocation of general or administrative costs of the head office is not deductible; only certified technical costs of the head office directly related to Saudi Arabian operations are permitted. Technical costs, generally expenses that relate to engineering, chemical, geological, or industrial work and research—even if incurred wholly abroad by the main office or other offices—are deductible if they can be substantiated by certain documents, such as technical services agreements, local employers' certificates, and head office auditors' certificates or invoices. If technical services are rendered by third parties in the Kingdom (including foreign shareholders, regardless of whether they are enjoying a tax holiday), payment for such services is subject to a deemed profit tax at a minimum rate of 15%. The DZIT may increase this profit percentage depending on the nature of the agreement; and a rate of 20% is now frequently applied.

Statutory maximum rates of depreciation are established by the DZIT. If rates used in the financial statements are greater, the excess is disallowed. If lower rates are used in the financial statements, an additional claim is not permitted. Rates up to 50% above the statutory depreciation rates may be negotiated for equipment, excluding computers, subject to abnormally high usage that can be verified.

When a Saudi mixed company deals with the head office or any affiliated company of foreign shareholders, it is expected to trade on an arm's length basis. The company is required to submit to the DZIT a certificate from the seller's auditors confirming that the materials and goods supplied to the Saudi Arabian company were sold at the international market price that prevailed at the date of dispatch. This requirement also is extended to foreign branches importing materials and goods from the head office for fulfillment of their Saudi contracts.

Capital Gains

Overall, capital gains from the sale of business assets and business interest are considered ordinary income and are taxed at regular corporate tax rates. Separate rules apply for the computation of taxable income arising from capital gains on the sale or transfer of ownership by a foreign shareholder in a limited liability company. The taxable gain is usually calculated by comparing the sale price of the share to the tax-adjusted net book value of the share, or by applying the average rate of net profit for the three years prior to the shareholders' funds.

Tax and Zakat Rates

The DZIT assesses corporate income tax on the share of profit attributable to interests owned by foreign persons and on the share attributable to the interests owned by Saudis and GCC nationals. Saudis and GCC nationals and their interests are subject to *zakat*, but not income tax. The 1999 corporate tax rates are described below.

Types of Tax	Rate (%)
Corporate Income Tax	45
Capital Gains Tax	45
Branch Tax	45
Withholding Tax	
Dividends	0
Interest	0
Royalties from Patents	0
Net Operating Losses (Years)	
Carry Back	0
Carry Forward	0

As can be seen from the table above, the maximum corporate tax rate is 45%. It applies to taxable income over SR 1,000,000 (US$267,000). However, the detailed rates of corporate income tax that are applicable to non-Saudis (excluding citizens of GCC states) follow.

Taxable Income		Tax on Lower Amount	Rate on Excess
Exceeding SR	Not Exceeding SR	SR	%
0	100,000	0	25
100,000	500,000	25,000	35
500,000	1,000,000	165,000	40
1,000,000	—	365,000	45

The earnings of employed individuals are not taxed. Foreign self-employed professionals and foreign partners in professional partnerships are subject to income tax on their business net income. The maximum individual tax rate of 30% applies to taxable business income over SR 66,000 (US$17,600).

Zakat is a religious wealth tax assessed on Saudi and GCC nationals and companies entirely owned by Saudi or GCC nationals. If companies or partnerships are owned by Saudis or GCCs nationals, or both, as well as by other foreigners, *zakat* is assessed in proportion to the equity interest of Saudis and GCCs nationals in the company. *Zakat* rates are 2.5% of capital employed, not invested in fixed assets, long-term investments, and deferred pre-incorporation expenses, adjusted by net results for the year.

Dividends, Interest, and Royalties

In general, joint stock companies and limited liability partnerships distributing dividends out of taxed income are not required to withhold tax on the distributions. Because Saudi companies pay dividends to shareholders out of income already subject to income tax or *zakat*, these dividends are not included in shareholders' taxable income. Interest paid to foreign affiliates or non-residents third parties is usually subject to a final withholding tax at a minimum 15% deemed profit rate. Interest paid to foreign banks that have no presence in Saudi Arabia is not subject to the deemed profit tax. Royalties, license fees, and management fees are deemed 100% profit. Consequently, withholding taxes are applied at the normal rates. Under the DZIT's current practice, management fees, royalties, license fees, and similar payments are taxed on a 100% deemed-profit basis.

All firms, Saudi and non-Saudi, are required to submit income tax or *zakat* returns each year to the DZIT. *Zakat* is assessed on the taxable income of joint stock companies, limited liability partnerships, contractors, or professionals. Foreign entities and individuals are subject to income tax on their share of profit from business entities, but they are not subject to *zakat*. Individuals are not subject to tax on their salaries or wages.

Income tax on business profits and *zakat* is the primary tax in Saudi Arabia. Capital gains on the sale of business assets and business interest are treated as ordinary business income. Both income tax and *zakat* may be collected through withholding by the payer, rather than through direct assessments on income recipients, especially if the recipients are not registered with the DZIT.

Most taxes in Saudi Arabia are direct taxes payable to the DZIT. The following direct taxes are imposed on income arising in Saudi Arabia: (1) corporate tax; (2) *zakat*; (3) tax on the income of foreign professionals; (4) withholding tax; (5) withholding *zakat*; and (6) capital gains tax. Sales tax, value-added tax, and estate or gift tax do not exist in Saudi Arabia.

Income tax is primarily imposed on business income earned through a business entity or on self-employment income. The most acceptable method for assessing tax liabilities is from audited financial statements. Foreign branches, after obtaining prior approval, may use an arbitrary method based on the assumption that the profit is a percentage of gross revenues, however, the minimum deemed profit acceptable to the DZIT is 15% of gross revenues. According to tax regulations, each company within a group is considered an independent entity and should file a separate tax return directly with the DZIT. Consolidation is not accepted by the DZIT.

Tax Incentives and Tax Holidays

A tax holiday is granted for a period of five or 10 years, depending on the industrial, agricultural, or other projects in which investment has been made by the foreign investor, only if Saudi participation in the invested capital is at least 25%. For industrial and agricultural projects, the tax holiday period is 10 years; otherwise, it is five years. Additional tax holidays are granted to foreign shareholders in industrial projects and banks if additional capital is invested and if certain other conditions are met. During the tax holiday period, the foreign shareholder is subject to tax if it carries out any activities not specifically covered by its license, which is issued by the Ministry of Industry and Electricity on the recommendation of the Foreign Capital Investment Committee (this license is known as the Foreign Capital Investment License [FCIL], or the Industrial License).

Saudi Arabia welcomes the contribution that foreign investments make to its economy, especially those that promote industrialization. Consequently, foreign investors may be eligible for incentives stipulated in foreign capital investment regulations if they obtain a FCIL. Another incentive available to local and foreign investors is the customs duty exemption. At present, certain machinery, tools, equipment, spare parts, raw material (primary or semi-manufactured), and packaging materials (including cases and cylinders) imported for industrial establishments are exempt from customs duties. Other customs duties are low or nominal by international standards.

SUMMARY AND CONCLUSIONS

This chapter examines the tax systems and regulations of the selected five Middle East countries: Egypt, Israel, Jordan, Kuwait, and Saudi Arabia. The purpose of this chapter is fourfold: (1) to understand the taxation systems and regulations of the selected countries of the Middle East; (2) to guide MNCs and foreign businesspersons in how to invest and manage their businesses successfully with Middle East tax regulations and to end up with the highest rate of return on their invested capital with the lowest possible business and political risks; (3) to help potential investors determine the most favorable country for a particular investment; and (4) to look at regional opportunities for cost savings and improvements in efficiency in tax affairs.

First, the chapter discussed taxation in general and emphasized the essential need for successful, effective tax planning for MNCs before they begin investing in selected Middle East countries to take advantage of tax differences, holidays, tax treaties, and other incentives. Second, the characteristics of the taxation systems of selected Middle East countries in general were analyzed. Regional tax coordination and trends and most of the potential advantages of well-designed regional tax planning were discussed. Third, the tax system of each country was discussed separately. MNCs and any potential investors can be very successful in investing their capital and in managing their businesses in the Middle East if they design an appropriate tax planning strategy that fits the Middle East tax environment. In doing so, tax planning should be done in advance, and should include the following five major steps:

1. Get access to all up-to-date tax information in the region and in the selected country.
2. Start your tax planning as soon as your project is initiated.
3. Involve your local partner(s) in your tax planning.
4. Minimize your tax burden by:
   a. choosing the most appropriate investment tools such as joint ventures or wholly owned subsidiaries;
   b. structuring contracts in the most convenient, appropriate manner;
   c. taking advantage of all tax holidays and other incentives available;
   d. coordinating the tax burden in the Middle East with that in your home country to take advantage of any tax treaty provisions and other tax credit opportunities
5. Design your pricing policy, including transfer pricing strategies, after considering all tax and custom issues.

REFERENCES

Abdallah, Wagdy. "Accounting Standards in Saudi Arabia and International Accounting Standards." *International Review of Accounting* 2 (1997), 27–41.
———. "American Joint Ventures in the Middle East: The Case of Amoco-Egypt—Managerial, Financial, and Tax Implications." *Middle East Business Review* 3 (1999), 49–64.
Bartlett, Sam. "Middle East Low Tax Myth Dispelled." *International Tax Review* (March 1997), 19–22.
Ernst & Young. *Doing Business in Kuwait.* New York: Ernst & Young International, 1993.
———. *Doing Business in Saudi Arabia.* New York: Ernst & Young International, 1993.
Ernst & Young International. "Doing Business in Egypt." http://www.eyi.com/Egypt, September 6, 1999.
———. "Doing Business in Israel." http://www.eyi.com/Israel, September 6, 1999.
———. "Doing Business in Jordan." http://www.eyi.com/Jordan, September 6, 1999.
———. "Doing Business in Kuwait." http://www.eyi.com/Kuwait, September 6, 1999.
———. "Doing Business in Saudi Arabia." http://www.eyi.com/SaudiArabia, September 6, 1999.

Gordon, Michael. "No Representation without Taxation." *Middle East* (March 1999), 19–20.

Jerusalem.newsroom@reuters.com, 1999.

Price Waterhouse. *Doing Business in Egypt.* New York: Price Waterhouse World Firm Services, 1995.

———. *Doing Business in Israel.* New York: Price Waterhouse World Firm Services, 1995.

———. *Doing Business in Saudi Arabia.* New York: Price Waterhouse World Firm Services, 1995.

Robins, Don and Michael Bishko. "Minimizing Taxes for Americans in the Gulf." *Middle East Executive Reports* (May 1991), 20–22.

Chapter 9

Transfer Pricing Policies for Multinationals Operating in the Middle East

This chapter discusses the importance of establishing well-designed transfer pricing policies for MNCs investing and operating in the Middle East and the dilemma of implementing the correct strategy. It analyzes the process of designing and establishing a transfer pricing system for global operations of MNCs. It also examines the requirements that should be satisfied to establish an efficient and effective transfer pricing system. The system will maximize the MNC's profits and minimize its international transaction costs, and can be used as an adequate profit yardstick to evaluate Middle East subsidiary managers' performance and the profit-center concepts and their applications in the Middle East environment.

MNCs are highly motivated to go to the Middle East region by many factors that vary from one industry to another and even from one firm to another within the same industry. They may export to or import from a subsidiary in Egypt, Israel, or Saudi Arabia owned by another MNC. In this case, a MNC may manufacture its products at home and then export them to a Saudi Arabian market to achieve higher profits. On the other hand, a MNC may find it less costly to manufacture its products where labor costs are the lowest, such as in Egypt or Jordan, and sell them where selling prices are the highest, such as in Europe or Japan.

MNCs may start to look for new markets in the Middle East for many reasons. These include: (1) improving their competitive position in both domestic and international markets; (2) exploring new markets in the Middle East; (3) maximizing profits; (4) meeting tariff and quota restrictions in foreign countries; (5) securing otherwise unobtainable raw materials for the home country, such as oil products; (6) exploring the scarce economic resources in the Middle East countries; (7) choosing countries with low tariff and quota restrictions; (8) choosing countries with low income taxes on foreign companies or foreign investments to minimize the sum of its U.S. and foreign taxes; and (9) manufacturing their products in the least cost-producing countries, especially the less developed countries (LDCs), and selling the products in the best-selling markets.

The rapid increase in business globalization means that MNCs, U.S. (e.g., the Internal Revenue Service), U.K. (e.g., Inland Revenue), Middle East, and other foreign tax authorities must consider transfer pricing carefully. MNCs should ensure that their transfer pricing policies achieve certain objectives and at the same time are fair. IRS and foreign tax authorities must ensure that they collect a fair amount of corporate income tax from MNCs operating in their jurisdiction (Elliot 1998a).

Moreover, Middle East governments, like others, may impose high tariffs on all imports going into their countries, either to protect their local industries from competition against foreign companies or to increase revenues for the government. MNCs must keep abreast of the changes and developments to ensure that they are able to demonstrate compliance with relevant U.S. and Middle East countries' tax regulations. They should avoid any transfer pricing misstatement for tax reporting with the IRS. The U.S. court case of *DHL Corp.* (1969) re-affirms that MNCs should plan to properly document and defend the transfer pricing method used to transfer intangible assets to their controlled parties. The courts will be willing to uphold the assessment of the 20%–40% penalties in appropriate situations, because the IRS will carefully scrutinize situations involving transfers of intangible assets from the United States to any related foreign parties, including the Middle East (Shapland and Major 1999).

The growth of MNCs has created new issues for Middle East national economies as well as international economies. These include the international location of production and distribution territories, their effect on national and international stock and commodity markets, their significant effects on both home and host governments' revenues, and the balance of payments of both foreign and home countries.

However, to maximize profits, a MNC should produce in the least cost-producing countries and sell in the best market countries. To achieve this, top management must have an attitude of globalism that makes it as concerned and involved with each of its foreign operations around the world as with home-country operations, and that makes it attempt to rationalize and manage its operations on a global rather than a domestic basis within the constraints of its social, economic, political, legal, and educational conditions. Consequently, the production and marketing operations in all foreign countries are integrated and coordinated on a global basis within the host and home national governments' restrictions.

One of the major characteristics of a successful MNC in the Middle East is having a highly efficient organizational tool for utilizing scarce economic resources on a worldwide basis and using a cost-effective alternative for allocating internal resources (Scharge 1999). Moreover, if the headquarters at the home office is to achieve the goals in the strategic plan, the international activities of all of its foreign, including Middle East operations, and domestic subsidiaries need to be planned, organized, coordinated, integrated, and controlled on a global basis.

THE PROBLEM OF INTRACOMPANY PRICING IN THE MIDDLE EAST

One of the most important and complex considerations in coordinating and integrating the production and marketing strategies of MNCs is intracompany pricing of their operations in the Middle East. Should the product be transferred among a company's own subsidiaries in and outside of the Middle East at the world market or at arm's-length price? Should each manager of Middle East subsidiaries be given freedom in making his or her production and marketing decisions and consequently in maximizing his or her own profits? How much tax will be paid to both the IRS and Middle East tax authorities? Is there an acceptable transfer pricing policy for all Middle East tax regimes? How does one secure compliance with complex rules operated by different accountants in Middle East locations? Do we assume that the arm's-length price will lead domestic, foreign, and Middle East subsidiaries to make production and marketing decisions in the best interest of the MNC as a whole? Or should full costs, variable costs, costs plus a percentage for markup, the profit split method, marginal costs of production, or marginal costs plus opportunity costs be used when there is neither an intermediate price nor a competitive market in the Middle East?

MNCs are usually organized into different subsidiaries in the Middle East and other foreign subsidiaries, and their managers are allowed considerable autonomy in day-to-day decision making. Each Middle East subsidiary transfers goods or services to others located in different countries under different political, legal, taxation, and governmental systems. The prices at which these goods are transferred affect subsidiary managers in making their divisional decisions, and some decisions may achieve divisional profits in the short run at the expense of the global profits in the long run when factors such as transportation costs, taxes paid to either home- or host-country governments, import duties, cash movement restrictions, or governmental rules, among others, are ignored.

Making pricing decisions for MNCs' products or services, in general, is an important, complex, flexible, and complicated task, because these decisions affect other major functions of MNCs, such as marketing, production location, transportation, and finance, which directly affect its total sales and profits. Moreover, there is no clear-cut or easy way to establish an effective pricing policy. MNCs cannot merely add a standard percentage as a markup to a full, variable, or marginal cost to come up with a price they have to charge for goods sold externally or transferred internally among their own subsidiaries. In reality, the transfer pricing policies of most MNCs have evolved as international businesses "have grown either organically or by acquisition in response to a number of competing and often conflicting commercial considerations. The minimization of direct tax is one of such consideration" (Elliott 1998a).

A transfer price is defined as the price at which a local, foreign, or Middle East subsidiary of a MNC transfers products or intangible properties or provides services to a related party (another foreign, Middle East, or local subsidiary of the same MNC). For all domestic activities of MNCs, intracompany transfers of goods or services can be determined by one of the traditional techniques: (1) full actual cost method, (2) full standard cost method, (3) actual variable cost method, (4) standard variable cost method, (5) cost plus method, (6) market or arm's-length price method, or (7) negotiated price method. Under the cost method, the transfer price can be determined on the basis of actual or standard full costs, actual or standard variable costs, or variable or fixed costs, plus a fixed amount or a percentage of cost.

Under the market or arm's-length price method, the transfer price is the price at which significant quantities of goods and services are generally sold to third parties who are external to the firm and who deal at arm's length with one another. The market or arm's-length price is the only price the IRS would accept if it is available. A negotiated transfer price is determined by bargaining between buyer and seller subsidiaries, presuming that both sub-units have the freedom or equal power or authority to bargain.

The choice of the appropriate technique for transfer pricing should be based on the following four criteria: (1) how well it promotes goal congruence and consequently profit maximization, (2) how well it provides an adequate profit yardstick for the performance evaluation of subsidiaries and their managers, (3) how well it guides top management in making decisions, and (4) how well it promotes increased autonomy for divisional or subsidiary managers in decision making (Benke and Edwards 1980; Atkinson, Banker, Kaplan and Young 1997).

MNCs face a major problem as they transfer goods and services between their subsidiaries—that of deciding at what price to transfer goods and services between them or between the parent company and its foreign subsidiaries. A survey on transfer pricing practice, sponsored by the Chartered Institute of Management Accountants (CIMA) and supported by Deloitte and Touche, was conducted to discover more about the way in which MNCs approach international transfer pricing (Elliott 1998a, 1998b). In the survey, it was found that the most important factors impacting the determination of MNCs' transfer pricing policies were the maximization of global profit, simplicity and ease of use, aggressiveness of tax authorities, market penetration, and stability of transfer price over time.

FACTORS AFFECTING INTERNATIONAL TRANSFER PRICING POLICIES IN THE MIDDLE EAST

International transfer pricing of a MNC is the process of setting prices for intracompany transactions when the buying subsidiary is in a country other than the selling subsidiary. Many factors affect international transfer pricing policies in the Middle East and make them more complicated than those used for domestic operations.

The most important factors can be grouped into two categories: (1) the internal factors that have an impact on several functions inside the firm, such as performance evaluation, motivation, stability over time, simplicity, ease of use, and goal harmonization; and (2) Middle East environmental variables that are external to the firm. Examples of external factors are Middle East and U.S. income taxes, tariffs, the aggressiveness of Middle East tax authorities, cash movement restrictions, foreign currency exchange risks, Middle East market penetration strategies, and the conflict with Middle East governments' policies.

If a MNC uses its transfer pricing policies for a performance evaluation of its domestic and Middle East subsidiaries and their managers, its pricing method must be at market or competitive prices, which is an essential factor of decentralization. The resulting net income or loss should be the yardstick for the measurement of the Middle East subsidiary manager's ability to manage and control his or her area of responsibility (or profit center). However, when the worldwide market for the transferred product is not competitive or does not exist for the intermediate product transferred, any transfer price other than the negotiated price will either maintain autonomy or freedom in decision making or motivate managers to adhere to the objectives of the company as a whole, which in turn will impair goal harmonization.

Of the Middle East environmental or external variables that affect MNCs in deciding on the appropriate transfer pricing policy to be used, one of the most important is the taxes to be paid to both Middle East and home governments as a result of transferring the goods or services across the borders of two different countries. The tax authorities in Middle East countries and the IRS of the United States are quite aware of the effect of the transfer price set by a MNC on taxes paid to each of the two tax authorities as a result of the existence of different tax structures of different countries. For example, a MNC can set a low transfer price for goods transferred from a Jordanian subsidiary, which is assumed to have a high corporate income tax rate, to sell at cost to an Egyptian subsidiary, which is assumed to have a lower corporate income tax rate. The result is that a MNC's global tax liability is less than before and, consequently, the global profit will be higher.

However, when the performance of each Middle East subsidiary is evaluated as a separate profit center, this transfer price will show lower profits for the Jordanian subsidiary and higher profits for the Egyptian subsidiary, which will lead to conflicts between the goals of Middle East subsidiaries and the MNC (Choi, Frost and Meek 1999). Elliott (1998a: 49) concluded from the results of a CIMA-sponsored survey about the transfer pricing practices of both U.K. and non-U.K. MNCs that transfer pricing policies have evolved as businesses have grown either organically or through acquisition in response to a number of competing and often conflicting commercial factors. The minimization of direct tax is only one such factor.

Another factor considered important when a MNC is setting up its international transfer pricing policies in the Middle East is the cash movement restrictions of Middle East governments on moving cash outside of the country. When a Middle East country is suffering from a problem of foreign exchange, the government may prohibit such a movement or may impose strong controls that limit the amount of cash, profit, or dividends that can be repatriated. This problem can be illustrated by assuming that Jordan, which is suffering from a lack of American dollars, imposes controls on all dollar transactions. A seller which is an American subsidiary in Kuwait, where there are no restrictions on cash movement of the dollar or other currency convertible into dollars, sells to a buyer which is an American subsidiary in Jordan, at a higher price than the cost. The outcome of the transaction is to transfer the profits from Jordan to Kuwait, and then from Kuwait to the U.S. parent company.

Import duties, tariffs, or customs of Middle East countries can be high or low from one country to another and can complicate the policies to establish the appropriate international transfer prices. If either Egypt, Israel, Jordan, or Kuwait imposes import duties at the rate of 20% on the invoice (transfer) price, a subsidiary selling its goods from Saudi Arabia to another subsidiary in Egypt could reduce the import duties paid by lowering the transfer price below cost. However, the Egyptian government may intervene, because it may believe that lowering transfer prices is tax evasion, and at the same time, the customs authorities in Egypt believe that there are foregone revenues.

As can be seen from this discussion, the appropriate international transfer price used by a MNC in the Middle East and the one required to achieve certain objectives, such as performance evaluation and motivation, income tax minimization, avoidance of foreign exchange controls, or competitiveness, may or may not be the same. It is important to note that five criteria must be met when establishing an efficient international transfer pricing system for Middle East operations:

1. The international transfer pricing policy should provide an adequate profit measurement to evaluate the performance of Middle East subsidiaries and their managers in terms of their controllable divisional contributions to global profits.

2. It should provide adequate information to top management to be used as guidelines in managerial decision making.

3. It should increase the overall profit rate of the MNC; in other words, the MNC's overall performance must be improved by the use of the international transfer pricing system.

4. It should motivate Middle East subsidiary managers to increase their efficiency and maximize their divisional profits in harmony with the objectives of top management.

5. It should minimize the international transaction costs for a MNC by minimizing border

and income tax liabilities, foreign exchange risks, currency manipulation losses, and conflict with the Middle East government's policies.

ESTABLISHING INTERNATIONAL TRANSFER PRICING SYSTEMS IN THE MIDDLE EAST

A transfer price is set and used by MNCs to quantify the goods transferred from one subsidiary domiciled in a specific Middle East or other country to another Middle East or foreign subsidiary in another country. The dynamic growth of most MNCs by going abroad and exploring more and more business opportunities in Middle East or other countries necessitated increased delegation of authority and responsibility with more autonomy for Middle East subsidiary managers, which opened the door for further decentralization and intracompany pricing problems.

Since the transfer price for the product has an important effect on the performance evaluation of individual Middle East subsidiary managers, their motivation, divisional profitability, and global profits, top management should devote special attention to designing international transfer pricing policies. A soundly developed policy could lead to better goal congruence, better performance evaluation measures, less taxes and tariffs, more motivated managers, less exchange risks, and better competitive positions in Middle East countries and international markets.

Another important issue is the transfer pricing policy review. How often do MNCs need to review their transfer pricing systems? What are the main pros and cons of the current transfer pricing system? In a survey by Jamie Elliott (1998b: 49), it was evident that a large proportion of the sample either had a very recent internal review of their transfer pricing system, or that the review was done on a continuous basis. Moreover, one of the problems encountered by MNCs in reviewing their transfer pricing systems included lack of comparable systems and concerns about the acceptability of their pricing systems by all Middle East and foreign tax authorities. A main advantage of an internal review of the transfer pricing system is increased confidence in the MNC's policy and documentation (Elliott 1998b: 50).

In designing international transfer pricing systems to be used in Middle East countries, four major characteristics should be considered: (1) input; (2) process; (3) objectives; and (4) output. The relationship among the four components of the system is illustrated in Figure 9–1.

The input stage includes relevant cost information, differential income tax rates in Middle East countries, exchange risks, restrictions on cash transfers, import and export tariffs, competition in Middle East markets, and inflation rates in Middle East countries. The process of an international transfer pricing system includes three components: (1) requirements for an international transfer pricing system, (2) factors affecting the system, and (3) the methods that can be used for international transfer pricing. Finally, the output of a well-designed inter-

Figure 9–1
The Relationship among the Components of the International Transfer Pricing System

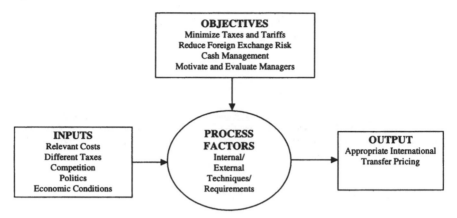

national transfer pricing system would be an appropriate international transfer price that would achieve all management objectives and be the optimal one.

THE INPUTS OF AN INTERNATIONAL TRANSFER PRICING SYSTEM

The inputs of an international transfer pricing system (ITP) consist of seven factors considered as inputs for deciding what is the appropriate price to be charged for goods transferred through the border from one Middle East country to another. The inputs are: (1) relevant cost information, (2) differential Middle East countries' income tax rates, (3) exchange risks, (4) restrictions on cash transfers, (5) tariffs, (6) competition, and (7) inflation rates of Middle East countries.

In this chapter, the effect of each input variable will be considered as if all other variables are held constant. In a later chapter, the effect of all input variables will be considered in a real world model for the established appropriate international transfer pricing system.

The relationship between the input factors and the international transfer pricing system is illustrated in Figure 9–2.

Relevant Cost Information

ITP policies need information about the costs and revenues of all goods and services transferred for coordination and integration purposes. Cost information is needed as a major input for the ITP system; it is considered one of the major factors in making decisions about transfer pricing. The question is, what cost

Figure 9–2
The Input Factors of the International Transfer Pricing System

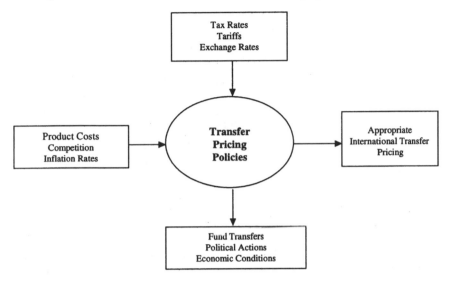

information is relevant to the Middle East manager's decision on the pricing of goods transferred out of the Middle East subsidiary?

Relevant costs are defined as those expected future costs that will make the difference between charging a higher or a lower price for goods transferred between subsidiaries of the same MNC in different countries.

A Middle East subsidiary manager must have relevant cost information, the ability to use it in the decision-making process, and the understanding of its effect on both the subsidiary's profitability and the global profits of the firm as well.

A cost objective is the product whose cost is to be determined. It includes direct materials, direct labor, and manufacturing overhead. Other costs include selling and administrative expenses that are related to a Middle East subsidiary, plus other costs allocated by the headquarters of the MNC. Those costs are classified into variable and fixed. Variable costs vary directly and proportionately with the activity level, while fixed costs do not change with the activity level. Variable costs include items such as direct raw materials, direct labor, sales commissions, and transportation costs. Fixed costs include items such as factory rent, salaries for supervisors, and depreciation of factory equipment.

Some costs cannot be described by a single cost behavior pattern, because they are partially variable and partially fixed. Many techniques have been developed for identifying the variable portion and fixed portion, including industrial engineering, account analysis, visual fit, high-low, and regression analysis.

In designing an ITP system, managers must decide upon which inventory-costing alternative to choose. This decision will have an effect on the net income

Table 9–1

The Income Statement Using the Absorption Costing Method for the Egyptian Subsidiary (in U.S. dollars)

Sales 20,000 at $10		$200,000	
Less: Cost of goods sold and transferred			
Beg. Inventory	0		
Direct materials 25,000 x $2 =	50,000		
Direct labor 25,000 x $1 =	25,000		
Factory overhead			
Variable 25,000 x $0.50 = 12,500			
Fixed 25,000 x $1.00 = 25,000	37,500		
	112,500		
Ending inventories (25,000 - 20,000) 5,000 x $4.50	(22,500)		
Cost of goods sold		(90,000)	
The foreign subsidiary gross profit		110,000	
Less: selling and administrative expenses	10,000		
Variable $0.50 x 20,000 =	7,000		
Fixed =		(17,000)	
The Egyptian subsidiary net income			**$93,000**

of both the Middle East subsidiary unit and the global net income, on the evaluation of foreign subsidiary managers' performance, and on international transfer pricing decisions (Horngren, Foster and Datar 2000).

Two inventory-costing methods are used in practice: absorption and variable costing. The absorption (or full) costing method includes direct materials, direct labor, and both variable and fixed factory overhead as the cost of a product (i.e., product costs include both direct and indirect manufacturing costs). Under this method, fixed manufacturing costs are absorbed by the product transferred, and are part of costs of goods sold or transferred and ending inventories.

The variable (or direct) costing method includes only variable manufacturing costs as the cost of a product (i.e., product costs include direct materials, direct labor, and variable manufacturing costs). All fixed manufacturing costs are excluded from the inventoriable costs and expensed during the fiscal year in which they are incurred, along with all selling and administrative expenses.

As an example, let us assume that a Middle East subsidiary of an American MNC in Egypt produced 25,000 units of its product. Fixed manufacturing costs were $25,000, variable manufacturing costs were $3.50 per unit, ($2 for direct material, $1 for direct labor cost, and 50 cents for variable factory overhead), variable selling costs were 50 cents per unit sold, and fixed selling and administrative expenses were $7,000. Sales for 1999 were 20,000 units at $10 per unit. The net income of the Egyptian subsidiary for the year under both absorption and variable costing methods can be seen in Table 9–1 and Table 9–2.

The difference in net income for the Egyptian subsidiary in 1999 between the two costing methods is caused entirely by the fixed factory overhead of $5,000 (5,000 units @ $1 per unit). This $5,000 is absorbed by the unsold products and is included in the ending inventory when absorption costing is used and

Table 9–2
The Income Statement Using the Variable Costing Method for a Middle East Subsidiary (in U.S. dollars)

Sales 20,000 at $10		$200,000	
Less: Total variable costs			
Manufacturing			
Direct materials 25,000 x $2 =	50,000		
Direct labor 25,000 x $1 =	25,000		
Variable factory overhead 25,000 x $0.50	12,500		
Variable mfg. cost of goods available for sale	87,500		
Less: Ending inventory 5,000 x $3.50	(17,500)		
= Variable cost of goods sold	70,000		
+ Variable selling and adm. exp. $0.50 x 20,000	(10,000)		
= Total variable manufacturing costs		(80,000)	
Total foreign subsidiary contributions margin		120,000	
Less: Total fixed costs			
Manufacturing	25,000		
Selling and administrative	7,000	(32,000)	
The Egyptian subsidiary net income			$88,000

expensed only when the products are sold or transferred out. Therefore, the ending inventory includes current fixed factory overhead costs of $5,000 that are not expensed until a future year.

Under the variable costing method, as can be seen in Table 9–2, fixed factory overhead is not inventoried (i.e., the $5,000 is included in the net income of 1999 and switched the net income of $93,000 under absorption costing to $88,000 under variable costing for the Egyptian subsidiary).

Generally, the absorption costing method is the accepted method of product costing for external reporting, and the variable costing method is used to prepare internal purpose financial reports to assist in making economic decisions.

Does it make any difference which method the firm chooses? Realistically, it depends on which transfer pricing technique the MNC is using or intends to use, assuming that the transfer pricing decision is made at the parent company's level. If the intention was to use unit variable actual (or standard) cost or unit variable cost plus a markup, the variable costing method would be more appropriate. However, with the use of the unit full cost (actual or standard) or unit full cost plus, the absorption costing method would be preferable.

Differential Income Tax Rates in the Middle East

The income tax policies and regulations of different governments of Middle East countries are not the same or even close to one another. International taxation has a significant effect on MNCs in making their management decisions. Taxation affects where a MNC invests, how it markets its products, what form of business organization it selects, when and where it remits cash, how it finances, and of course its transfer price (Mueller, Gernon, and Meek 1997: 181). If the tax rates of different countries were the same, there would be no impact of preferring a higher country's transfer price over a lower one for the global profits of a MNC.

Both the Middle East and U.S. governments are interested in profits realized by a MNC, and transfer prices make a big difference between the amount of income tax paid to either government. The tax authorities in both countries have become quite aware of the significant impact of the differences in the two tax structures on MNCs in deciding at what price to transfer goods or services from one Middle East country to another. From a MNC's point of view, the transfer of goods and services from one subsidiary to another in a different country generates taxable revenues and tax-deductible costs.

Section 482 of the U.S. Internal Revenue Code gives the Internal Revenue Commissioner the authority to reallocate gross income, deductions, credits, or allowances in intracorporate transactions to prevent tax evasion or to reflect more clearly a fair allocation of income. The correct price, from the IRS's perspective, is the market or arm's-length standard. Because it is difficult to prove that the transfer price was equal to the market price, MNCs often find themselves in disputes with the IRS regarding the transfer pricing methodology and an acceptable range of results. Therefore, the IRS's Advance Pricing Agreement (APA) Program, in its eight-year existence, has evolved from a dream approach to resolving transfer pricing disputes into the forum of choice for the resolution of the most dramatic, challenging issues (Wrappe and Soba 1998).

Exchange Risks in the Middle East

Foreign exchange risk is defined as "the risk of a change (gain or loss) in the company's future economic value resulting from a change in exchange rates" (Oxelheim 1985: 61). For a MNC, the exchange risk is connected with the firm's cash flows in different currencies, and any change in exchange rates between two different currencies has a direct effect on the value in the base currency of funds to be converted from one foreign currency to another (ibid.: 61). Devaluation of the currency of the home country pushes the foreign sale of goods up and pushes the home country sales down. This directly affects MNCs, because it increases the foreign currencies they are holding.

Since MNCs' activities involve many countries, they must deal with many currencies. The value of currencies frequently changes, either through devaluation or appreciation. Foreign exchange risk affects both companies with international operations and those with receivables and payables to be collected or paid in foreign currencies (Robock and Simmonds 1983: 536).

Restrictions on Cash Transfers in the Middle East

Host governments, especially in Middle East countries, devise different policies, such as profit repatriations and/or tax exchange controls, on a MNC's activities to protect their own local industries. MNCs set international transfer pricing policies to overcome these restrictions (Kim and Miller 1979: 72). Sidney Robbins and Robert Stobaugh (1973: 72), in their interview with 39 U.S.-based MNCs, concluded that although income tax minimization is a major objective in using transfer pricing, avoiding exchange controls is more important.

Exchange controls with profit repatriation restrictions have been ranked as one of the most important factors in setting international transfer prices by MNCs. Most developing countries have been using exchange control restrictions to avoid outflows of foreign funds outside of the country (Kim and Miller 1979: 72). However, MNCs use their international transfer pricing policies to overcome these restrictions imposed by host governments and to decide how much cash would be sent out of the host countries or to the home country as part of their profits.

Tariffs in the Middle East

The words tariffs, customs, and import duties are used interchangeably. Transfer pricing policies can be used to reduce the tariffs of Middle East countries imposed on imports into the country or exports on goods to be transferred out of the country. Low transfer prices for imports reduce the payments of high tariffs.

In Middle East countries, using low transfer pricing on imports may significantly affect the balance of payments of a particular country, especially when it imports huge quantities from the same MNCs. On the other hand, MNCs may impose a higher transfer price for goods transferred to subsidiaries of foreign countries with low duty rates.

However, combining both Middle East tariffs and income taxes complicates the decision in setting up the appropriate transfer prices, as will be discussed in the next chapter, especially in countries where there are low duties with high income tax rates. In addition, both export duties and income taxes of the country where the foreign subsidiary (the seller) should be considered with the import duties of the country where the buying subsidiary is located, which in turn will never coincide with the transfer pricing strategies of MNCs.

The trade-off between Middle East tariffs and income taxes is more difficult than it looks. A MNC cannot charge two different subsidiaries of the same country, two different transfer prices for the same goods. Host governments have begun to look more closely at the transfer pricing policies of MNCs investing in their countries until they ensure that the tax revenues of the countries are not affected significantly and consequently the balance of payments.

Competition in the Middle East Market

When a new Middle East subsidiary starts a new business, competition is another factor that should be considered in establishing international transfer pricing policies. A MNC can set a low transfer price for goods shipped to the new foreign subsidiary to strengthen its financial and competitive position in the first years of business. However, this may open the door for the intervention of Middle East host governments to protect their local industries if the selling price of the new subsidiary is much lower than other domestic industries of the host country. A MNC can charge high international transfer prices for imported goods to report lower profits on its foreign subsidiaries to avoid host governments' interference when it shows higher profitability or charges low transfer prices to discourage any new firms from entering the market to compete with it.

International transfer pricing policies have become the most controversial issues in MNCs in reporting the results of their Middle East business transactions. The top management of a MNC tries to accomplish the following:

1. To minimize their Middle East exchange losses.
2. To avoid exchange control restrictions on cash outflows.
3. To pay less tariffs on both imports and exports.
4. To minimize total income tax liability to be paid for both home and Middle East countries' governments by charging low international transfer prices for goods and services transferred into low income tax rate countries for the buying subsidiaries and charging high prices for goods and services transferred into high income tax rate countries.
5. To help Middle East subsidiaries compete with other firms in foreign countries. MNCs at the same time try to achieve goal congruence between foreign subsidiary objectives and overall MNC objectives to provide subsidiary managers with relevant information for decision making, to evaluate the performance of Middle East subsidiaries and their managers on an objective basis, and to allocate their financial, economic, and human resources efficiently.

A MNC, when trying to establish its ITP policies for Middle East activities, may find a great degree of conflict among all of these factors. Countries with low income tax rates may impose higher tariffs on goods transferred into the country. Countries with serious problems with foreign exchange may use restrictive monetary policies to completely prohibit or place restraints on cash movements that can be repatriated. Moreover, there is a conflict between charging low international transfer prices to help newly established foreign subsidiaries compete or survive in that country by showing more artificial profits, and then by using them for performance evaluation of Middle East subsidiary managers.

THE PROCESS OF INTERNATIONAL TRANSFER PRICING SYSTEMS

A process can be a series of actions, changes, or functions that brings about a particular result. The process of an ITP system includes a series of factors affecting the decision to choose the appropriate ITP technique to meet specific requirements to achieve the MNC's objectives.

In discussing the process of the ITP system, four elements are included: (1) the factors affecting the decision, (2) different techniques to choose from, (3) specific requirements that need to be met, and (4) the objectives of the ITP system. Items 1 and 3 are discussed in detail in this chapter, and items 2 and 4 will be discussed later in two different chapters.

Factors Affecting the International Transfer Pricing System in the Middle East

Many factors have a significant effect on designing an appropriate ITP system for Middle East business activities. These factors can be classified into internal and external ones. In designing ITP policies, all internal as well as external factors should be considered, otherwise many problems such as sub-optimal decisions, disruption in the operating process, and negative behavioral actions may result.

Internal factors are behavioral, organizational, managerial, and motivational issues. The degree of decentralization, interdependence, management control system, goal congruence, motivation, and performance evaluation are just examples. These and other related issues that have an effect on establishing a well-designed ITP system that fits the Middle East business units are discussed next.

First, the degree of decentralization or centralization of managerial decision making for transfer pricing is an important issue. Complete decentralization, which includes the delegation of authority for decision making of production and sales, is used only when Middle East subsidiaries buy and sell on the market. Foreign or domestic subsidiary managers are assumed to have freedom in making their decisions regarding productions and sales, making their decisions faster, relieving top management from making operating decisions, and being evaluated on the basis of operational measurement performance.

However, decentralization has its own drawbacks or side effects for a MNC. The biggest problem is "dysfunctional decision making," which may result as a conflict between Middle East subsidiary and corporate objectives. Another problem is that relevant information for making decisions is gathered at the subsidiary level for transfer pricing than at the home country level; however, because of the independence of each Middle East or U.S. subsidiary from another, the relevant information is not fully communicated among subsidiary managers (Knowles and Mathur 1985: 18).

Second, the degree of interdependence among Middle East and U.S. subsidiaries is another issue that affects the establishment of a well-designed ITP system. If the decisions or actions of one American subsidiary, for example, affect the business of one or more other American subsidiaries in the Middle East, a high degree of interdependence of international operations exists. With highly interrelated international operations, subsidiary managers may make their decisions without considering the effects on other subsidiaries of the same MNCs. As a result, these managerial decisions may optimize the individual manager's profits at the expense of others, which in turn will not lead to optimal global profits.

Third, many MNCs, as the main basis of domestic performance evaluation, have used the profit center concept. A Middle East subsidiary manager, under this concept, makes the major decisions relating to profit center costs and revenues. Since he or she is able to influence the results of operations, he or she is accountable for and evaluated on the basis of those results, which are the profits of his or her subsidiaries.

Independence, autonomy, and freedom in decision making usually characterize a profit center. A Middle East subsidiary manager should try to achieve the highest possible profits for his or her subsidiary by buying from other subsidiaries of the same MNC or from the market at the lowest price and selling to others at the highest price. Managers are actually using the international transfer prices that maximize their profits, and consequently they show better performance for their Middle East subsidiaries. However, the profit center concept in MNCs may not work well, for the following reasons:

1. Transfer pricing policies are usually set in MNCs to facilitate cash movements in the Middle East where currency restrictions exist and to minimize taxes. Therefore, transfer pricing policies are not complementary to the profit center concept, and performance evaluation cannot be achieved properly using traditional management techniques.

2. With different inflation rates and other sociological, economic, legal, political, social, and educational conditions among Middle East countries, top management may have trouble understanding each Middle East country's situation and thus may be less able to evaluate good or bad profit performance abroad. Profit centers are likely, therefore, to have more applicability for domestic than Middle East subsidiaries.

3. Domestic company activities are often organized by independent profit or investment centers. Under these decentralized systems, subsidiary managers are given the authority to make decisions directly affecting their activities. Under these conditions, ROI, as a measure of performance, may be acceptable. However, such performance evaluation systems may not function well for MNCs, because Middle East operations are often established for strategic marketing and economic reasons rather than for profit maximization, thus many cannot be measured precisely or quantitatively by ROI.

4. Many times the units of a MNC are integrated and managed as a coordinated whole, which means that the major decisions affecting Middle East profits are made centrally for all international units. Therefore, the profit center concept may not be relevant for Middle East activities.

If no high degree of independence exists and the Middle East subsidiary has no control over the transfer price, then the pseudo-profit center concept is used. A pseudo-profit center is "a responsibility center in which profit is based on internal sales or purchases at artificial prices" (Benke and Edwards 1981: 385).

Middle East managers of the pseudo-profit center use artificial profits and have control only over costs, and it is more likely considered a cost center. In this case, international transfer prices are used only for performance evaluation.

Fourth, the management control process (MCP) is another factor affecting ITP systems. Two major objectives of the process are to: (1) guide Middle East subsidiary managers to achieve the MNC's objectives; and (2) measure the results of a Middle East subsidiary's performance against the MNC's objectives. It is essential for a MNC to operate and manage its Middle East operations within the objectives of its management control process and to ensure that the objectives of both the management control and ITP process are consistent (Knowles and Mathur 1985: 17).

The main purpose in designing the MCP is to achieve goal congruence which is the equality between the sum of individual goals and the MNC's goals. The international transfer price should help both the buying and selling Middle East subsidiaries to make the right decision to maximize their own profits and at the same time the global profits of the MNC as a whole. However, it is more likely that transfer prices may create conflicts between the buying and selling Middle East subsidiaries, because the buying subsidiary tries to use the lowest possible transfer price to maximize its profits, while the selling subsidiary tries to sell at the highest possible price.

Fifth, the use of ITP systems may motivate Middle East subsidiary managers to work in their own divisional self-interest, because they are motivated by the "presumed behavioral advantage" of operating with a high degree of autonomy. At the same time, organizational objectives should be achieved by motivation to work for the best interests of the MNC as a whole. However, subsidiary managers may choose transfer pricing methods that are not compatible with a MNC's long-term objectives (Knowles and Mathur 1985: 17).

Finally, the performance evaluation of a Middle East subsidiary and its managers is among the important factors affecting ITP policies. Subsidiary managers who manipulate their costs or profits to create "the illusion of better or worse performance" than has actually happened should not use transfer pricing techniques (Benke and Edwards 1980: 21).

Performance evaluation reports, based on a transfer price set by top management, do not reflect the degree to which the foreign or domestic subsidiary or its manager contributes to the global profits, unless the international transfer price among subsidiaries is identical to the market or arm's-length price of the intermediate product. Under these circumstances, the contribution of the subsidiary, measured by the market price, will be important for managers and central management who use each subsidiary's contribution for the evaluation of the subsidiary's profitability and make decisions either to continue or discontinue their investments in these subsidiaries.

However, when there is no market for the intermediate products transferred internally among the subsidiaries, conflict is likely to arise in MNCs between subsidiary managers because of the conflict of interest between the buying subsidiary, who wants to be charged with the lowest possible transfer price, and the selling subsidiary, who wants to achieve the highest possible divisional profits by charging the highest possible transfer price.

The problem is more complicated when we look at all of the factors affecting transfer pricing policies. Different income tax rates and the rules of various Middle East countries, different tariffs, market penetration strategy, and different cash flow restrictions on the one hand, and motivation, performance evaluation, goal congruence, profit center or pseudo-profit centers on the other hand, are leading into conflicting results, and both require different transfer prices for the same goods or services transferred across the border.

It is obvious that international transfer prices as used now in practice, at which goods or services are transferred internally among different subsidiaries of different countries of MNCs, can significantly distort the profitability of Middle East subsidiaries and their managers.

In addition to internal factors, as discussed above, external factors can effect the decision regarding which transfer price should be charged. These are: (1) market conditions in Middle East countries, (2) economic conditions, and (3) currency appreciation or devaluation.

Middle East countries' governmental intervention puts many restrictions on MNCs as they do business there. Middle East governments can intervene in the business of MNCs in many ways. They may increase or decrease the price of imports and exports through tariffs, quotas, and taxes, or they may intervene through foreign exchange rates. They also may restrict the amount of profits a MNC can transfer to reduce pressure on the balance of payments of the host country. All of these factors have a significant effect on MNCs in setting the appropriate transfer prices.

Transfer prices also are affected by the competitive position of subsidiaries in Middle East countries, either to be strengthened by charging low transfer prices for the input or high prices for the output, or to be weakened to avoid any potential governmental intervention.

Requirements for International Transfer Pricing Policies in the Middle East

An ITP policy in the Middle East should meet specific requirements if a MNC wants to achieve its objectives. These requirements are discussed below.

Any transfer pricing method should provide an adequate measurement of the performance of both Middle East subsidiaries and their managers. It should measure the manager's controllable contribution toward the global profit in an objective, operational way that must be consistent with the global objectives of the MNC and, at the same time, must motivate managers toward instituting better performance.

It should provide top management with relevant information when deciding to expand, continue, or discontinue its operation in specific Middle East countries. International intracompany pricing information plays a major role, which is considered input for the decision-making process and presents a realistic profit picture of Middle East subsidiary performance.

It should minimize the income tax liability that MNCs pay for both Middle East and U.S governments and/or tariffs (import/export duties). In this case, the appropriate international transfer price should come up with the lowest possible total tax liability of MNCs to be paid, including combined income taxes and tariffs.

Finally, it should reduce or alleviate the conflict between MNCs' objectives and foreign governments' objectives. MNCs should understand the needs of Middle East governments, and they should try to utilize the total economic and human resources in their own and in Middle East governments' best interests to avoid the possibility of profit repatriation, restrictions on cash movements or exchange control, expropriations, or any limitations imposed on MNCs' Middle East activities that have a significant negative effect on global profits over the long run.

SUMMARY AND CONCLUSIONS

Four major characteristics of ITP systems for Middle East countries are identified in this chapter: (1) input, (2) process, (3) objectives, and (4) output. The input of an ITP system consists of seven factors in deciding the appropriate price to charge for goods transferred across the border from one country to another. The inputs include: (1) relevant cost information, (2) differential Middle East income tax rates, (3) foreign exchange risks, (4) restrictions on cash transfers, (5) tariffs, and (6) competition and the inflation rates of foreign countries.

The process of an ITP system in the Middle East includes a series of factors affecting the decision to choose an appropriate ITP technique, which should meet specific requirements to achieve the MNC's objectives. In discussing the process of an ITP system, four elements should be considered: (1) the factors affecting the decision; (2) different techniques to choose from; (3) specific requirements that need to be met; and (4) the objectives of ITP systems. Factors 1 and 3 were analyzed and discussed in detail in this chapter, and items 2 and 4 will be discussed in later chapters.

The most important factors in establishing an appropriate transfer pricing policy for Middle East businesses are maximization of global profits, avoidance of foreign exchange risks, simplicity, ease of use, reduction of restrictions on cash transfers, and performance evaluation. These factors include the trade-offs that MNCs must consider when establishing or revising their transfer pricing policies. To be successful in their Middle East business activities, MNCs should put more emphasis on designing their transfer pricing policies to fit the Middle East cultural, legal, and economic environment. Moreover, it is important for MNCs to prepare social responsibility reports to show their degree of contribution to the welfare and social and economic conditions of Middle East countries.

REFERENCES

Atkinson, Anthony A., Rajiv D. Banker, Robert S. Kaplan, and Mark S. Young. *Management Accounting*, 2nd ed. Upper Saddle River, N.J.: Prentice Hall, 1997.

Ball, Donald A. and Wendell H. McCulloch, Jr. *International Business*, 2nd ed. Plano, Tex.: Business Publications, 1985, 443–444.

Benke, Ralph L., Jr. and James Don Edwards. "Should You Use T.P." *Management Accounting* (February 1981), 36–39, 43.

———. *Transfer Pricing Techniques and Uses*. New York: National Association of Accountants, 1980.

Choi, Frederick D. S. "Global Finance and Accounting Uniformity." *University of Michigan Business Review* (September 1976), 48.

Choi, Frederick D. S., Carol Ann Frost, and Gary K. Meek. *International Accounting*, 3rd ed. Upper Saddle River, N.J.: Prentice Hall, 1999.

Elliot, Jamie. "International Transfer Pricing: A Survey of UK and Non-UK Groups." *Management Accounting* (November 1998a), 48–50.

———. "International Transfer Pricing: A Survey of UK and Non-UK Groups: Part 2." *Management Accounting* (December 1998b), 48–50.

Horngren, Charles T., George Foster, and Srikant M. Datar. *Cost Accounting: A Managerial Emphasis*, 10th ed. Upper Saddle River, N.J.: Prentice Hall, 2000.

Kim, H. Seung and Stephen W. Miller. "Constituents of the International Transfer Pricing Decisions." *Columbia Journal of World Business* (Spring 1979), 72.

Knowles, Lynette L. and Ike Mathur. "Factors Influencing the Designing of International Transfer Pricing Systems." *Management Finance* 11 (1985), 17–20.

Mueller, Gerhard G., Helen Gernon, and Gary Meek. *Accounting: An International Perspective*, 4th ed. Homewood, Ill.: Richard D. Irwin, 1997.

Oxelheim, Lars. *International Financial Market Fluctuations*. New York: John Wiley & Sons, 1985.

Robbins, Sidney M. and Robert B. Stobaugh. *Money in the Multinational Enterprise*. New York: Basic Books, 1973.

Robock, Stefan H. and Kenneth Simmonds. *International Business and Multinational Enterprises*, 3rd ed. Homewood, Ill.: Richard D. Irwin, 1983.

Scharge, Michael. "Smart, Works Hard, in Mint Condition." *Fortune* (July 19, 1999), 134–135.

Scott, George M. "Planning, Control and Performance Evaluation Systems in International Operations." *Cost and Management* (January–February 1977), 8.

Shapland, Rick and Bill Major. "40% Transfer Pricing Penalty Upheld." *The Tax Adviser* (April 1999), 224–225.

Wrappe, Steven C. and George H. Soba. "A Practical Guide to the U.S. Advance Pricing Agreement Process." *Tax Executive* (November/December 1998), 454–464.

Chapter 10

Objectives and Strategies of Transfer Pricing Policies in the Middle East

Theoretically, MNCs have the ability to use their Middle East transfer pricing policies to maximize their global profits. Practically, developing these policies is the most difficult pricing problem, one more complicated than developing domestic transfer pricing policies. A MNC has to manage its Middle East production and marketing policies in a world characterized by different international tax rates, Middle East exchange rates, governmental regulations, currency manipulation, and other economic and social problems. Such market characteristics create high transaction costs for a MNC when it uses its regular marketing policies. It is important for MNCs to create an internal market if they want to avoid these problems and any costs associated with them. The allocation of resources among domestic, foreign, and Middle East subsidiaries requires the central management of a MNC to set up the appropriate transfer price for Middle East activities to achieve certain objectives.

The top management of MNCs and both domestic and Middle East subsidiary managers must understand the objectives for using transfer pricing policies within their organizations. They need to know how these usually interrelated objectives can affect each other (Knowles and Mathur 1985: 12).

An international transfer pricing (ITP) system in the Middle East should achieve two different groups of objectives. The first group includes: (1) consistency with the system of performance evaluation of Middle East subsidiaries; (2) motivation of Middle East subsidiary managers; and (3) achievement of goal harmonization. The second group consists of certain objectives that are more relevant to Middle East operations. These objectives include: (1) reduction of income taxes, (2) reduction of tariffs on imports and exports, (3) minimization of foreign exchange risks, (4) avoidance of a conflict with Middle East countries' governments, (5) management of cash flow, and (6) competitiveness in the international markets.

However, any manipulation of transfer pricing systems by MNCs may have a significant impact on many areas of the worldwide economy, including both home and Middle East countries. The impact of transfer pricing systems includes effects on balance of payments and Middle East and domestic formation of capital investment. By charging higher transfer prices on goods transferred into or services performed to a Middle East subsidiary, the MNC can limit a subsidiary's export abilities or avoid controls on foreign remittance by "tapping-off excess profits" (Greenhill and Herbalzheimer 1980: 232). Imposing low transfer pricing on sales of Middle East subsidiaries will reduce customs duty payments and help subsidiaries compete in Middle East markets against other local competitors (ibid.). Jamie Elliott (1998: 50) conducted a survey and found that local management may be remunerated, in part, by results and artificial transfer prices that would undermine the objective of this and possibly damage the business by demoralizing management.

The purpose of this chapter is to identify, at the international level, different objectives for establishing transfer pricing systems for Middle East business activities, to investigate how MNCs can achieve all, most, or a few of these objectives, and to point out significant problems MNCs might face when they try to achieve these objectives. The second group of objectives will be discussed first because of their significant impact on Middle East operations.

REDUCTION OF INCOME TAXES IN THE MIDDLE EAST

One of the most important objectives of an international transfer pricing policy is believed to be reducing the global income tax liability of a MNC. Tax reduction can be achieved by transferring goods to countries with low income tax rates at the lowest possible transfer prices and by transferring goods out of these countries at the highest possible transfer prices. In countries with high income tax rates, goods transferred into the country should be at the highest possible prices.

International transfer pricing policies are generally set to maximize the after-tax profitability of worldwide business transactions. The minimization of income tax liabilities for a MNC has been considered the most significant factor or objective in designing ITP policies in the Middle East and, consequently, if a transfer price shifts profits from a country with high tax rates to a country with low tax rates, the global profits will be maximized. However, the IRS and the tax authorities of other countries are concerned that MNCs could use these transfer prices to shift profits between related parties through the cost of goods sold.

MNCs often have at their disposal several alternative methods of structuring and financing their Middle East investments, arranging transactions between related parties located in different Middle East countries and returning profits

Table 10–1a
The Tax Effect of High versus Low International Transfer Pricing

LOW TRANSFER PRICE	Egyptian Subsidiary	Kuwaiti Subsidiary	The MNC
SALES			
20,000 @ $10	$200,000		
20,000 @ $20		$400,000	$400,000
LESS: COST OF GOODS SOLD	(90,000)	(200,000)	(90,000)
GROSS PROFIT	110,000	200,000	310,000
LESS: S, A, & G EXP.	(17,000)	(75,000)	(92,000)
NET INCOME BEFORE TAX	93,000	125,000	218,000
LESS: INCOME TAX			
(30% AND 50%)	(27,900)	(62,500)	(90,400)
NET INCOME	$65,100	$62,500	$127,600

S = Selling; A = Administrative; G = General.

to investors in the home country. These alternatives have important tax implications, and there is considerable evidence that tax considerations strongly influence the choices that firms make. International tax avoidance typically entails reallocating taxable income from countries with high tax rates to countries with low tax rates, and may also include changing the timing of income recognition for tax purposes. Many of these methods are quite legal (Hines 1999: 315).

To illustrate the income tax effects on setting international transfer prices for Middle East activities, let us assume that an Egyptian subsidiary produces 25,000 units and sells 20,000 units to a Kuwaiti subsidiary at US$10 a unit. The Kuwaiti subsidiary, in turn, sells these units for US$20 a unit to an unrelated customer.

As can be seen in Table 10–1a, Egypt's income tax rate is 30% and Kuwait's is 50%. As a result of using different transfer prices, there is a significant change in the net income of both Middle East subsidiaries and the consolidated net income of the MNC as a whole. With the low transfer price, the Egyptian subsidiary sells at $10 a unit and pays income taxes of $27,900. The Kuwaiti subsidiary pays an income tax liability of $62,500, and the MNC pays a total tax liability of $90,400. Under the high transfer price policy of $14 a unit, as seen in Table 10–1b, the Egyptian subsidiary's income taxes rise to $51,900, while the Kuwaiti subsidiary's taxes fall to $22,500. The combined tax liabilities of the MNC go from $90,400 to $74,400, and the consolidated net income goes from $127,600 to $143,600. The consequences of charging a higher transfer price are a decrease in total tax liabilities by $16,000 ($90,400 – $74,400) and an increase in the consolidated net income by the same amount.

Table 10–1b
The Tax Effect of High International Transfer Pricing

HIGH TRANSFER PRICE	Egyptian Subsidiary	Kuwaiti Subsidiary	The MNC
SALES			
20,000 @ $14	$280,000		
20,000 @ $20		$400,000	$400,000
LESS: COST OF GOODS SOLD	(90,000)	(280,000)	(90,000)
GROSS PROFIT	190,000	120,000	310,000
LESS: S, A, & G EXP.	(17,000)	(75,000)	(92,000)
NET INCOME BEFORE TAX	173,000	45,000	218,000
LESS: INCOME TAX			
(30% AND 50%)	(51,900)	(22,500)	(74,400)
NET INCOME	$121,100	$22,500	$143,600

S = Selling; A = Administrative; G = General.

The general rule for the pricing strategy of MNCs is that if the sole corporate objective is to minimize total tax liability, it should transfer most of the profits to the foreign subsidiaries in the tax-haven countries, as seen in Figure 10–1. However, the manipulation of ITP policies for reducing income taxes has caused the governmental tax authorities, including the U.S. IRS, the Inland Revenue of the United Kingdom, and other industrial countries' tax authorities, to intervene to ensure that there is no tax evasion and that the country does not lose its tax revenue under the transfer pricing shield.

Moreover, many factors besides Middle East income tax minimization should be considered by MNCs in designing their ITP systems, such as motivation and performance evaluation of Middle East subsidiary managers, competitiveness in Middle East markets, and foreign exchange risks.

A survey by H. Seung Kim and Stephen W. Miller (1979) indicated that, in the past, MNCs considered the reduction of income taxes the most important objective in designing their ITP systems. Now tax reduction is only a minor factor among many others, and the company's overall objective rather than income tax liability should be a major concern (71). Another survey by Jamie Elliott (1998) found that an important factor that places constraints on a group's freedom to minimize direct taxes by fixing artificial transfer prices is the possible knock-on effect that this could have on indirect taxes (50).

The evidence of tax-motivated transfer pricing comes in several forms. While it is possible that high tax rates are correlated with other location attributes that depress the profitability of Middle East investment, competitive conditions typically imply that after-tax rates of return should be equal in the absence of tax-

Figure 10–1
Transfer Pricing Strategies under Different Tax Rates of Different Countries

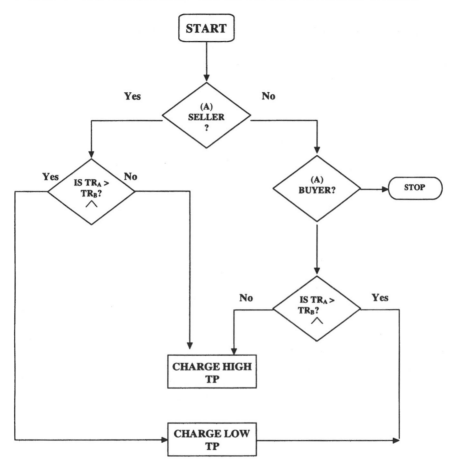

TR_A = tax rates of Country A; TR_B = tax rates of Country B; TP = transfer prices.

motivated income shifting. The fact that before-tax profitability is negatively correlated with local tax rates is strongly suggestive of active tax avoidance (Hines 1999: 311).

Along with the reduction of global income tax liability, a major problem is how to coordinate the tax effect of transferred goods among Middle East countries to arrive at the optimal transfer price. To set the appropriate transfer price for tax reduction, it is very important to determine the tax effects of different ways of taxing imports and exports by imposing duties and customs on them and different tax rate structures and the methods of taxing MNCs' profits used by Middle East countries.

It is not an easy task to determine the results of these effects on MNCs' global profits, because they are frequently and rapidly changed by Middle East and home country governments to achieve certain economic, political, or social objectives for their own countries. In the United States, the IRS is concerned that MNCs may rescue their tax liabilities by using transfer prices to shift profits from multinational local businesses to businesses in countries with low tax rates. Section 482 of the Internal Revenue Code gives the IRS the power to reallocate income and deductions among subsidiaries of a MNC if it finds that this is necessary to prevent an illegal reduction of taxes (i.e., tax evasion). Under this section, all transfer prices should generally be established according to arm's-length market values on any transactions between affiliates.

MNCs, under Section 482 of the Internal Revenue Code, are not allowed to use a transfer price that will maximize their global profits, other than an arm's-length—the comparable uncontrolled price method, the resale price method, and the cost-plus method. However, if the ITP policies of a MNC were designed only to comply with Section 482, there would be no effective systems to measure Middle East managers' performance, to motivate them to control the costs of their Middle East subsidiaries, or to maximize the global profits of the MNC as a whole.

In general, contractual arrangements between related parties in Middle East countries with different tax rates offer several possibilities for tax avoidance. Multinational firms typically can benefit by reducing prices charged by affiliates in high-tax countries for goods and services provided to affiliates in low-tax countries. Almost all countries require firms to use transfer prices that would be paid by unrelated parties, but enforcement is difficult, particularly when pricing issues concern distinct items, such as in pharmaceutical companies, where products may even be patented. Given the looseness of the resulting legal restrictions, it is entirely possible for firms to adjust transfer prices in a tax-sensitive fashion without violating any laws (Hines 1999).

REDUCTION OF TARIFFS

Tariffs are the most widely used trade restrictions by the Middle East and can be imposed on either imports or exports. Tariffs on imports are used to reduce the volume of imports coming into the country and to protect local industries. MNCs use transfer pricing policies to reduce import or export tariffs and to avoid paying high tariffs to governments and, consequently, to reduce their global costs and maximize their global profits. However, the use of transfer pricing for both reduction of income taxes and tariffs at the same time complicates the transfer pricing system.

As an example, let us assume that a foreign subsidiary in Kuwait must pay tariffs at the rate of 15%, and that the income tax rates of Egypt and Kuwait are 30% and 50%, respectively. Increasing the transfer price then would increase the tariffs the Kuwaiti subsidiary would have to pay, assuming that the tariffs were imposed on the invoice transfer price. The combined effect of tax and

Table 10–2a
The Effect of Low Transfer Pricing, Income Taxes, and Tariffs on Net Income

LOW TRANSFER PRICE	Egyptian Subsidiary	Kuwaiti Subsidiary	The MNC
SALES			
20,000 @ $10	$200,000		
20,000 @ $20		$400,000	$400,000
LESS: COST OF GOODS SOLD	(90,000)	(200,000)	(90,000)
IMPORT CUSTOMS @ 15%	=====	(30,000)	(30,000)
GROSS PROFIT	110,000	170,000	280,000
LESS: S, A, & G EXP.	(17,000)	(75,000)	(92,000)
NET INCOME BEFORE TAX	93,000	95,000	188,000
LESS: INCOME TAX			
(30% AND 50%)	(27,900)	(47,500)	(75,400)
NET INCOME	$65,100	$47,500	$112,600

S = Selling; A = Administrative; G = General.

tariff with the increased transfer price is shown in Tables 10–2a 10–2b, and 10–2c.

Under the low transfer price policy of $10 a unit, import tariffs of $30,000 (15% of $200,000) are paid to the Kuwaiti government, while the income tax paid will decline by a $15,000 tax shield (50% of $30,000), since import tariffs are assumed to be tax-deductible in Kuwait. Global income taxes and import tariffs to be paid are $105,400 ($75,400 + $30,000, respectively), and the global net income is $112,600 (65,100 + $47,500), as can be seen in Table 10–2a.

Under the high transfer price policy of $14, the import tariffs increased from $30,000 to $42,000 (a difference of $12,000), while at the same time the Egyptian subsidiary's income increased by $56,000 (from $65,100 to $121,100), and the Kuwaiti subsidiary's net income and income taxes decreased by the same amount, $46,000, as can be seen in Table 10–2b. However, global tax liability and tariffs decreased by the net difference of $10,000, from $105,400 to $95,400, and the global net income increased from $112,600 to $122,600. Therefore, the high transfer price policy is still preferable because of the $10,000 increase in global profits.

As a result of a $4 increase in the transfer price, tariffs to be paid to the Kuwaiti government will be increased by $12,000 (15% of $80,000). Since the tax rate in Kuwait is higher than in Egypt, the tax shield will be $6,000, to be subtracted from the difference of avoiding paying 20% more of $80,000, which is $16,000. Therefore, the global profits will be increased by $10,000 (tax savings of $16,000 – net cost of tariffs after tax of $6,000). We can conclude from

Table 10–2b
The Effect of Both Taxes and Tariffs of High International Transfer Pricing

HIGH TRANSFER PRICE	Egyptian Subsidiary	Kuwaiti Subsidiary	The MNC
SALES			
20,000 @ $14	$280,000		
20,000 @ $20		$400,000	$400,000
LESS: COST OF GOODS SOLD	(90,000)	(280,000)	(90,000)
IMPORT CUSTOMS @ 15%	════	(42,000)	(42,000)
GROSS PROFIT	190,000	78,000	268,000
LESS: S, A, & G EXP.	(17,000)	(75,000)	(92,000)
NET INCOME BEFORE TAX	173,000	3,000	176,000
LESS: INCOME TAX			
(30% AND 50%)	(51,900)	(1,500)	(53,400)
NET INCOME	$121,100	$1,500	$122,600

S = Selling; A = Administrative; G = General.

this analysis that as long as the tax rate differential—which is 20% in our case, as the difference between the tax rates of the two countries is higher than the net effect of tariff rates (which is 15% of the cost of goods transferred, reduced by the tax shield of 50% of the 15% = 15% − 50% of 15% = 7.5%) imposed by the country with the higher tax rate, the higher transfer price will always generate net savings for the MNC (12.5% for each $4 increase in the transfer price per unit).

However, if management (either the Egyptian subsidiary manager or the head-quarters of the MNC) increases the price for goods transferred from the Egyptian subsidiary to the Kuwaiti subsidiary by $1 more (from $14 to $15), it will have a negative effect on both the global profits of the MNC and on the net income of the Kuwaiti subsidiary, as can be seen in Table 10–2c. For the Egyptian subsidiary, the net income increased by $14,000, which is the increase in the transfer price after tax (20,000 units × [$15 − $14] = $20,000 × [1 − income tax rate in Egypt] 1 − 30% = $14,000).

For the Kuwaiti subsidiary, the negative effect includes: (1) an increase in the cost of goods sold by $20,000, as a result of being charged a higher transfer price by $1 for 20,000 units; (2) an increase in tariffs paid on imports to Kuwait ($3,000) at a 15% rate of the difference in the transfer price ($20,000); and (3) no income tax liability, since items (1) and (2) will result in net loss before tax, and hence in a reduction of income tax paid to the Kuwaiti government from $1,500 to zero. The net negative effect will be $20,000 + 3,000 − 1,500 =

Table 10–2c
The Effect of Both Taxes and Tariffs of High International Transfer Pricing

HIGH TRANSFER PRICE	Egyptian Subsidiary	Kuwaiti Subsidiary	The MNC
SALES			
20,000 @ $15	$300,000		
20,000 @ $20		$400,000	$400,000
LESS: COST OF GOODS SOLD	(90,000)	(300,000)	(90,000)
IMPORT CUSTOMS @ 15%	=====	(45,000)	(45,000)
GROSS PROFIT	210,000	55,000	265,000
LESS: S, A, & G EXP.	(17,000)	(75,000)	(92,000)
NET INCOME BEFORE TAX	193,000	(20,000)	173,000
LESS: INCOME TAX			
(30% AND 50%)	(57,900)	=====	(57,900)
NET INCOME (LOSS)	$135,100	($20,000)	$115,100

S = Selling; A = Administrative; G = General.

$21,500, a reduction in the net income of the Kuwaiti subsidiary. The global net income will be decreased by $7,500, because the decrease in the net income of the Kuwaiti subsidiary ($21,500) exceeded the increase in the net income of the Egyptian subsidiary. Therefore, if the transfer price goes over $14, as illustrated in Table 10–2c, the effect on the net income of both the transferee and the MNC as a whole will be detrimental. In general, the higher the import tariffs relative to the difference in net income tax rates between different countries, the more likely it is that a low transfer price is preferable.

In concluding this section, it is important to note that there is a limit for any increase in the transfer price. When the higher transfer price results in showing a net loss for the buying subsidiary, the global profits of the MNC will decrease by the difference between the maximum tax savings the MNC could get, which is the tax shield of 50% of the increase in the cost of the goods transferred (50% of $20,000 = $10,000), plus the 50% tax shield of the increase in the tariffs (50% of $3,000 = $1,500), and the maximum tax reduction allowed (which is $1,500) because of achieving net loss and paying zero tax. Assuming that no losses are allowed to be carried forward to the next year according to the tax regulations of Kuwait, the net effect, as indicated in the example, will be a $7,500 decrease in the global profits, resulting from paying more tariffs ($45,000 − $42,000 = $3,000) and more income taxes of $4,500 ($57,900 − $53,400).

MINIMIZATION OF EXCHANGE RATE RISK

The risk of the foreign exchange rate arises from doing international business denominated in currencies other than the domestic currency. High fluctuations in foreign exchange rates cause high risk of loss or gain. International transfer prices may be used to reduce a MNC's foreign exchange risk, which is the risk of a gain or loss in the MNC's future economic value resulting from a change in the foreign exchange rate (Oxelheim 1985: 61).

Transfer pricing is one of the best means to minimize foreign exchange losses from currency fluctuations or to shift the losses to another subsidiary by moving assets from one country to another under the floating exchange rate system. This can be done by determining what currency is to be used for payment and whether the buying or selling subsidiary has the foreign exchange risk. If this is done, the appropriate transfer price for Middle East activities will have a significant effect on the net exposure of the Middle East subsidiary. In this case, funds in weak currency countries are moved through transfer pricing, especially when the foreign currency is not allowed to move out of the country.

As an example, let us assume that an American subsidiary sold $20,000 in merchandise in January 1999 to an Egyptian subsidiary, and that the payment was in American dollars within 60 days, at a time when the exchange rate was U.S. $1 = Egyptian pound (EP). Let us also assume that the MNC headquarters imposed a transfer price of $22,000. The American subsidiary would receive $2,000 (or EP 2,000) more, but the assets of the Egyptian subsidiary would have been reduced by EP 2,000, or $2,000. The difference in the price does not affect the global profit of the MNC.

Funds in weak currency countries can be siphoned off by using international transfer price adjustments. To use international transfer pricing effectively in achieving gains through the use of the exchange rates, it must be coordinated with the currency-hedging techniques of "leading" or "lagging," which allow MNCs to avoid exchange risks and to extract more funds out of a weak currency for conversion into a strong currency (Plasschaert 1981).

At the time of payment, March 1999, if the exchange rate was $1 = EP 1.50, the Egyptian subsidiary had to pay the American subsidiary $22,000, which is equivalent to EP 33,000 at the time of payment. In this case, the MNC moved the profits from Egypt (which has a soft currency) to the U.S. currency. Subsidiary A, the American, received EP 11,000 more than the original transfer price and EP 2,000 more than the original market price. The result was EP 11,000 foreign exchange loss for the Egyptian subsidiary on a relatively small transaction.

Generally, assets in weak currency countries are moved through the use of international transfer price adjustments. A MNC can change the transfer price to take advantage of expected movements in the exchange rate. This allows it to charge high transfer prices when the currency is expected to decline. By doing so, it maintains the gross profit margins in terms of U.S. dollars, even though in local currencies, the gross profit margin has increased. However, price controls or government intervention may limit the use of this technique.

AVOIDING A CONFLICT WITH MIDDLE EAST
COUNTRIES' GOVERNMENTS

The transfer pricing policies of MNCs have a direct effect on Middle East countries' economies where there are foreign subsidiaries. MNCs must set their transfer pricing policies to charge for goods and services transferred into and out of Middle East countries on a basis that Middle East governments will consider justified. To avoid a conflict with the Middle East country's government, a MNC should not charge high transfer prices for any goods and services transferred, because high prices mean more cash or fund outflows from the country than cash inflows, which will have a direct impact on the country's balance of payments and, consequently, on its economy. Therefore, MNCs must determine "what price" to charge for their own products manufactured in one country and transferred to another country to achieve reasonable global profits.

Middle East governments, on the other hand, may concentrate on devising different tools, techniques, or regulations to minimize the effect of the transfer pricing policies of MNCs on their countries. Host-country governments want to ensure that the long-term cash or fund outflows, such as dividends, royalties, and especially intracompany pricing manipulations, do not significantly exceed the value of goods, services, funds, or cash inflows. Therefore, MNCs must strike a balance between maximizing their global profits by charging very high transfer prices and avoiding conflict with the host-country government by charging low transfer prices.

MANAGEMENT OF CASH FLOW IN THE MIDDLE EAST

MNCs may need to withdraw funds from their Middle East subsidiaries, either because it is expected that a new political group is moving into the foreign government and an expropriation of most investments is anticipated, or because there are restrictions on moving cash out of the country, due to balance of payments or exchange rate problems. International transfer pricing, dividends, royalties, interest on loans, and management service fees are the most important techniques for withdrawing cash from foreign countries. A MNC may raise transfer prices on goods or services transferred to a Middle East subsidiary within the same organization by withdrawing funds from countries. Charging high transfer prices may be the only way to shift funds out of the country, as stated by an officer of a large MNC: "If I cannot get dividends out and my royalty rate is fixed, and I want to remit more money, then I do this on an uplift of my transfer prices" (Robbins and Stobaugh 1973: 91). Another officer indicated that his firms, even though they did not use transfer pricing for tax purposes, would push transfer prices up or down if exchange restrictions blocked the transfer of funds (ibid.).

MNCs can control their cash flow in Middle East countries through transfer pricing techniques. In cash flow management, the transfer pricing strategy of MNCs comes into play. For example, if a U.S. corporation has a subsidiary in Jordan and an IRS examination is required to shift $400 million of income from the Jordanian subsidiary to the U.S. parent corporation, then there obviously would be major tax and cash flow effects.

Tax liabilities and foreign tax credits would change, and the company might need to pay a dividend. When this enormous shift in income happens, cash flow planning goes out the window. The idea that all this could be controlled through an APA so a company could plan makes sense not only from a tax perspective but from a corporate management perspective as well. (Wrappe, Milani, and Joy 1999: 40)

COMPETITIVENESS IN THE MIDDLE EAST MARKET

A MNC must help its subsidiaries in their first stages of business in Middle East countries. ITP systems can be used to help them compete against other businesses through a low transfer price for goods shipped into those countries to keep Middle East subsidiaries competitive with other local businesses.

Competition can be in the final selling markets, the raw materials market, the intermediate market, or the parent company's market. However, a conflict may arise between Middle East governments and MNCs that charge very low transfer prices for goods transferred into the Middle East country, especially when import customs or duties are imposed on the invoice price of goods, and/or the low transfer price helps Middle East subsidiaries compete against local firms, and may drive them out of the market. In this case, foreign governments may intervene to protect their domestic industries and their tax or tariff revenues as well.

PERFORMANCE EVALUATION OF MIDDLE EAST
SUBSIDIARY MANAGERS

MNCs set up their international transfer pricing policies at the central management (or top management) level to facilitate cash movements in the Middle East where currency restrictions exist and to minimize taxes. A conflict between ITP techniques and the performance evaluation measurement of a Middle East subsidiary manager is to be expected and, in general, transfer pricing policies are not complementary to the profit center concept.

At the second-quarter meeting of the Consortium for Advanced Manufacturing–International (CAM–I), it was emphasized that performance measurement consists of an integrated, comprehensive set of measures that flows from management's vision and strategy. It also was suggested that firms should try to understand investors' non-financial performance concerns. One presentation focused on Caterpillar, Inc.'s performance measurement system, which utilizes a market-based transfer pricing system and a balanced scorecard of nine top-tier performance measurements (Daly 1996).

Unfortunately, the traditional profit center concept for the performance evaluation of a Middle East subsidiary manager is inappropriate for MNCs, because there is no clear distinction between operating subdivisions of MNCs. With integrated, centrally coordinated operations, Middle East subsidiary management does not have the authority to make major decisions that affect its reported profits. Differences between Middle East countries, such as social, economic, political, legal, and educational differences, have a considerable effect on a Middle East subsidiary manager's performance. There is an urgent need for further research to introduce additional elements into traditional management accounting evaluation techniques.

In judging the performance of a Middle East subsidiary, it is appropriate to evaluate its contribution to the objectives and goals of the entire MNC. It is also important to evaluate the contribution of Middle East subsidiary managers to the performance of the MNC. David Solomons (1965: 59) has stated, "In the absence of evidence to the contrary, the presumption is that the success of one implies the success of the other. But circumstances outside a manager's control may dictate success or failure of the venture."

The headquarters enforces a specific transfer price to be used by its own Middle East subsidiaries to achieve certain objectives such as domestic, foreign, and Middle East income tax minimization, foreign exchange risk reduction, and Middle East exchange control avoidance, among others. To achieve these objectives, international transfer pricing may result in some Middle East subsidiaries showing higher artificial profits, while others may show much lower ones.

A Middle East subsidiary manager may have the operation of his or her area evaluated as though it were a completely autonomous, independent subsidiary. Middle East subsidiary managers may have the greatest degree of freedom in making decisions related to the short run. However, they have a lesser degree of freedom in making decisions directly affecting other foreign subsidiaries and the global market.

With the frequent fluctuation of currency values, combined with the floating exchange rate system, MNCs face the problem of distorted performance measurements of their domestic and foreign subsidiaries as profit centers (Malmstorm 1977; 25). Performance of foreign subsidiaries in U.S.-based MNCs is usually adjusted for any fluctuation in currency exchange rates (Benke and Edwards 1980: 118).

At Honeywell, Inc., Duane Malmstorm (1977: 25) implemented a simple solution to this problem. His technique is called "dollar indexing," which has the same impact as local currency invoicing, including two basic objectives: (1) to allow a realistic performance evaluation; and (2) to reflect the real economic

Table 10–3
The Effect of Transfer Pricing on Performance Evaluation

	A		B		The Globe
	U.S.$	JOD	U.S.$	NIS	U.S.$
SALES					
20,000 @ $10	$200,000	$142,000			
20,000 @ $20			$400,000	1,700,000	$400,000
LESS: COST OF GOODS SOLD	(90,000)	(63,900)	(200,000)	(850,000)	(90,000)
GROSS PROFIT	110,000	78,100	200,000	850,000	310,000
LESS: S, A, & G EXP.	(70,000)	(49,700)	(95,000)	(403,750)	(165,000)
NET INCOME BEFORE TAX	40,000	28,400	105,000	446,250	145,000
Net Income as % of Sales	20%	20%	26%	26%	36%
U.S.$1 = JOD 0.71					
U.S.$1 = NIS 4.25					

S = Selling; A = Administrative; G = General.

cost of the product transferred. Malmstorm used the following indexed formula for U.S.-dollar transfer prices:

$$NTP = OTP \times \frac{CER}{PER}$$

where

NTP = New transfer price
OTP = Old transfer price
CER = Current exchange rate
PER = Planned exchange rate

Using this formula will result in applying a uniform transfer price for all goods transferred out of the same subsidiary.

To illustrate, let us assume that a Jordanian subsidiary transferred 20,000 units of its products at a transfer price established by the parent U.S.-based MNC at $10 a unit to another subsidiary in Israel owned by the same MNC. The foreign exchange rates on October 19, 1999, were Jordanian Dinar (JOD) 1.00 = US$1.412, or US$1 = JOD .708, and New Israeli Shekel (NIS) = US$0.2353, or US$1 = NIS 4.25. As can be seen in Table 10–3, the Jordanian subsidiary achieves a net income of US$40,000, or JOD 28,400 in Jordanian dinars, while the Israeli subsidiary achieves a net income of $105,000, or NIS 446,250 in Israeli new shekels.

If we assume that the U.S. dollar was depreciated equally against both the

Table 10–4
The Effect of Transfer Pricing with Changes in Foreign Exchange Rates on Performance Evaluation

	A U.S.$	JOD	B U.S.$	NIS	The Globe U.S.$
SALES					
20,000 @ $10	$200,000	$106,280			
			$533,120	1,700,000	$533,120
LESS: COST OF GOODS SOLD	(120,196)	(63,900)	(200,000)	(627,200)	(120,196)
GROSS PROFIT	79,804	42,480	333,120	1,072,800	412,924
LESS: S, A, & G EXP.	(93,486)	(49,700)	(126,616)	(403,750)	(220,102)
NET INCOME BEFORE TAX	(13,682)	7,320	206,504	669,050	192,822
Net Income as % of Sales	(7%)	(7%)	39%	39%	36%
U.S.$1 = JOD 0.5314					
U.S.$1 = NIS 3.136					

S = Selling; A = Administrative; G = General.

Jordanian and Israeli currencies to JOD 1.00 = US$1.8818, or US$1 = JOD 0.5314 and NIS 1 = US$0.3136, or US$1 = NIS 3.136, the income statements for both subsidiaries and the MNC measured in U.S. dollars and local currencies would be as shown in Table 10–4. Since the transfer price ($10 a unit) was set centrally by the U.S.-based MNC, the operating results of the Jordanian subsidiary would show a net loss of $13,682, or JOD7,320, while the Israeli subsidiary would achieve a net income of $206,504, or NIS669,050, because of the devaluation of the U.S. dollar in international markets.

The effect of using the $10 as a transfer price for international operations when there was a devaluation in the parent company's currency resulted in switching the operating results of the selling subsidiary from a net income of 20% of sales to a net loss of 7% of sales. On the other hand, the operating results of the buying subsidiary would be the opposite, switching from a net income of 26% to a higher net income of 39%. That is, this transaction not only transferred goods from the Jordanian subsidiary to the Israeli subsidiary but also transferred $53,682 ($40,000 + $13,682) of profits and a translation gain of $47,822, a total of $101,504. In this case, the MNC as a whole should show a profit of $192,822 (higher than before by $47,822), because of the translation gain resulting from the devaluation of the U.S. dollar. For performance evaluation the manager of the Jordanian subsidiary was negatively affected by the change in the exchange rate and by the imposed transfer price, while the Israeli subsidiary's manager did nothing more than before yet showed a 39% net income percentage (13% higher than before the change occurred).

Table 10–5
The Effect of Transfer Pricing Adjusted for Changes in Exchange Rates

	A U.S.$	A JOD	B U.S.$	B NIS	The Globe U.S.$
SALES					
20,000 @ $13.33	$266,600	141,671			
			$533,120	1,700,000	$533,120
LESS: COST OF GOODS SOLD	(120,196)	(63,900)	(266,600)	(836,058)	(120,196)
GROSS PROFIT	146,404	77,771	266,520	836,942	412,924
LESS: S, A, & G EXP.	(93,486)	(49,700)	(126,616)	(403,750)	(220,102)
NET INCOME BEFORE TAX	52,918	28,071	139,904	433,192	192,822
Net Income as % of Sales	20%	20%	26%	26%	36%
U.S.$1 = JOD 0.5314					
U.S.$1 = NIS 3.136					

S = Selling; A = Administrative; G = General.

Using the indexed formula for U.S.-dollar transfer prices suggested by Malmstorm, the adjusted transfer price would be

$$NTP = OTP \times \frac{CER}{PER}$$

$$NTP = \$10 \times \frac{1.882}{1.412} = \$13.33$$

$$NTP = \$10 \times \frac{0.3189}{0.2353} = \$13.33$$

Table 10–5 shows the effect of transfer prices adjusted for changes in exchange rates. The new transfer price is $13.33, which is higher than the old one. For the Jordanian and Israeli subsidiaries, the net income percentage as related to sales is the same as before there were any changes in the exchange rate, and both had the same measured performance as before. The MNC had higher global profits with a dollar devaluation of $47,822, which is a translation gain. However, the translation gains were divided in such a way that the Israeli subsidiary received $34,904 out of total translation gains of $47,822, while the Jordanian subsidiary received only $12,918 (20% of $66,500, which is the increase in the transfer price), due to the extent that the U.S. dollar was devalued in relation to the local currency. Therefore, the adjusted transfer price helps avoid any distortion in the financial results and ratios and reflects the effect of the exchange rate fluctuations.

MOTIVATION

Motivation is considered one of the objectives of setting an international transfer pricing policy for domestic, foreign, and Middle East subsidiaries. Middle East subsidiary managers need to be motivated to maximize (or increase) their subsidiary's profits and transfer their products or services in and out of their areas of responsibility within the MNC at appropriate transfer prices. Transfer prices, in this case, can be used to motivate Middle East subsidiary managers to achieve their subsidiaries' goals (by maximizing their own local profits) and at the same time achieve their MNC's goals (by maximizing the global profits).

For an ITP system to be a motivator, it must be tied to the performance of Middle East subsidiary managers. To be used as a measure of performance, an ITP system must meet the following four criteria:

1. It must be a result of the Middle East manager's behavior.
2. It must include all of the actions or activities that need to be performed.
3. It must be accepted by Middle East subsidiary managers as a valid measurement of their performance.
4. It must include practical, attainable goals for Middle East subsidiary managers.

Does the transfer price measure completely the Middle East subsidiary manager's performance? That is, does the transfer pricing system reflect all of the actions that should be performed by the Middle East subsidiary manager in selling his or her products to another subsidiary? Certainly the answer is no, because a Middle East subsidiary manager does not have control over the fluctuations of the exchange rate of the local currency of the country in which he or she is doing business. The manager can easily achieve translation gains or losses to be included in his or her performance report because of political, legal, economic, or social factors over which he or she does not have control. The manager's profits can rise or fall because of sudden increases in inflation rates and/or commodity or stock prices, and the outcome will be an increase or a decrease in the market price when it is used as a transfer price.

MNCs must analyze the potential impact of using a transfer pricing system as a motivator for a Middle East subsidiary manager's performance. Actions or decisions made by managers to improve their performance can have a negative effect on the global goals or profits of the MNC as a whole. Whenever international transfer pricing objectives lead to conflicting consequences, MNCs are forced into trade-offs between achieving different objectives, and they must accept lower global profits when one objective has priority over another, especially for achieving long-term objectives.

GOAL HARMONIZATION

Goal harmonization exists when the goals of the MNC's Middle East subsidiary managers, as long as they are feasible, are consistent with the global goals of the MNC. In establishing the correct transfer pricing policy, top management should motivate Middle East subsidiary managers to achieve the subsidiary's goals by contributing toward the achievement of the MNC's goals. It is almost impossible to obtain perfect congruence between Middle East subsidiary managers' goals and the MNC's goals. However, at least the ITP policies should not motivate Middle East subsidiary managers to make decisions that may conflict with the MNC's goals.

Motivation and goal harmonization are important factors in designing ITP systems. If a MNC wishes to have its Middle East subsidiary manager strongly motivated toward achieving congruent goals, it is necessary to consider the effect of the transfer pricing policy on its divisional profitability or performance. However, if there is a conflict between Middle East subsidiary managers' goals and global goals, it may be preferable for managers to have as little motivation and autonomy as possible.

Generally, an ITP system should be designed in such a way that a Middle East or a domestic subsidiary manager is motivated to make decisions that are in the best interest of the MNC as a whole. When Middle East subsidiary managers increase their subsidiaries' profits and at the same time increase global profits, then they are in the MNC's interest if the ITP system does not mislead managers about what the MNC's interests really are. However, both subsidiary managers and central management must be aware that the measurement of a subsidiary's net income (or contribution) under this ITP system is inherently imperfect, and that the limited usefulness of that performance measure is further complicated by the existence of common resources used within the MNC.

SUMMARY AND CONCLUSIONS

This chapter has identified and discussed nine different objectives of establishing an ITP policy for Middle East operations, including (1) reduction of income taxes, (2) reduction of tariffs, (3) minimization of foreign exchange risks, (4) avoidance of a conflict with host countries' governments, (5) management of cash flow, (6) competitiveness, (7) performance evaluation, (8) motivation, and (9) goal harmonization. For the first two objectives, as long as the tax rate differential is higher than the net effect of the tariff rate imposed by the country with the higher tax rate, the higher transfer price will always generate net savings for the MNC. However, if the higher transfer price results in showing artificial losses for the buying subsidiary, the net effect will be detrimental for the MNC as a whole.

With the fluctuations in Middle East exchange rates, assets in weak currencies can be moved through the use of higher transfer prices. However, host-government intervention with or without price controls will certainly limit the MNC's use of this technique. When performance evaluation systems combine with fluctuations in foreign exchange rates, transfer pricing policies will lead to misleading, imperfect financial measures of performance. An adjusted transfer pricing system (dollar-indexing technique) was suggested, which is believed to help in evaluating Middle East subsidiary managers' performance and to avoid any distorted financial results for performance evaluation.

Motivation, goal harmonization, and autonomy of Middle East subsidiaries and their managers always lead to conflicting results with performance evaluation, reduction of income taxes, reduction of tariffs, and avoidance of foreign exchange risks. However, when different objectives lead to conflicting consequences, MNCs have to make trade-offs between achieving these different objectives, and they must be satisfied with lower global profits when one objective has priority over another, especially in achieving long-term goals.

In designing an ITP policy to fit the Middle East, the business literature, especially accounting, does not provide MNCs with a unique technique or model to help them arrive at the appropriate transfer price. Therefore, MNCs are in urgent need of a practical and an objective technique or model that can avoid conflicts between different objectives of the system and, at the same time, achieve their global goals to continue doing their Middle East business activities under various political, economic, and social environmental conditions.

REFERENCES

American Accounting Association. "Report of the Committee on International Accounting." *Accounting Review* 49 (1974 Supplement), 252–257.

Arpan, Jeffrey S. *International Intracompany Pricing: Non American Systems and Views*. New York: Praeger, 1972, 70.

Benke, Ralph L., Jr. and James Don Edwards. *Transfer Pricing Techniques and Uses* New York: National Association of Accountants, 1980, 118.

Daly, Dennis C. "Performance Measurement and Management." *Management Accounting* (September 1996), 65.

Elliot, Jamie. "International Transfer Pricing: A Survey of UK and Non-UK Groups." *Management Accounting* (November 1998), 48–50.

Greenhill, C. R. and E. O. Herbalzheimer. "International Transfer Pricing: The Restrictive Business Practice Approach." *Journal of World Trade Law* (May–June 1980), 232.

Hall, L. le Van. *The Multinational Corporation: Accounting and Social Implications*. Urbana: Center for International Education and Research in Accounting, University of Illinois, 1977.

Hines, James R., Jr. "Lessons from Behavioral Responses to International Taxation." *National Tax Journal* (June 1999), 305–322.

Kim, H. Seung and Stephen W. Miller. "Constituents of the International Transfer Pricing Decisions." *Columbia Journal of World Business* (Spring 1979), 71.

Knowles, Lynette L. and Ike Mathur. "International Transfer Pricing Objectives." *Managerial Finance* 11 (1985), 12.

Malmstorm, Duane. "Accommodating Exchange Rate Fluctuations in Intercompany Pricing and Invoicing." *Management Accounting* (September 1977), 25.

Oxelheim, Lars. *International Financial Market Fluctuations*. New York: John Wiley & Sons, 1985, 61.

Plasschaert, Sylvain R. F. "The Multiple Motivations for Transfer Pricing Modulations in Multinational Enterprises and Governmental Counter Measures: An Attempt at Clarification." *Management International Review* 1 (1981), 49–63.

Robbins, Sidney M. and Robert B. Stobaugh. *Money in the Multinational Enterprise* New York: Basic Books, 1973, 91.

Solomons, David. *Divisional Performance: Measurement and Control.* Homewood, Ill.: Richard D. Irwin, 1965, 59.

Wrappe, Steven C., Ken Milani, and Julie Joy. "The Transfer Price Is Right . . . Or Is It?" *Strategic Finance* (July 1999), 38–43.

Chapter 11

Transfer Pricing Techniques in the Middle East and Section 482 of the IRC

This chapter discusses the transfer pricing methods that are appropriate to achieve certain internal objectives of MNCs in managing their Middle East activities. It analyzes Section 482 of the U.S. Internal Revenue Code (IRC) and its impact on the Middle East activities of MNCs, and it examines the Internal Revenue Service's (IRS) Advanced Pricing Agree (APA) program and its effect on the transfer pricing policies regarding Middle East activities. Finally, the Organization for Economic Cooperation and Development (OECD) guidelines for transfer pricing policies will be discussed.

MNCs use transfer pricing policies to achieve certain objectives in managing their Middle East business operations. Two sets of objectives are known in the business literature: internal and external. Internally, MNCs use transfer prices as accounting prices to account for transactions transferred between different subsidiaries within the same organization. They are also used for decision making regarding the allocation of resources between different subsidiaries in different countries, and to help top management in managing a decentralized organization by integrating and coordinating autonomous (or pseudo-autonomous) subsidiaries all over the world. Motivation, control, and performance evaluation of Middle East subsidiaries within MNCs are other objectives for using transfer prices. At the top of the objectives stands goal harmonization, which requires that all actions and decisions made by Middle East subsidiary managers be in the best interest of the MNCs as a whole.

The second set of objectives relates to factors outside of the home country. From the viewpoint of a MNC, transfer prices are used to allocate net income among different subsidiaries in different countries under different legal, social, and economic regulations. Externally, MNCs face other problems, such as different income tax rates for various countries, tax structures and regulations, quotas and import duties, cash movement restrictions, currency exchange control, and conflicts with Middle East governments. From the viewpoint of the U.S. government or any other foreign government, transfer pricing policies create problems with the belief that they do not reflect open market prices. Middle East governments, like others, believe that MNCs set their own transfer pricing policies to avoid paying taxes. Therefore, MNCs are in conflict with both home and Middle East governments.

The two sets of objectives are not directly related to each other, and there is no evidence that a single transfer price is designed for only one of its objectives that will satisfy all others. No practical evidence has been found regarding the best or most appropriate transfer price for MNCs to use in managing their businesses in the Middle East. There are three reasons for this problem, discussed below.

First, changing Middle East environmental factors, such as market conditions, governmental attitudes, political issues, legal considerations, economic conditions, and different global strategies, force MNCs to use different transfer prices at different times under different circumstances. Second, the balance of payments, tax revenues, and market structures of different Middle East countries, among other factors, are affected by the use of transfer prices.

There is no easy way to "ascertain ex post whether a given transfer price level was practiced ex ante with a view to minimize taxes or regulations or primarily on business grounds" (Plasschaert 1979: 12). Third, if the transfer price does not reflect the Middle East market conditions, or if it deviates from the arm's-length price between unaffiliated companies, then it is unacceptable. "The extent of the deviation depends on the yardstick used; . . . the implementation of the yardstick is difficult and frequently gets enmeshed in the issue of the fair price, whatever that concept may mean" (ibid.).

To choose the appropriate transfer pricing policy for Middle East activities, it is essential to look at both of the appropriate transfer pricing techniques used for internal use of management and the appropriate transfer pricing method for tax purposes. Therefore, this chapter is divided into the following sections: (1) economics and accounting-oriented analysis, (2) mathematically oriented analysis (including linear and nonlinear), (3) Section 482 of the IRC, (4) the IRS' APA program, and (5) the OECD guidelines on transfer pricing policies.

ECONOMICS AND ACCOUNTING-ORIENTED ANALYSIS

The economic and accounting-oriented techniques fall into one of the following subgroups: (1) market price; (2) cost-based and cost-plus methods, including full production cost, full production cost plus profit margin, variable production cost, and variable production cost plus profit margin; (3) marginal cost-based; and (4) negotiated price.

Market/Arm's-Length Price

The market price is the price that would prevail when a manufacturing subsidiary sells its products to an external customer, or when the manufacturing subsidiary charges the same price to the buying subsidiary as it would to an external customer in arm's-length transactions. However, four criteria should be satisfied to use the market price as a transfer price: (1) the existence of a competitive intermediate market, (2) subsidiary managers have freedom in decision making, that is, they can decide either to buy or sell internally or in the open market without interference from top management, (3) subsidiary managers have autonomy or at least a minimal degree of interdependence among profit centers, and (4) a known market price can be quoted at any time.

Using the market price has several advantages. First, if a market price can be determined, it is the best price to be used for the performance evaluation of the profit centers, since it motivates managers to act as though they were managing their own business, and consequently it reduces the costs of production and increases divisional profits. Second, market prices correspond to the arm's-length price, which is the right price from the IRS's perspective. Using the market price may help MNCs avoid conflict with either home or host country governments. Third, subsidiary managers, especially in foreign countries, may be well qualified to make quick decisions under certain circumstances to avoid any negative consequences such as interference from the government.

However, some problems may result from using market prices. First, the appropriate market price may be difficult to determine—it may be different from one country to another, even if it is in the same currency. Second, in the international market, transportation costs are significant, and also are different from one location to another, which makes it impossible to establish a uniform market price for the same product of the same MNC sold in different countries. Third, the supply and demand in foreign markets requires establishing a price that will prevail in that market and will help foreign subsidiaries compete with other subsidiaries. Therefore, no unique market price can be quoted.

Cost-Based and Cost-Plus Methods

Cost-based transfer pricing may be used when market prices do not exist or are not available for MNCs to use for international transfer pricing. Under the cost-based method, cost may mean different things and have different effects on performance evaluation, motivation, decision making, divisional profits, income tax liability, and global profits.

The cost-based method includes full costs (actual or standard) and variable costs (actual or standard). Full costs include direct material, direct labor, and factory overhead. This method offers three major advantages: (1) Availability of cost information is provided by the accounting system currently in use by the MNC, (2) It is in conformity with U.S. Generally Accepted Accounting Principles concerning inventory valuation and income determination, and (3) It may motivate foreign subsidiary managers to increase their divisional contribution as long as the full absorption cost exceeds the variable cost and there is additional capacity to accommodate incoming orders.

However, use of the full absorption costing method can create many problems, which can be summarized as follows:

1. If the selling subsidiary is assured of covering all full production costs on all goods transferred internally, there is little incentive for foreign subsidiary managers either to have control over their divisional costs, produce efficiently, or make rational decisions related to their area of responsibilities as long as the cost of their inefficient use of resources is passed on to the buying subsidiaries. This can be avoided by using standard costs rather than actual costs for transfer pricing.
2. If the full cost exceeds the market price, the buying subsidiary manager would be motivated to buy from the market outside of the MNC; consequently, this would create idle capacity for the MNC as a whole.
3. It leads to suboptimal, short-run decisions for the MNC as a whole when the buying subsidiary treats the fixed costs of the selling subsidiary as variable costs.

A variable cost–based transfer price leads the buying subsidiary to make optimal decisions in the best interest from the MNC's viewpoint. The MNC's variable actual or standard cost is considered the buying subsidiary's variable cost as if it acts in the international market. However, using the variable cost-based transfer price forces the selling subsidiary to report a zero profit or a loss equal to its fixed costs.

For making long-run pricing decisions, variable cost-based transfer pricing will mislead buying subsidiary managers when making the appropriate pricing decisions to compete in the international market from the MNC's viewpoint. In other words, a subsidiary manager's decision may not be in the best interests of the MNC as a whole.

Cost-plus transfer pricing may use actual or standard costs that should be marked up to allow the selling subsidiary to realize a profit. A markup can be a flat percentage of the cost (actual, standard, full, or variable). A markup should allow the foreign subsidiary to recover its normal operating costs, plus an appropriate markup to earn a return on investment equal to that earned in the domestic market (Nagy 1987: 35).

A major reason for the common use of cost-plus transfer pricing is its simplicity, clarity, and approximation of the market price, especially when the intermediate product has an international market and when it is a justifiable, reasonable transfer price when there is no market for the product. However, this may lead to suboptimal decisions for the MNC as a whole when not related to an economic reality.

Marginal Cost-Based Method

Marginal cost is the change in total cost that results from an increase in production by an additional unit.

Under the marginal cost-based method, the transfer price is set at the marginal cost of the selling subsidiary. The selling subsidiary should produce when its marginal cost (the transfer price) is equal to its marginal revenue, which will lead to maximization of the profits of the MNC. The marginal cost-based transfer pricing method is presumed to result in optimal production for the MNC.

This method is appropriate when there is neither an external market for the intermediate product nor an agreeable negotiated transfer price between the two subsidiaries. However, information on marginal cost cannot be practically collected from the MNC accounting system. Several empirical studies have shown that the marginal transfer pricing method, which is a theoretical technique, is of little use in practice and is not a realistic technique to be used.

Negotiated Transfer Pricing Method

A negotiated transfer price is used when the buying and selling subsidiaries are free to negotiate the acceptable transfer price for both. It retains the independence of each manager to make the correct decision for his or her subsidiary, and it makes each manager accountable for the outcome of his or her decisions. Therefore, it motivates subsidiary managers to maintain control over their costs and to increase their divisional contribution to the MNC.

However, this may lead to suboptimal decisions, especially when the final product is sold in a different country and when other factors, such as different tax rates, different government regulations, different tariff, and competition, are ignored. Another problem is that negotiations may require too much time, therefore, it is a lengthy process and may require top management intervention for settlement.

MATHEMATICALLY ORIENTED ANALYSIS

Mathematical programming techniques were introduced after the failure of traditional economic models to solve transfer pricing problems. The mathematical programming models allocate resources efficiently and at the same time evaluate the efficient use of resources under a decentralized organization (Abdel-Khalik and Lusk 1974; Baumal and Fabian 1964). These techniques include (1) linear programming models that deal with allocation problems in which the objective (or goal) and all of the requirements imposed are expressed by linear functions; (2) nonlinear programming models that are used when the goal and/or one or more of the requirements imposed are expressed by nonlinear functions; and (3) a goal programming model used when there are multiple goals for a MNC. Under all of these techniques, the mathematical model sets transfer prices at the opportunity costs (or shadow prices) of the intermediate product.

However, the suggested mathematical programming techniques have the following drawbacks:

1. The MNC must obtain suboptimal divisional information in order to maintain "efficient decentralized operations" (Bailey and Boe 1976: 561). When transfer prices are set centrally, the autonomy of foreign subsidiary managers is ignored completely, and the profit center concepts are not applicable under these conditions.

2. The problem is enlarged with MNCs because of the existence of different economic, political, and social variables, which may require setting a different transfer price in each country where a foreign subsidiary is located. In other words, different tax rates, foreign exchange risks, expropriation risks, governmental intervention, and avoiding any conflicts with host country governments are examples of the many problems that MNCs face when doing business abroad, and they may make the development of a mathematical programming model for MNCs much more difficult, if not impossible, for domestic firms. Therefore, experimental or empirical studies are badly needed to validate the use of these models within MNCs.

3. These models do not consider the behavioral implications of using transfer pricing, therefore they do not achieve the objectives of establishing international transfer pricing, as described above.

4. In evaluating Middle East managers' performance as one of the objectives of international transfer pricing policies within these models, performance evaluation is assumed to be a function of profits. However, performance evaluation may be affected by divisional costs, variations between the budgeted and actual cost, or any other factors that should be incorporated into the system (Khalik and Lusk 1974: 20).

THE U.S. TAXATION OF INTERNATIONAL TRANSFER PRICING TRANSACTIONS AND SECTION 482 OF THE IRC

For the past three decades, MNCs have not had a business function that goes as deeply into nearly all international operations, including manufacturing, marketing, management, and financing, as transfer pricing. International transfer pricing decisions have a great impact on Middle East operations of MNCs, directly affecting their global revenues and profits, and they can help or limit MNCs' abilities to operate, manage, and utilize their economic resources on a global basis to achieve their ultimate goals.

Recent U.S. tax changes reflect the importance of global competition and devote considerable effort to revising provisions that affect the taxation of Middle East income (Hines 1999: 306). Tax regulations in the United States are different from those in Middle East countries in many respects, such as tax rates, tax treaties, tax bases, foreign tax credits, and taxes imposed on any profits resulting from using intercompany transfer pricing policies for goods and services that cross a country's border. Among Middle East countries, great differences exist in many aspects of their tax regulations and laws. Developed countries, such as the United Kingdom, Canada, Germany, France, Japan, and Switzerland, have objectives in their tax structure, policies, and regulations different from those of developing countries such as Egypt, Kuwait, Saudi Arabia, Bahrain, and Jordan, among many others.

The significant growth of the global market means that both MNCs and tax authorities should consider transfer pricing policies carefully. MNCs should ensure that their transfer pricing policies and strategies can be supported and that they are deemed fair and acceptable. Middle East tax authorities should also ensure that they collect a fair and reasonable amount of corporate tax revenue from MNCs investing and operating in their countries (Elliott 1998: 49).

Developed countries impose taxes on their multinational and foreign corporations for four main purposes:

1. to raise revenues
2. to provide tax incentives
3. to avoid or minimize double taxation
4. to curb tax abuses

Developing countries (DC), including the Middle East, use their tax systems to achieve, to some extent, different objectives:

1. to achieve certain rates of economic growth
2. to establish industrial priorities
3. to encourage new investments in new industries
4. to maintain political and social stability by sustained development of the economy
5. to monitor all foreign exchange transactions and enforce stringent control

However, some Middle East countries relax governmental restrictions on the repatriation or remittance of profits, capital, or income of foreign investments to encourage more inward investment in their countries.

It is estimated that almost 60% of all international business transactions takes place between related partners, so tax authorities worldwide developed four main ways to monitor and reduce tax evasion by transfer pricing (Lermer 1998: 30):

1. Including provision in the legislation with formal, detailed, and binding regulations, similar to the ones in the U.S. tax code.
2. Including provision in the legislation with detailed guidelines on reasonable and acceptable techniques of transfer pricing, such as in Germany.
3. Providing in the legislation arm's-length standards that will help establish acceptable transfer pricing practices based on the guidelines of the OECD, such as in the United Kingdom.
4. Having no specific transfer pricing legislation, where the ordinary tax laws and eva-

sion prohibition are relied on to prevent transfer pricing understatement, such as in the Netherlands.

Transfer pricing is becoming increasingly important as Middle East countries become more accessible to the rest of the world, and vice versa. Tax authorities in Middle East countries are not well prepared to deal with the complicated issues involved in the transfer pricing policies of large MNCs. Different countries do things differently—no specific regulations control transfer pricing issues in most of Middle East countries. Some Middle East countries' tax authorities make less stringent inspections of MNCs investing in the area than others, depending on the political party at the time of the inspection, the tax officer, and the economic conditions of the country.

As the peace process between Israel and Palestine moves forward, MNCs face a great challenge, because both political risk and business risk in the Middle East will decline, and the rate of return on investments will increase. Under the new environmental conditions, MNCs expand their activities; consequently, more and more of their products and services will be transferred in and out of Middle East countries. The governments there will notice a significant increase in their transfer pricing activities. It is expected that these governments will implement enforcement, documentation, and penalty regimes similar, although never quite identical, to the regime now familiar in the United States.

Over the long run, different tax structures, different tax rates on foreign investments and subsidiaries, and different foreign exchange control policies may constitute the most basic reason for using the correct strategy for international transfer pricing policies in the Middle East. This can be combined with long-range global tax planning to achieve the global objectives of MNCs within different environmental conditions in the Middle East market.

SECTION 482 OF THE IRC

International transfer pricing decisions have a significant impact on the global sales, tax liabilities, and profits of MNCs. The tax authorities in most countries of the world, including the Middle East, require that the transfer pricing policies between related entities be at arm's length. Their objectives are: (1) to prevent MNCs from reducing their tax liabilities by shifting profits from one entity to another; (2) to allow tax authorities to adjust income and deductions to reflect clearly the correct taxable income within their territories; and (3) to counter abusive transfer pricing policies. Most of the legislation in different countries has focused on the concept of comparing intercompany prices to arm's-length, third-party prices.

In the United States, Section 482 of the U.S. IRC provides that the IRS may allocate gross income, deductions, credits, or allowances among related entities to prevent the evasion of taxes and to reflect clearly the income of each entity of a corporate group. Related entities under Section 482 are defined as two or more trades, organizations, or businesses owned or controlled, either directly or indirectly, by the same group or interests. The purpose of Section 482 is to prevent the shifting of income or profits from one commonly controlled entity to another by a MNC.

Section 482 deals with the following five types of transactions:

1. interest charged on intercompany loans
2. services performed for a related party
3. use of tangible property by a related party
4. intercompany transfers of intangible property
5. intercompany sales of tangible property

Intercompany pricing on sales of tangible property is the most widely known problem, therefore, it will be discussed the most in this book.

The application of Section 482 of the U.S. IRC of 1986 tended to focus on the concept of comparing intragroup transfer prices with arm's-length, third-party prices. The arm's-length standard is defined by the IRC as "the amount, which would have been charged in independent transactions with unrelated parties under the same or similar circumstances." In other words, Section 482 insists that intercompany transactions be priced at arm's length, or as though they involved unrelated parties in the open market.

Currently there is evidence of tax-motivated transfer pricing, which comes in several forms. While it is possible that high tax rates correlate with other location attributes that depress the profitability of foreign investment, competitive conditions typically imply that after-tax rates of return be equal in the absence of tax-motivated income shifting. Before-tax profitability negatively correlated with local tax rates is strongly suggestive of active tax avoidance (Hines 1999: 313).

Many problems may arise in translating Section 482 into practice by MNCs, because regulations are ambiguous and vague. Consequently, facts and circumstances of what constitutes the appropriate arm's-length price to be used among related entities can provide plenty of scope for debate and negotiations. Thus, most cases between the IRS and MNCs require courts to settle disputes, and there is no general rule arrived at among courts.

A study performed by Jane D. Burns (1980) concluded that 53% of the sample group of MNCs had Section 482 reallocations in at least one year and that the average annual deficiency proposed by the IRS was about $1 million, of which 70% was agreed to and paid, 16% was reduced, and 14% was being disputed.

Section 482 prescribes three specific methods for determining arm's-length prices, to be used in order, and a fourth method that may be used for all other situations in which none of the first three are considered appropriate and reasonable. The three methods set forth in the regulations, to be used in order, are: (1) comparable uncontrolled price method, (2) resale price method, and (3) cost-plus method.

The IRS, in allocating profits or income, should look first for an uncontrolled transaction, second for a resale price, and third for the cost of a tangible property, plus a reasonable profit.

If none of these three methods apply, a fourth is used. This method was included in the regulations after great objections by businessmen. It allows MNCs to use an alternative method to the three methods if they can fully justify the appropriateness and reasonableness of the method selected for their circumstances. In allocating the income or profits of foreign subsidiaries, MNCs have the responsibility of justifying their international transfer pricing methods and proving that they are reasonable. Otherwise, income reallocation made by the IRS must be accepted by the courts unless the MNC proves them unreasonable or arbitrary allocations (Burns 1984: 140).

Generally, it is not necessary for a MNC to use only one pricing method for all of its products under all circumstances. It may be acceptable for it to sell various products at different stages of completion in other markets using dissimilar pricing methods. The methods prescribed in Section 482 of the IRC are discussed below.

Comparable Uncontrolled Price Method (CUP)

An uncontrolled sale is defined in the IRC regulations as a sale in which the seller and buyer are not members of the same controlled group. In other words, it uses prices charged in comparable sales to third, unrelated parties as the appropriate prices for intercompany transactions.

Uncontrolled sales can be comparable to the conditions surrounding the sale that are either identical to the controlled sales or nearly identical so that differences can be reflected by adjustments to the price. Adjustments are made when they reflect differences that have a definitive, reasonable effect on price. The uncontrolled sale, as adjusted, makes up the comparable uncontrolled sale price.

A comparison of sales to third parties is deemed the most appropriate method. However, a major problem that opens the door for disputes is, how can a MNC validly prove a comparable uncontrolled price? Factors in doing so would include the terms of the sale, the timing of the sale, the conditions prevailing in the marketplace, transportation costs, and different qualities of products (Liebman 1987: 4). Generally the most important issue under this method is whether the sale is truly comparable.

The transfer pricing system requires that MNCs certify their tax returns in accordance with the arm's-length price. However, two problems exist: (1) MNCs are not confident that foreign tax authorities would necessarily be in accordance with their view of arm's-length pricing and (2) It is difficult to obtain support from senior management assigned to overseas locations for short periods of time (Elliott 1998: 49).

Several problems are encountered in applying the CUP method in practice (Schindler 1987). One of the most serious is the absence of unrelated transactions in industries such as the petroleum industry, where there is vertical integration of global operations handling exploration, production, shipping, and refining. It is seldom practical to find unrelated parties that handle some of these major transactions. Another problem is that intercompany transfers of intangible property do not fit into the arm's-length standard required by the regulations. It is difficult, if not impossible, for a firm to sell its valuable advanced technology, marketing know-how, or any intangible asset, such as a patent, to both their own foreign subsidiaries and to unrelated parties that may be competitors.

An excellent example of some of the problems associated with the use of comparable prices is cited in the survey conducted by Jamie Elliott (1998: 50). The survey stated that to use the prescribed transfer pricing guidelines by the tax authorities, pharmaceutical companies had to conduct comparability studies; however, it was almost impossible for pharmaceutical companies to find comparable transactions between independent parties, since products and ingredients of pharmaceutical MNCs are unique and patented.

The Resale Price Method (RPM)

If an arm's-length price cannot be determined through the comparable, uncontrolled price, the regulations specify that the resale price method must be used. Arm's-length price is computed by looking at a sale by a related buyer to its customers, reduced by an appropriate markup percentage.

The RPM is appropriate when a sales transaction is made to a controlled party that then resells to an unrelated party and there is no comparable, uncontrolled price. A portion of the resale price may be attributable to value added by the related party. In that case, adjustments must be made to the resale price.

Different guidelines regarding the appropriateness of a markup may be used, however, the appropriate markup percentage can be determined from uncontrolled sales made by other resellers under similar circumstances. Generally two methods exist to compute the markup percentage: the gross profit percentage and the net profit percentage. The regulations prescribe that the gross profit percentage method be used in allocating the income of subsidiaries, but the net profit percentage can be used as a fourth method.

Cost-Plus Method (CPM)

The seller's price is computed by multiplying the cost of production by an appropriate gross profit percentage to cover the functions it carries out. The appropriate gross profit percentage can be determined from comparable, uncontrolled sales of the seller, another party of the uncontrolled sale, or unrelated parties. This method is usually used by MNCs with major activities in exports of manufacturing components or unfinished goods that have substantial values added to them by the purchasing foreign subsidiaries.

However, the term *cost of production*, as prescribed in the regulations, should be consistent with sound accounting practices for allocating costs. According to the regulations, if the seller used its full costs to compute its gross profit percentage, then the cost of production would be the full production cost. If the seller used direct costs to compute its gross profit percentage, the cost of production would be equal to the direct costs.

The manner in which direct costs are computed may be inconsistent with the regulations' definition of cost of production. In management (or cost) accounting practices, direct costs are defined as those that can be traceable into and identified specifically with a particular product or process for a specific purpose. However, direct costing, sometimes called variable costing, is a method of product costing that charges only the variable costs of manufacturing to the product. Variable manufacturing costs include direct materials, direct labor, and variable manufacturing overhead.

Section 482 of the IRC does not clarify what is meant by direct costs. Is it "direct costs," which includes direct materials and direct labor costs only, or is it the product costing method "direct costing"? The difference between the two is variable manufacturing overhead, which may be between 10% to 30% of production costs.

The Alternate Method

The regulations provide that when none of the three methods can reasonably be applied under the usual circumstances of a particular case, an alternate method should be used. The alternate method can be a variation of one of the three, or it can be an entirely different method, appropriate under certain circumstances.

For many years, Section 482 of the IRC has been used as the standard tax treatment of intercompany transfers. It was first adopted in the Revenue Act of 1921 and has remained essentially unchanged since then. A few clarifications and some additional authorities have been given to the IRS during a period of more than 65 years of statutory history.

Today, U.S.-based and non-U.S. corporations and their international activities have expanded from only imports and exports to increasingly direct involvement in different international markets using various methods. The growth of U.S.-based and foreign MNCs has brought significant changes to the structure of international markets and has created significant economic interdependence between most nations (Schindler 1987: 9). Elliot's (1998: 50) survey indicated that the most applicable transfer pricing methods for U.K., U.S. and European-owned companies were cost-plus, the CUP method, and resale price.

The U.S. Tax Reform Act of 1986 reduced U.S. corporate tax rates. The act significantly affected international operations of U.S.-based MNCs and U.S. taxation of foreign MNCs with subsidiaries in the United States. While the act changed corporate tax rates, it also made international transfer pricing policies more complicated than before. The majority of accounting practitioners and

MNCs' key top executives believed that lowering U.S. corporate tax rates below those of other industrial developed and developing countries would encourage U.S.-based MNCs to minimize their global tax liability and consequently maximize their global profits. This could be done by bringing more and more of their taxable income to the United States, however, Section 482 of the IRC still insists on the use of arm's-length pricing for intercompany transactions.

While MNCs do not deal with their foreign subsidiaries as though they were unrelated, proving the reasonableness of their international transfer pricing policies in dealing with the IRS may be nearly impossible, especially if their production and marketing techniques are not comparable to any other techniques used throughout the world.

Another problem with the U.S. Tax Reform Act of 1986 created regarding the transfer price for goods imported into the United States was that a U.S. importer could not claim a transfer price for income tax purposes on goods purchased from a related party that was higher than that claimed for U.S. custom purposes. This restriction prevented companies from reporting a lower transfer price for customs purposes and, consequently, from paying a lower custom duty than reported for income tax purposes. On the other hand, the higher the cost of goods sold used for transfer pricing, the lower the U.S. taxable income that would be used as a basis for income tax liability.

It may be concluded from the above analysis that as long as tax rate differentials arc higher than the net effect of tariff rates imposed by the higher tax rate country, the higher transfer price will always generate net savings for the MNC.

However, if top management increases the price for goods transferred from one subsidiary to another by a specific amount of money, the higher transfer price may have a negative effect on both the global profits of the MNC and on the net income of the buying subsidiary. Generally, the higher the import tariffs relative to the difference in net income tax rates between different countries, the more likely that a low transfer price is preferable.

THE IRS's ADVANCED PRICING AGREEMENT (APA) PROGRAM

The expansion of global business activity in recent years made a significant increase in transfer pricing enforcement by tax authorities around the world inevitable. The United States was the first country to adopt substantial penalties relating to transfer pricing and to require that companies maintain detailed documentation of their transfer pricing systems. Many MNCs, fearful of penalties, responded by seeking to reduce risk exposures in the United States (Durst 1999).

On March 1, 1991, the IRS released its official procedures for obtaining an APA in Revenue Procedure 91–22. The IRS's APA program is designed to provide MNCs with the opportunity to avoid costly audits and litigation by allowing them to negotiate a prospective agreement with the IRS regarding the facts, the transfer pricing methodology, and an acceptable range of results. The program is aimed at MNCs interested in avoiding penalties, managing risk, and determining their tax liability with a high degree of certainty (Wrappe, Milani, and Joy 1999).

On May 24, 1995, the IRS explained the general objectives of the APA program in its proposed revenue procedure, as follows:

1. To enable taxpayers to arrive at an understanding with the IRS on three basic issues:
   - the factual nature of the intercompany transactions to which the APA applies;
   - an appropriate transfer pricing methodology (TPM) applicable to those transactions; and
   - the expected range of results from applying the TPM to the transactions. However, in appropriate cases, the IRS will consider APAs that set forth a TPM without the specification of any range.
2. To do so in an environment that encourages common understanding and cooperation between the taxpayer and the IRS and that harmonizes and incorporates the opinions and views of all of the IRS's functions involved with the taxpayer.
3. To come to an agreement in an expedited fashion, as compared to the traditional method, which entails separate and distinct dealings with the examination, appeals, and competent authority functions and/or possible subsequent litigation.
4. To come to an agreement in a cost-effective fashion for both the taxpayer and the IRS.

Therefore, the APA program's goal is to agree on the best method to calculate market-driven prices, which allows MNCs to determine the acceptable transfer price and, ultimately, one's tax liability with certainty. An APA will result in no surprises for the MNC. Because the IRS has agreed prospectively, MNCs will not find themselves involved in transfer pricing disputes later, as long as they comply with the agreement, which can cover as many as five years and can also be applied to prior years.

Some MNCs have suffered over not getting the right transfer price from the IRS's point of view. In December 1998, DHL, a package delivery service, lost a transfer pricing battle with the IRS over the valuation of its trademark. DHL valued the trademark at $20 million, while the tax court concluded that $100 million was the correct price. Unfortunately, DHL was fined a 40% penalty for this error in judgment. The APA program not only allows MNCs to avoid the payment of such penalties, it also lets them gain certainty regarding their expected tax liability (Robak 1999).

The APA process may be long and tedious, however, it has many benefits to both taxpayers and to the IRS, as explained in the program description released by the IRS.

1. MNCs can avoid penalties and gain substantial certainty with respect to how the desired transfer pricing activities will be treated for U.S. tax purposes and, in the case

of a bilateral APA program, how U.S. transfer pricing activities will be treated by foreign tax authorities as well.

2. The APA process provides an environment in which the taxpayer, the IRS, and, where appropriate, the competent authorities cooperate to determine which transfer pricing method should apply to transfer pricing activities. The APA process stimulates a free flow of information between all parties involved in the process to come to a legally correct, practical, and workable result.

3. The APA process can reduce taxpayers' record-keeping burden. Taxpayers must keep records to substantiate only one reasonable methodology (the TPM agreed upon), and generally they do not have the burden of keeping all documents potentially relevant to other methodologies that the IRS could consider in an examination.

4. The APA process may help taxpayers avoid extended litigation, subjects the TPM to extensive review, and retains legal merit.

5. The APA process provides the opportunity to resolve open years by rolling back the APA pricing provides the opportunity to resolve open years by rolling back the APA pricing methodology to resolve transfer pricing issues in prior years, with the consent of the appropriate district, appeals, or competent authority.

In summary, the advantages of APA program include friendly collaboration between the MNC and the IRS, possible avoidance of costly, time-consuming audits and litigation, and reduction of uncertainty about the tax treatment of international transfer pricing activities.

However, MNCs expose themselves to the following risks by applying for an APA (Tang 1997: 102):

1. The IRS may scrutinize the industry and taxpayer-specific information submitted and the annual reports for each taxable year of a MNC covered by the APA.

2. An APA does not shelter the taxpayer from the IRS's subsequent scrutiny regarding transfer pricing activities of the business entity.

3. The significant assumptions may change. What was an acceptable TPM at the time the APA was signed may be quite disadvantageous in later years.

4. The cost of obtaining an APA may be significant.

MNCs are the target of tax authorities of all governments worldwide. Most MNCs are based in highly industrialized and developed countries such as the United States, the United Kingdom, Japan, Germany, and Canada.

The United States was the first country to respond to domestic political pressures for tax enforcement of MNCs in the 1980s and early 1990s, and it adopted new regulations designed to make enforcement easier, to adopt substantial penalties relating to transfer pricing, and to require that companies maintain detailed documentation of their transfer pricing policies. Many MNCs, fearful of penalties, responded by seeking to reduce their risk exposures in the United States (Durst 1999; 57).

Initially, the other tax authorities generally perceived the increased U.S. enforcement as a potential assault on their own tax bases, which the non-U.S. countries feared that they could not realistically counter with increased enforcement regimes of their own. Other countries, therefore, did not agree on the U.S. initiatives, but the major developed countries, including the trading partners of the United States, felt that global political and economic realities called for an appropriate uniform international approach to transfer pricing enforcement. Today, an international environment exists in which many countries are implementing enforcement, documentation, and penalty regimes similar to the regime now implemented in the United States (Durst 1999: 57).

The APA programs in Canada, Germany, Japan, the United States, and the United Kingdom vary in their degree of complexity and formality. A survey examined the status of APAs in five countries, and it found that APA programs are more popular with tax authorities than with MNCs. The principal reasons cited by MNC's for nonparticipation involve documentation, the costs involved, and confidentiality concerns about the information contained in the documentation (Borkowski 1996: 23–34).

Tax authorities from all industrialized countries tend to consider transfer pricing a soft target because of the difficulties involved and the fact that most MNCs are ready to pay. The simultaneous increase in the scrutiny of transfer pricing by governments around the world places new pressure on the tax executive of the MNC. More than ever before, the effective management of a company's transfer pricing policies requires a global approach in which perhaps the greatest danger consists of focusing too closely on the enforcement risks in a single country, or a small group of countries, while ignoring equally significant risks in others (Durst 1999: 57).

In the United Kingdom, all U.K.-based MNCs are liable for a tax rate of 35% on their worldwide profits. A foreign tax credit is allowed for foreign income taxes paid on foreign income taxable in the United Kingdom, with the U.K. tax actually charged on that foreign income as a maximum. Branches of non-U.K. MNCs are liable for income tax at a rate of 35%, the same as the domestic rate, on British source income. A few years ago, the Inland Revenue decided that an advance ruling system would be too time consuming and too costly to operate. However, a reasonably comprehensive ruling system is now springing up in the United Kingdom (Symons 1998: 62). At this time, the U.K. government has no statutory arrangements in place to help taxpayers participate in APAs. In 1999, the U.K. Inland Revenue published a Statement of Practice describing how APAs are administered. The Inland Revenue encourages applications for bilateral APAs in relation to cross-border transfer pricing considerations. The APA process will typically consist of four stages: expression of interest, formal submission of application for clarification, evaluation, and agreement (Tax Planning International Review 1999).

In the United Kingdom, the objective of a ruling system is to give MNCs certainty about their tax obligations. The system will work only if the tax authorities are able to deal with the rulings in a helpful, efficient, businesslike, and non-hostile way. That will cost money. This comparison is particularly stark if one looks at the opportunity cost of diverting highly trained inspectors away from compliance work, however, anything less could lead to a serious culture clash that would be contentious and confusing (Symons 1998: 62).

Japan requires its MNCs to aggregate the loss or income of foreign branches with the income or loss of the corporation and to pay the Japanese corporate income tax of 33.3% on distributed income, or 43.3% on undistributed income on their worldwide income. Branches of foreign MNCs are taxed only on the Japanese source income in the same manner as the Japanese corporations. The allowed methods for determining an arm's-length price are the classic transaction-based methods of the comparable uncontrolled price method, the resale price method, and the cost-plus method. None of these methodologies is preferable over another. Japanese transfer pricing rules prescribe a fourth method in the event that none of the above methods can be used. Specifically, this is a method that corresponds to one of the above three methods or a method pre-scribed by the official tax authority. The Tax Administration does not recognize the comparable profits method, the transactional net margin method, or similar profit methods as permissible transfer pricing methods (Anonymous 1998: 25). The Tax Administration recently prepared a series of questions and answers regarding the profit split method. The first series clearly states that the Tax Administration does not accept, in current form, the comparable profit method or modified resale price method being used in APAs (ibid.).

For MNCs, the goods and services transferred between two countries may be priced using two different approaches by two different tax authorities for the same item. In addition, the various objectives and policies of the tax regulations of the two countries could lead to completely conflicting results.

Despite the tax treaties among countries, MNCs are still required to pay high income tax liabilities over their global profits as a cost of doing business across the border. Every tax revenue authority tries to come up with the arm's-length price, which may not be in existence when the product is unique in the inter-national market.

However, tax treaties are applied only to dividends, interest, rent, or royalties. Business profits, which do not include the above four items, are taxable at corporate tax rates applicable by the host country to business profits in general. Tax treaties do not eliminate double taxation completely; in most cases, they only reduce the tax rate on income. Dividends, for example, are taxed by both host and home countries, which are parties to tax treaties, but at different lower rates.

THE OECD GUIDELINES ON INTERCOMPANY TRANSFER PRICING

In May 1979, the OECD issued a report on intercompany transfer pricing prepared by its Committee on Fiscal Affairs and adopted the recommendation included in the report. The report, "Transfer Pricing and Multinational Enterprises," includes two major issues on intercompany transfer pricing, including:

1. Considerations to be taken into account in determining the appropriate international transfer prices for tax purposes.
2. A description of the generally agreed-upon practices of transfer pricing policies in developed countries for tax purposes.

The report concentrated on the major problem of determining transfer prices, however, it did not discuss specific applicable cases or circumstances to a country, an industry, a MNC, or a geographical area.

The OECD report significantly affected the views and attitudes of tax revenue authorities throughout the world. The report is similar to Section 482 of the U.S. IRC. The U.K. tax revenue authorities participated in the preparation of the report. Canada, Japan, and Germany, among other members of the OECD committee, have tax laws, tax regulations, and guidelines similar to those adopted by the United States and outlined in the OECD 1979 report on transfer pricing (OECD 1979).

While the OECD 1979 report had no binding authority in the OECD member countries, it provided an indication of the rules and approaches adopted by a tax revenue authority in a country, the United States, with a well-developed tax system. The acceptance of the report by the Business and Industry Committee, representing business interests in major countries, is evidence of significant support for the worldwide adoption of U.S. tax rules on transfer pricing (Helmers 1980: 141).

The OECD, on July 27, 1995, released its final guidelines in "Transfer Pricing Guidelines for Multinational Enterprises and Tax Administration," which included the 1979 report, "Transfer Pricing and Multinational Enterprises" and the 1984 report, "Transfer Pricing and Multinational Enterprises: Three Taxation Issues" (OECD 1984). The 1995 guidelines are not laws, but member countries are encouraged to follow them. Most member countries do not have their own detailed transfer pricing regulations and have been following prior OECD guidelines on transfer pricing.

Despite some differences, the guidelines are generally consistent with Section 482 of the IRC on transfer pricing regulations. American MNCs that comply with Section 482 regulations should not be exposed to a significant risk of double taxation in OECD member countries. The guidelines emphasize the arm's-length standard and the use of transaction-based methods that rely on comparable uncontrolled transactions. The Section 482 regulations require taxpayers to select the "best method rule," which under the facts and circumstances will provide the "most reliable measure" of an arm's-length result relative to the other potentially applicable methods. Under the guidelines, MNCs must select the method that provides the "best estimate" of an arm's-length standard (Greenhill and Bee 1996).

The guidelines discussed important issues related to transfer pricing policies, including the arm's-length standard, transfer pricing methods, transfers of intangible property and services, and guidelines on documentation and penalties. They are discussed in detail below.

The Arm's-Length Standard

According to the 1995 OECD guidelines, similar to Section 482 regulations, no adjustment should be made to a MNC's transfer pricing results if those results are within an arm's-length range derived from the use of two or more comparable uncontrolled transactions or more than one pricing method. However, if a MNC's transfer pricing results are outside of the arm's-length range, those results may be adjusted to within the range. Under Section 482, such an adjustment would normally be in the mid-point range; under the 1995 guidelines, the adjustment would be to the point that best reflects the facts and circumstances.

Transfer Pricing Methods

The 1995 guidelines explain the following transfer pricing methods in detail: (1) the three traditional transaction methods, which include the comparable uncontrolled price method (CUP), the resale price method (RPM), and the cost-plus method (CPLM); (2) the transactional profit methods, which include the profit split method (PSM) and transactional net margin method (TNMM); and (3) the global formulary apportionment method (GFA). In several cases, the three traditional transaction methods (CUP, RPM, and CPLM) and the two transactional profit methods (PSM and TNMM) can be used as arm's-length standards, however, the GFA is considered a non-arm's-length method and is rejected by the OECD.

The OECD guidelines, similar to Section 482 regulations, provide standards of comparability that emphasize functions performed, risks assumed, and assets used. Both permit the use of inexact comparables "similar" to the controlled transaction under review. The types of risks that must be taken into account under both sets of rules include market risks; risks of loss associated with the investment inland use of property, plant, and equipment; risks associated with the success or failure of research and developmental activities; and financial risks such as those caused by currency exchange rate and interest rate variability.

The 1995 guidelines express a strong preference for the use of transactional methods for testing the arm's-length character of transfer prices for transfers of tangible property. These methods include the comparable, uncontrolled price method, the resale method, and the cost-plus method, all "specified methods" under Section 482 regulations.

No substantive differences exist between Section 482 regulations and the 1995 guidelines in the concepts underlying these methods, the manner in which these methods are to be applied, or the conditions under which these methods would likely be the best. Section 482 regulations and the 1995 guidelines differ only in their evaluation of the probability that comparable, uncontrolled transactions can be identified and that adequate and reliable data about the transactions can be reasonably obtained. The guidelines state that the inability to apply the transactional methods will be the exception, not the norm (Greenhill and Bee 1996).

Both the Section 482 regulations and the 1995 guidelines provide for the use of other methods when the transactional methods cannot be used. Under Section 482 regulations, a taxpayer may use the CPM or the PSM; under the 1995 guidelines, a taxpayer may use the PSM or the TNMM. Unlike Section 482 regulations, which limit the use of the PSM, the 1995 guidelines express a strong preference for the use of the PSM over the TNMM. It should be noted that the PSM would produce a very different result than that obtained under any of the other methods specified in either the Section 482 regulations or the 1995 guidelines.

The OECD 1995 guidelines would allow a MNC to base its profit split analysis on projected profits, seemingly without regard to actual profits realized; such an approach would not be permitted under Section 482 regulations. The TNMM is substantially equivalent to the CPM under Section 482 regulations. Some OECD members rejected the use of the CPM, mainly because they could not understand the requirements in Section 482 of the IRC. Some OECD countries perceive the CPM only as the imposition of industry-wide average returns to a taxpayer's entire business activity, without regard to comparability and to factors other than transfer pricing that might ignore profit margins. However, Section 482 regulations have explicit comparability standards that apply to all pricing methods. Thus, when properly used, the CPM and the TNMM should produce to a large extent the same result (Greenhill and Bee 1996).

Transfers of Intangible Property and Services

In the OECD 1995 guidelines, intangible property is divided into three groups, as follows:

1. the right to use industrial assets, such as patents, trade names, trademarks, models, or designs;
2. literary and artistic property rights; and
3. intellectual property, such as know-how and trade secrets.

These intangible assets may or may not have any book value on the MNC's financial statements, but many may be quite important to the company. On the contrary, some may be associated with high risks (such as product liability or environmental or air pollution). The 1995 guidelines do not address the arm's-length principle for either the transfer of intangible property or cost sharing, or the provision of intercompany services. On April 11, 1996, the OECD updated its guidelines for the transfer of intangible property and services (Greenhill and Bee 1996).

Guidelines on Documentation and Penalties

The OECD 1995 guidelines provide extensive discussion on the documentation to be obtained from MNCs in connection with a transfer pricing inquiry. The guidelines suggest that MNCs should make reasonable efforts when establishing their transfer-pricing policies to determine whether their transfer pricing results meet the arm's-length standard. The OECD also recognizes that tax authorities should have the right to obtain the documentation to verify compliance with the arm's-length standard. The guidelines encourage member countries to administer penalty systems in a manner that is fair and not unduly onerous for MNCs. Thus U.S. MNCs are not relieved of the need for contemporaneous documentation required under Section 6662(e) to avoid the risk of U.S. transfer pricing penalties.

SUMMARY AND CONCLUSIONS

This chapter discussed transfer pricing methods appropriate to achieve certain internal objectives of MNCs in managing their Middle East activities. It also analyzed Section 482 of the U.S. IRC and its impact on the Middle East activities of MNCs. In addition, it examined the IRS's APA program and its effect on the transfer pricing policies of Middle East activities. Finally, the OECD 1995 guidelines and similarities to Section 482 of the IRC for transfer pricing policies were discussed.

The objective of an appropriate ITP technique for either internal or external reporting, or both, is determined largely by the objectives of establishing an ITP policy. Transfer pricing methods are divided into two groups: (1) economic and accounting-oriented analysis, including the market price, cost-based, cost-plus, marginal cost-based, and negotiated price methods; and (2) mathematically oriented analysis, including linear, nonlinear, and goal programming models.

When different tax authorities of two countries adjust the appropriate transfer price based on the appropriate arm's-length price, a MNC may be liable for more than double the tax liability on the same item.

A technique or method useful for one group of objectives or for one purpose may not be the best choice for another. The two sets of objectives, as discussed in this chapter, are not directly related to each other, and there is no evidence that a single transfer price designed for only one of the ITP objectives will satisfy all others. No practical evidence has been found concerning the appropriate (or optimal) transfer price for MNCs to use, based on the following reasons:

1. The significance of and fast change in Middle East environmental conditions, such as market conditions, governmental attitudes, and different global strategies, force MNCs to use different transfer prices at different times under different conditions.

2. Middle East and host countries' balance of payments, tax revenues, and Middle East market structures, among other factors, are affected by the use of transfer pricing policies.

3. The use of any transfer price other than the arm's-length one is more likely unacceptable to tax authorities.

4. Foreign exchange risks, expropriation risks, governmental interventions, and avoiding any conflict with host countries' governments are examples of many problems facing MNCs in developing an appropriate ITP policy and make it much more difficult, if not impossible, for domestic firms.

5. The most important key factors in deciding which transfer pricing method to use are the global strategy of MNCs, exchange controls, income tax liability, and performance evaluation of Middle East subsidiaries and their managers.

6. MNCs, the IRS, and Middle East tax authorities will receive great benefits from APA programs, including friendly collaboration between the MNC and the IRS, the possible avoidance of costly, time-consuming audits and litigation, and less uncertainty regarding the tax treatment of ITP activities.

REFERENCES

Abdel-Khalik, A. Rashad and Edward J. Lusk. "Transfer Pricing: A Synthesis." *Accounting Review* 69 (1974), 3–23.

Anonymous. "Acceptable Transfer Pricing Methodologies." *International Tax Review* 7 (February 1998), 25.

———. "Transfer Pricing—United Kingdom: Revenue Practice on APAs Announced." *Tax Planning International Review* 18 (October 1999), 16–18.

Bailey, Andrew D., Jr. and Warren J. Boe. "Goal and Resource Transfers in the Multigoal Organization." *The Accounting Review* (July 1976), 559–573.

Baumal, W. J. and T. Fabian. "Decomposition, Pricing for Decentralization, and External Economies." *Management Science* (1964), 1–32.

Borkowski, Susan C. "Advance Pricing (Dis)agreements: Differences in Tax Authority and Transnational Corporation Opinions." *The International Tax Journal* (Summer 1996), 23–34.

Burns, Jane O. "How IRS Applies the Inter-company Pricing Rules of Section 482: A Corporate Study." *Journal of Taxation* (May 1980), 308–314.

———. "The Multinational Enterprise: U.S. Taxation of Foreign Source Income." In H. Peter Holzer et al. (eds.), *International Accounting*. New York: Harper and Row, 1984, 140.

Durst, Michael C. "United States." *International Tax Review* (February 1999), 56–62.

Elliot, Jamie. "International Transfer Pricing: A Survey of UK and Non-UK Groups." *Management Accounting* (December 1998), 48–50.

Greenhill, Mitchell and Charles W. Bee, Jr. "Transfer Pricing Guidelines Issued by the OECD." *The Tax Adviser* (May 1996), 265–266.

Helmers, Dag. "BOAC's Response to the OECD Report on Transfer Pricing and Multinational Enterprises." *Intertax* (August 1980), 286–293. In Jane O. Burns, "Multinational Enterprises: U.S. Taxation of Foreign Source Income," in H. Peter Holzer et al. (eds.), *International Accounting*. New York: Harper and Row, 1984, 141.

Hines, James R., Jr. "Lessons from Behavioral Responses to International Taxation." *National Tax Journal* (June 1999), 305–322.

Lermer, David. "Pitfalls of Transfer Pricing." *Finance Week*, December 4, 1998, 30.

Liebman, Howard. "International Transfer Pricing and Recent Development: Part I." *Tax Planning International Review* (August 1987), 4.

Nagy, Richard J. "Transfer Price Accounting for MNEs." *Management Accounting* (January 1987), 35.

Organization for Economic Cooperation and Development (OECD). *Transfer Pricing and Multinational Enterprises: Three Taxation Issues*. Paris: OECD, 1984.

———. *Transfer Pricing Guidelines for Multinational Enterprises and Tax Administrations*. Paris: OECD, 1995.

Organization for Economic Cooperation and Development. Committee on Fiscal Affairs. *Transfer Pricing and Multinational Enterprises*. Paris: OECD, 1979.

Plasschaert, Sylvain R. F. *Transfer Pricing and Multinational Corporations: An Overview of Concepts, Mechanisms and Regulations*. New York: Praeger, 1979.

Robak, Epsen. "Son of Solomon: Tax Court Splits the Baby in DHL Corp." *Taxes* (September 1999), 20–31.

Schindler, Guenter. "Inter-Company Transfer Pricing after Tax Reform of 1986." *Tax Planning International Review* (November 1987), 9–10.

Symons, Susan. "US Corporate Tax: The Dawn of a New Era." *International Tax Review* (September 1998), 61–63.

Tang, Roger Y.W. *Intrafirm Trade and Global Transfer Pricing Regulations*. Westport, Conn.: Quorum Books, 1997.

Wrappe, Steven C., Ken Milani, and Julie Joy. "The Transfer Price Is Right . . . Or Is It?" *Strategic Finance* (July 1999), 38–43.

Part IV

Looking Ahead

Chapter 12

The Future of the Business Environment and Its Effect on the Future of Accounting Development in Middle East Countries

The purpose of this chapter is twofold: (1) to present a summary of the key factors in managing Middle East subsidiaries and investments by providing MNCs' executives with guidelines to help them in planning, managing, and controlling their Middle East business activities; and (2) to state general conclusions from the research on the future of the business environment and its effect on accounting development in the Middle East.

In Chapter 1, it was noted that the primary purpose of this book was to provide the latest information on managing MNCs in the Middle East. The cultural and economic issues of selected Middle East countries and their effect on accounting principles, harmonization of accounting standards, performance evaluation, and transfer pricing standards were emphasized. The economic, political, and legal characteristics of Middle East countries and accounting systems were covered in Chapter 2, while the effect of culture and religion on accounting systems and practices of selected Middle East countries compared to IAS and U.S. GAAP was discussed in Chapters 3, 5, and 6. Guidelines on the important issues for conducting and managing successful joint ventures in the Middle East were reviewed in Chapter 4.

Performance measurement and the evaluation of Middle East subsidiaries and their managers was discussed in Chapter 7. Tax systems in selected Middle East countries, ITP issues, and Section 482 of the U.S. IRC were covered in Chapters 8 through 11. In this last chapter, we take a global view of managing Middle East countries to summarize the major findings from research on the following topics:

- the effect of culture and religion on accounting in the Middle East;
- financial reporting of Middle East countries and IAS;

- performance measurement and evaluation of Middle East subsidiary managers of American and non-American MNCs;
- tax planning for investments in the Middle East;
- ITP policies; and
- business and accounting in the Middle East in the next century.

MAJOR FINDINGS FROM THE RESEARCH

The Effect of Culture and Religion on Accounting Systems and Practices in the Middle East

In Chapter 3, it was noted that prior research has shown that there are difficulties in harmonizing IAS because of the significant effect of different cultural values on the achievability of uniform ones. Religion, especially Islam, is one of the most significant cultural values that has a considerable effect on a country's accounting systems and practices, and it should it not be ignored. The major cultural and religious issues affecting accounting can be summarized as follows:

- Most prior researchers have claimed that national systems and practices are determined by environmental variables. Gray (1988) developed a model by identifying the mechanism by which societal-level values are related to the accounting subculture, which directly influences accounting practices. Gray used Hofstede's culture-based societal value dimensions as the basis for his analysis. He also identified four value dimensions of the accounting subculture, which are also related to societal values: Professionalism, Uniformity, Conservatism, and Secrecy.
- Recently, the effect of religion on the concepts and mechanisms of accounting in the Islamic world and its potential effect on the harmonization of IAS has been discussed by Hamid, Graig, and Clarke (1993).
- In the Middle East, culture is often considered one of the important environmental factors shaping accounting systems and practices. Baydoun and Willett (1995) adopted the Hofstede–Gray framework as an implied definition of cultural relevance and applied it to Lebanon, one of the Middle East countries, to see if the result would lead to conclusions relevant to its history, environment, and culture.
- Hofstede (1980, 1987, 1991) developed a commonly acceptable, well-defined, and empirically based terminology to describe cultures. He identified four different elements of culture: Individualism, Power Distance, Uncertainty Avoidance, and Masculinity. One can see the impact the basic tenets and practices of Islam—*salat* (prayer), *zakat* (contribution), *hajj* (pilgrimage), and *sawm* (fasting)—have had on Hofstede's four cultural values, in part by comparing the social actions of individuals and organizations of Western countries to those of Islamic countries.
- Significant cultural differences exist between Arabs, Israelis, and Americans Table 3–1 showed Hofstede's differences in the cultural values of Arab countries compared to the United States, and the cultural values of Israel compared to the United States. Unlike Israel and the United States, no direct assessment of Egypt's, Kuwait's, or Saudi Arabia's four cultural dimensions is available. However, Hofstede (1991) provides data

on Arab countries as a group, including the three Arab countries, which can be used as the starting point for the analysis.

- If the national cultural values of Islamic society shape and reinforce both accounting systems and practices, it will be a rational decision to harmonize the accounting standards of those countries as one subgroup of the international community. Therefore, it is time for the IASC to consider not harmonizing IAS but rather establishing Islamic IAS. IIAS will be helpful to South Asia Muslim countries (275 million), African Muslim countries (200 million), Arab countries (180 million), and the remaining Islamic adherents (545 million). IIAS should be based on the Holly Qur'an and on the Sunna of the Prophet Mohammed (PBU).

Financial Reporting of Middle East Countries and International Accounting Standards

In Chapters 5 and 6, the accounting systems and practices of selected Middle East countries and IAS were examined. Comparisons of financial reporting in the Middle East with IAS and the U.S. GAAP were included. The major issues of financial reporting can be summarized as follows:

- The selected Middle East countries are following the U.S. GAAP and IAS for seven out of 10 accounting issues, the only difference being that Israel is using the fair market value in short-term investments. Accounting for inflation, as one of the other three accounting issues, is treated differently by the selected Middle East countries. The Egyptian GAAP covers this and does not require it, even though the average inflation rate in the country was nearly 20% a year for the period 1995–1999. Saudi Arabia's GAAP does not cover the inflation issue, however, the inflation rate there is not significant. Israel, with the highest inflation rate in the Middle East, mandates the use of both general price level adjustments and current cost accounting. Of the remaining two accounting issues, equity accounting and consolidation, Saudi Arabia is the only country using the cost method for consolidated financial statements.

- The adoption of IAS by Middle East countries is likely to have a strong impact on the financial reporting practices of listed business entities in the Middle East, particularly since IAS 1, Presentation of Financial Statements, clearly rules out any "soft" application of IAS. Companies preparing financial statements under IAS now have to ensure not only that their accounting policies comply with them, but also that they present the financial information in the form and with all of the disclosures mandated by IAS (Khanna 1999).

- In the absence of both a local or a regional body of GAAP and a private regional professional organization, it is important for Middle East stock markets to adopt IAS as the financial reporting and disclosure framework for all companies listed or seeking a listing on the stock market. The acceptability of IAS is reinforced by the fact that the local banks may accept financial statements prepared under IAS, and the Big Five accounting firms operating in the Middle East have been encouraging their clients, with considerable success, to prepare their financial statements under IAS.

- Investors and creditors must be protected and encouraged to participate in the local stock exchange market. The Arab stock market must formulate a comprehensive, well-structured, and strictly enforceable regulatory mechanism that results in accountability and effective standards of responsibility.

- If Arab countries wish to have one regional standard setter and one set of international financial reporting standards in the future, the following four principles are essential in achieving this ultimate goal: (1) Arab countries who are involved in global financial reporting and stock markets must have a common mission or objective of their financial accounting and reporting systems; (2) they must have a complete process for developing financial reporting standards that is accepted and trusted by all constituents— one that ensures that the mission of the standard setter is fulfilled; (3) they should develop standards that achieve high quality; and (4) one regional standard-setting body should be formed and must have the power to enforce accounting standards for all national companies in the region.

- In Israel, IAS have been adopted by the ICPA. They apply in cases where there are no specific pronouncements issued by the ICPA. Therefore, the financial statements of Israeli or other companies are more likely to be prepared according to IAS and, consequently, will be comparable.

Performance Measurement and Evaluation of Middle East Subsidiary Managers of American and Non-American MNCs

Chapter 7 introduced, discussed, and analyzed the performance evaluation problem of MNCs in evaluating their Middle East subsidiaries and managers. The major issues of performance evaluation and measurement can be summarized as follows:

- Traditional management accounting techniques are inadequate to appropriately solve the problems of evaluating the performance of Middle East subsidiaries and their managers, and MNCs are unable to achieve satisfactory and desired levels of performance evaluation. Management accounting techniques have not adequately considered the distinct characteristics of the environment within which MNCs operate and manage their businesses.

- A suggested performance evaluation system for Middle East countries was presented. The proposed system estimates foreign subsidiary managers' relative performance after considering the effects of non-controllable Middle East environmental factors on the measured performance of Middle East subsidiaries.

- The suggested environmental model was applied to a Middle East subsidiary of an American MNC to illustrate how MNCs can implement it in practice.

- There are many implications of this proposed model for performance evaluation for Middle East subsidiary managers and decision making in allocating the limited resources (human and financial) of MNCs. One possible implication is that new advanced management accounting techniques should be developed and used to facilitate the measurement and evaluation of the performance of Middle East MNC subsidiary managers.

- The proposed Middle East environmental model is useful for MNCs in designing a system of performance evaluation of subsidiary managers. The proposed system incorporates the distinction of each Middle East environmental factor into its design. This new system will surely lead to improved systems, improved planning, and improved decision-making processes and outcomes.

Tax Planning for Investment in the Middle East

Chapter 8 discussed taxation in general and emphasized the essential need for a successful and an effective tax planning strategy for MNCs before they begin investing in selected Middle East countries to take advantage of tax differences, holidays, tax treaties, and other incentives. The most important issues of tax systems and regulations of Middle East countries and some guidelines for investors can be summarized as follows:

- American and non-American MNCs, and any potential investor, can be very successful in investing their capital and managing their businesses in the Middle East if they design an appropriate tax planning strategy that fits the Middle East tax, social, and economic environment.
- In doing so, tax planning should be done in advance and should include the following six major steps:
  1. Obtain access to all up-to-date tax information of the region and of the selected Middle East country.
  2. Start your tax planning as soon as your Middle East joint venture or project is initiated.
  3. Make a wise decision in selecting the correct, honest local partner(s) for your joint venture.
  4. Involve your local partner(s) in your tax planning.
  5. Minimize your tax burden by
     a. choosing the most appropriate investment tools, such as joint ventures or wholly owned subsidiaries;
     b. structuring contracts in the most convenient, appropriate manner;
     c. taking advantage of all available tax holidays and other incentives; and
     d. coordinating the tax burden in the Middle East with that in your home country to take advantage of any tax treaty provisions and other tax credit opportunities.
  6. Design your pricing policy, including transfer pricing strategies, after considering all tax and custom issues.

International Transfer Pricing Policies

International transfer pricing (ITP) issues are discussed in Chapters 9 through 11. The objectives, techniques, and strategies of using the appropriate ITP system were examined, analyzed, and illustrated. Two Middle East subsidiaries were used as examples. The most important issues of tax systems and regulations of Middle East countries and some guidelines for investors can be summarized as follows:

- The most important factors in establishing an appropriate transfer pricing policy for Middle East businesses are the maximization of global profits, avoidance of foreign exchange risks, simplicity, ease of use, reduction of restrictions on cash transfers, and performance evaluation of Middle East subsidiaries. These factors include the trade-offs MNCs must consider when establishing or revising their transfer pricing policies. To be successful in their Middle East business activities, MNCs should put more emphasis on designing their transfer pricing policy to fit the Middle East cultural, legal, and economic environment. Moreover, it is very important for MNCs to prepare social responsibility reports to show their level of contribution to the welfare and social and economic conditions of Middle East countries.

- Chapter 10 identified and discussed nine different objectives in establishing an ITP policy for Middle East operations: (1) reduction of income taxes, (2) reduction of tariffs, (3) minimization of foreign exchange risks, (4) avoidance of a conflict with host countries' governments, (5) management of cash flows, (6) competitiveness, (7) performance evaluation, (8) motivation, and (9) goal harmonization. For the first two objectives, as long as the tax rate differential is higher than the net effect of the tariff rate imposed by the country with the higher tax rate, the higher transfer price will always generate net savings for the MNC. However, if the higher transfer price results in showing artificial losses for the buying subsidiary, the net effect will be detrimental for the MNE as a whole.

- In designing an ITP policy to fit the Middle East, the business literature, especially accounting, does not provide MNCs with a unique technique or model to help them arrive at the appropriate transfer price. Therefore, MNCs are in urgent need of a practical, objective technique or model that can avoid conflicts between different objectives of the system and at the same time achieve their global goals to continue doing their Middle East business activities under various political, economic, and social environmental conditions.

- A transfer pricing technique or method useful for one group of objectives or for one purpose may not be the best choice for another. There is no evidence that a single transfer price designed for only one of the ITP objectives will satisfy all others. No practical evidence has been found concerning the appropriate (or optimal) transfer price for MNCs to use, due to:

  1. The significance of and fast change in Middle East environmental conditions, such as market conditions, government attitudes, and different global strategies, which force MNCs to use different transfer prices at different times under different conditions.

  2. Middle East and host countries' balance of payments, tax revenues, and Middle East market structures, among other factors, are affected by the use of transfer pricing policies.

  3. The use of any transfer price other than the arm's-length one is more likely unacceptable to tax authorities.

  4. Foreign exchange risks, expropriation risks, governmental intervention, and avoiding

a conflict with host countries' governments are examples of the problems facing MNCs in developing an appropriate ITP policy, making it much more difficult, if not impossible, for domestic firms.

5. The most important key factors in deciding which transfer pricing method to use are the global strategy of MNCs, exchange controls, income tax liability, and performance evaluation of Middle East subsidiaries and their managers.

- MNCs, the U.S. IRS, and Middle East tax authorities will receive great benefits by adopting APA programs, including friendly collaboration between the MNC and the IRS, possible avoidance of costly, time-consuming audits and litigation, and less uncertainty regarding the tax treatment of ITP activities.

Business and Accounting in the Middle East in the Twenty-First Century

In general, the Middle East countries that have been discussed in this book are dependent for their material strength and development potential on the ongoing success of their melding into the global economy. This melding is far from simple, given the cultural, political, and religious forces influencing these countries. Security and certainty in the economies of Middle East countries will not and will never be ensured unless the peace process agreement between the Israelis and Palestinians is fulfilled reasonably for Palestinians. My belief is that the Arab–Israeli conflict is nearing the end. Very soon, the Middle East will open widely for all MNCs. In the twenty-first century, business, not politics, will lead the Middle East to its most significant business success, as long as the peace process is fully in effect.

However, if the Arab countries and Israel are looking forward to having one of the best global markets, to attracting the best investors in the world, and to competing with the European Union market, then the following recommendations should be implemented seriously in the early years of the twenty-first century:

- Israel, Palestine, the participating Arab countries, and the United States must look forward to strong business growth with stable and strong economies rather than look to strong armies with the most sophisticated weaponry. The peace process can be speeded up only through the involvement of all parties, but it should be an accomplished only through acceptable conditions for all parties involved.
- If Arab countries are looking forward to having a regional standard setter, if possible, and a set of international financial reporting standards, the following major issues are essential in achieving this ultimate goal:

1. There is a growing trend in Arab countries about the urgency of enforcing a core set of internationally recognized standards to ensure that the information upon which investors and other stakeholders base their decisions is transparent, comprehensive, reliable, consistent, and internationally comparable. The Gulf Cooperation Council

(GCC) can be the leading organization by adjusting its constitution or bylaws to enforce the harmonization of accounting standards on its member countries to make financial reports comparable, consistent, and comprehensive, especially to protect foreign investors from any fraud or misleading financial data.

2. All Arab countries must have a common mission or an objective regarding financial accounting and reporting.

3. Arab countries must have a process for developing financial reporting standards that is accepted and trusted by all constituents, one that ensures that the mission of the standard setter is fulfilled.

4. Arab countries should develop standards that achieve high quality.

5. One regional standard-setting body should be formed and must have the power to enforce accounting standards on all national companies in the region. The accounting profession in Arab countries must play a positive role and should participate in the development of regional, high-quality accounting and auditing standards and cooperate with accounting firms serving the business community of the Middle East in implementing those standards.

• One of the real or recommended policy goals common throughout the Arab countries is the need for economic diversification of their industries. This is especially evident in the oil-based economies. Coupled with diversification is an urgent need for privatization. In the early 1990s, the Egyptian government admitted that state-owned enterprises are no longer the best way to foster economic development. Many major Egyptian companies have been sold to private Egyptian, American, and other firms to start a new, strong, private sector willing to participate in the development of the Egyptian economy and to create a successful business environment for investors.

In the twenty-first century, I expect the recommendations of this book, if used as practical guidelines, to have many implications for American and non-American MNCs, potential international investors, large accounting firms, Middle East local investors, Middle East professional accounting and management organizations, and last but not least, the governments in the Middle East, as a result of encouraging all different types of foreign investments.

REFERENCES

Baydoun, Nabil and Roger Willett. "Cultural Relevance of Western Accounting Systems to Developing Countries." *Abacus* 31, no. 1 (1995), 67–91.

Doupnik, Timothy S. and Stephen B. Salter. "External Environment, Culture, and Accounting Practice: A Preliminary Test of a General Model of International Accounting Development." *The International Journal of Accounting* 30 (1995), 189–207.

Gray, S. J. "Toward a Theory of Cultural Influence on the Development of Accounting Systems Internationally." *Abacus* (March 1988), 1–15.

Hamid, Shaari, Russell Graig, and Frank Clarke. "Religion: A Confounding Cultural Element in the International Harmonization of Accounting?" *Abacus* 29, no. 2 (1993), 131–147.

Hofstede, Geert. *Culture Consequences*. Beverly Hills, Calif.: Sage Publications, 1980.
———. *Accounting and Culture*. Barry E. Cushing (ed.). Sarasota, Fla: American Accounting Association, 1987.
———. *Cultures and Organizations—Software of the Mind*. London: McGraw-Hill, 1991.
Khanna, Nitin. "A Commercial Hub for the Middle East?" *Accountancy* 123 (February 1999), 78–79.

Index

Abdallah, Wagdy M., 3, 5, 11, 13, 31, 62, 63, 94, 150, 153, 162
Abdel-Khalik, A. Rashad, 241–242
Absorption (full) cost, 206–207, 248
Accountability, 4
Accounting changes, 76
Accounting control, 19, 34, 37, 65, 157, 162, 211, 213
Accounting policies, 33
Accounting profession/organizations, 11, 20, 29, 31, 35, 36, 45, 57, 75, 95, 100, 119, 124, 270
Accounting reports, 5
Accounting subculture, 6, 40, 44, 48, 52, 264
Accrual basis, 76, 98
Advance Pricing Agreement (APA) Program, 14, 208, 237–238, 249–253
Advanced technology, 9
Agars, Peter, 142
Aitkin, Robert, 137
AlHashim, Dhia D., 27, 31, 34, 35, 89
Allen, Brandt R., 106
Allocation, 4, 27, 32, 35, 133
Al-Omari, Ahmad, 98
Al-Rai, Ziad K., 99
America Online, 98

American Accounting Association (AAA), 5, 11, 95, 152
American Institute of Certified Public Accountants (AICPA), 94, 128, 130
American-Kuwaiti joint ventures, 12
American-Saudi joint ventures, 76, 80–81
Amoco-Egypt, 94
Arabs, 45
Arm's-length (market) price, 176, 180, 190, 213, 222, 238–239, 243–247, 249, 253, 255–256, 240
Asset valuation, 88, 92, 103, 106, 117
Association of Southeast Asian Nations (ASEAN), 3
AT&T, 8
Atkinson, Anthony A., 137, 200
Azzam, Henry T., 137

Bahrain, 3
Bailey, Andrew D., Jr., 242
Balance of payments, 2, 157, 198, 214, 218, 227, 238
Ball, Donald A., 158
Banker, Rajiv D., 200
Bankruptcy, 4, 57
Barkey, Henry J., 23
Bartlett, Sam, 171–173

Baumal, W. J., 241
Baydoun, Nabil, 40, 41, 51, 136, 264
Bechtel International, 12
Bee, Charles W., Jr., 254, 256
Belkaoui, Ahmed Riahi, 5, 40, 136
Benke, Ralph H., Jr., 200, 212–213, 229
Bethany World Prayer Center, 45
Bishko, Michael, 171
Blakeway-Philips, Matthew, 137
Boe, Warren J., 242
Borkowski, Susan C., 252
Brannan, Rodger, 8
Briston, Richard J., 89
British accounting systems, 74, 89
British multinationals, 2, 8, 62, 135
British standards, 31
Budget, fiscal, 90–91
Budgeting, 52, 89
Burns, Jane O., 245–246
Bursk, Edward C., 152–153
Business combinations, 108
Business risk, 171

Canada, 124
Capital investments, 2
Capital maintenance approach, 32
Cheney, Glen, 128
China, 3
Choi, Frederick D. S., 123, 201
Christianity, 7, 42, 44, 54
Chrysler, 8
Clarke, Frank, 40, 135–136, 264
Cole, Simon, 3, 21
Collectivism, 46–47, 53–54
Comparable Uncontrolled Price (CUP)
    Method, 245–247, 255–256
Compensations, 72
Conservatism, 6, 40, 48, 52–55, 264
Consolidation/consolidated income/con-
    solidated returns, 9, 75, 88, 92, 97,
    100, 102, 103, 108, 112, 116–119,
    179, 184, 219, 265
Contingent liabilities, 33
Control, 4
Control system, 2, 5, 8
Controllable factors. *See* Non-controllable
    factors
Convertible securities, 27

Cook, Stephanie, 101
Cost recovery, 79
Cost-Based and Cost-Plus Methods, 199–
    200, 239–240, 245, 247–248, 253, 255–
    256
Crossborder Monitor, 66, 88
Crude oil, 3, 22, 101, 189
Cultural distance, 8
Cultural factors, 2
Culture, 5, 6, 7, 8
Current rate method, 111
Customer satisfaction, 28

Dahmash, Naim, 99
Datar, Srikant M., 206
Decentralization, 13, 211
Deferred income taxes, 88, 103, 109, 110
Deloitte and Touche, 200
Department of Zakat and Income Tax, 76
Dessouki, Assem, 21
DHL Corp., 198
Diller, Daniel C., 3, 21
Dividends, 64, 72, 77, 82, 177, 180–181,
    184–185, 187–188, 191–192, 253
Divisional profitability, 13
Double taxation, 79, 175, 253
Doupnik, Timothy S., 5, 6, 10, 29, 40,
    50, 136
Durst, Michael C., 251–252
Dyncorp, 12

Eastern Europe, 3
Economic and Social Council
    (ECOSOC), 23
Economic differences, 2
Economic integration, 21
Economic leverages, 3
Economic stability, 22
Edwards, James Don, 200, 212–213, 229
Egyptian Generally Accepted Accounting
    Principles, 74, 89, 92–94, 104, 106,
    112, 113, 116–119, 265
Egyptian Society of Accountants and Au-
    ditors, 75, 94, 118, 136
Egyptian Stock Exchange, 177
El-Ashker, Ahmed A., 89
Elliot, Jamie, 198, 200, 201, 203, 218,
    243, 246, 247–248

El-Mahjoob, Rafaat, 4
Elmallah, Amin A., 123
Energy reserves, 3
Environmental accounting systems, 19, 20, 29, 32–37
Epstein, Barry J., 104, 106, 107
Equality, 4, 8
Equitable taxation, 57
Equity accounting method, 88, 92, 97, 108, 117, 119, 265
Equity investments, 27
Ernst & Young, 72, 136, 171, 174
Ethics, 4, 7, 34, 42, 56, 57, 131–132
European Accounting Standards Board, 134
European Economic Community (EEC/ EU/EC), 3, 21, 22, 26, 27, 31, 36, 133–134, 269
European multinational companies, 24
Exchange rates, 2
Expropriation risk, 61, 64, 74, 82, 215, 227, 242

Fabian, T., 241
Farag, Shawki M., 5, 28, 29
Farmer, Richard M., 40, 159
Fechner, Harry H. E., 5, 40, 136
Femininity, 46, 48
Ferris, Kenneth R., 106
Financial Accounting Standards Board (FASB), 9, 75, 94, 110, 117–118, 123, 125–129, 131–133
Financial performance, 5
Financial reporting and disclosure, 1, 13, 26, 27, 32, 33, 35, 61, 74, 81, 82, 88, 93, 117, 119, 127, 138–139, 266
Financial reports, 5, 124, 134, 207
Flexibility, 48
Foreign Capital Investment Law (FCIL), 80–81
Foreign currency translations and transactions, 88, 93, 99, 103, 111, 112, 117, 119
Foreign debt, 3, 21
Foreign exchange gains or losses, 63, 70, 72, 79, 82, 112, 231–232
Foreign exchange rate, 23, 26, 72, 74, 116, 155, 157–158, 214, 229–233

Foreign exchange risk, 13, 61, 201–202, 204, 217, 226, 242
Foreign tax credit, 78, 79, 182, 242, 252
Foster, George, 206
Foster-Wheeler Energy Group, 12
France, 124
Free zones, 65, 69, 82, 178
French uniform accounting system, 74
Frost, Carol Ann, 123, 201
Functional currency, 111

General Agreement on Tariffs and Trade (GAAT), 23, 36
General Motors, 8
General price index, 112
General purchasing power, 105, 117
Geographical strategies, 1
German multinationals, 2, 8
Gernon, Helen, 123, 208
Goal (congruence) harmonization, 13
Going-concern assumption, 98
Gomez-Mejia, Luis R., 7, 8
Goodwill, 107, 116
Gordon, Michael, 173, 183
Graig, Russell, 40, 135–136
Gray, Sidney J., 5, 6, 23–26, 28, 39, 40, 41, 42, 44, 48–50, 56, 57, 136, 264
Green, Ronald F., 47, 52, 53, 137
Greenhill, C. R., 218
Greenhill, Mitchell, 254, 256
Gress, Edward J., 89
Gross domestic product, 90–91
Gulf Cooperation Council (GCC), 3, 21, 22, 27, 36, 78, 103, 137, 173, 269, 270
Gulf War. See Persian Gulf war

Hamid, Shaari, 40, 44, 45, 56, 135–136, 264
Harding, Frank, 132
Harmonization, 22, 173, 217, 234
Harmonization of accounting standards, 3, 14, 19, 26, 27, 29, 31, 35, 36, 39, 40, 44, 46–47, 51, 55–57, 87–88, 123, 132, 135, 137, 263–265, 270
Hart, Michael H., 44
Hassan, Naim, 30, 33, 104, 109
Herbalzheimer, E. O., 218
Hinduism, 42

Hines, James R., Jr., 221–222, 242
Historical cost principle, 74, 95, 118
History, 1
Hofstede, Geert, 5, 6, 39–42, 45, 46, 48, 50, 52, 53, 55–57, 136, 264
Honeywell, Inc., 229
Horngren, Charles T., 206
Hughes Aircraft International, 12
Hyperinflation economies, 117

Incentives, 61, 65, 69, 77, 82, 172–173, 185, 188, 193
Income tax laws, 63–64
Income taxes, 3, 77, 80, 96
Income taxes, accounting for, 93, 117, 119, 215, 218–220, 244, 239
Individualism, 43, 46, 47, 51, 53, 56, 264
Inflation, 2, 11, 23, 27, 66, 90–91, 97–98, 106, 155, 157–158, 204, 212, 233, 265
Inflation, accounting for, 93, 97, 103, 112, 116, 117, 119, 265
Institute of Certified Public Accountants in Israel (ICPA), 75, 95, 96, 97, 143, 266
Interest, 177–178, 180, 182, 184–185, 187–188, 191–192, 253. See also Usury (riba)
Interest rate, 4, 23, 155
Internal Revenue Code (IRC), 110, 208
Internal Revenue Service (IRS), 198–201
International Accounting Standards (IAS), 10, 12, 13, 19, 30, 31, 35, 36, 74, 75, 87–88, 92–93, 97, 99–101, 103, 104, 106, 116–120, 124–137, 139, 142, 263–265
International Accounting Standards Committee (IASC), 10, 26, 29, 30, 56, 87, 94, 97, 110, 119, 127–135, 265
International Federation of Accountants (IFAC), 26, 96, 123–124, 131–132, 136
International Monetary Fund (IMF), 11, 23, 70, 98
International Organization of Securities Commissions (IOSCO), 26, 123, 125–126, 129–131, 133
Inventory valuation, 88, 92, 105, 116, 117, 119, 175–176

Investment, accounting for, 88, 104
Investment risk, 10
Iqbal, M. Zafar, 123
Iran, 20
Iraq, 3, 12, 20, 70, 99
Islam, 4, 7, 8, 12, 20, 22, 32, 39, 41, 54, 55, 264
Islamic banking, 32
Islamic International Accounting Standards, 39, 56–57
Islamic Sharia (regulations), 53
Israeli Generally Accepted Accounting Principles, 92–93, 95, 96, 105–106, 108, 113, 116–119, 143

Jahmani, Yousef, 98, 99
Japan, 22, 28, 72
Japanese multinationals, 2, 8, 24, 135
Joint ventures, 2, 6, 8, 9, 14, 22–25, 52, 61, 62, 64, 65, 67–70, 72, 76–78, 81–83, 175
Jordanian Association of Certified Public Accountants, 75, 118
Jordanian Generally Accepted Accounting Principles, 92–93, 99, 105, 118
Joy, Julie, 228
Judaism/Jewish/Jewish state, 42, 44, 46, 54

Kantor, Jeffrey, 138–141
Kaplan, Robert S., 200
Kavoossi, M., 2
Keller, Donald, 150, 153
Kemper, Cynthia L., 44
Kesselman and Kesselman, 95, 142
Khanna, Nitin, 119, 265
Kieso, Donald E., 113
Kilborn, Robert, 101
Kilgore, Alan, 5, 40, 136
Kim, H. Seung, 209, 220
Knowles, Lynette L., 211, 213, 217
Kuwaiti Generally Accepted Accounting Principles, 92–93, 100, 105, 136
Kuwaiti Stock Exchange, 76, 100

Labor costs, 62, 71–72
Landau, Philip, 142
Lermer, David, 243

Lessig, Van, 152–153
Lusk, Edward J., 241–242

Major, Bill, 198
Malmstorm, Duane, 229
Management accounting techniques, 4
Management control. *See* Accounting
    control
Mansfield, Peter, 3
Masculinity, 43, 46, 48, 51, 53, 54, 57,
    264
Mathur, Ike, 211, 213, 217
Mauriel, J. J., 151
McCulloch, Wendell H., Jr., 158
McGregor, Warren, 126–128, 131–134
Meek, Gary K., 123, 201, 208
Melcher, Trini U., 123
Mergers and acquisitions, 24, 27
Milani, Ken, 228
Miller, Stephen W., 209, 220
Mirza, Abbas Ali, 104, 106, 107
Moore, John L., 3, 21
Moral values, 4
Morsicato, Helen G., 151
Motivation, 64, 211, 213, 217, 220, 233–
    234
Mueller, Gerhard G., 5, 39, 123, 208
Murtuza, Athar, 11

Nagy, Richard J., 240
Natural gas, 2, 22
Net realizable value, 106
New York Stock Exchange (NYSE), 26,
    27, 131
Nichols, Judy, 101
Nobes, C. W., 5, 40, 136
Noncontrollable environmental factors,
    162–165, 214
Non-financial information, 32, 37, 50
Nydell, Margaret K., 45, 46, 48–50

Oil, 2, 12, 62, 67–68, 79, 94, 98, 99
Oil export countries, 21, 101
Oil prices, 3, 101
Oil production, 22, 79, 197
Oil reserves, 12, 20
Oil wealth, 21
Oman, 1, 3, 21

OPEC, 101, 237–238, 243, 253–257
Organization for Economic Cooperation
    and Development (OECD), 23, 26, 36,
    130
Oxelheim, Lars, 208, 226

Page, John, 21
Palestine, 66, 72, 89, 142, 244, 269
Palich, Leslie E., 7
Payroll costs, 72
Peace agreements/process, 1, 66, 269
Pension plans, 27
Per capita income, 12
Perera, M.H.B., 5, 6, 40, 53, 136
Performance evaluation/measurement, 10,
    13, 14, 28, 32, 36, 132, 149, 150–154,
    156–160, 162–163, 165, 197, 200–203,
    210–214, 217, 220, 228–234, 239, 242,
    263–264, 266
Persen, William, 152–153
Persian Gulf, 98, 99
Persian Gulf War, 22, 89, 101
Picur, Ronald D., 5, 136
Plasschaert, Sylvain R. F., 226, 238
Political instability, 20
Political Islam, 4
Political leverage, 3
Political risk, 24, 74, 88, 171, 244
Pooling-of-interests method, 107–108
Power, Carla, 42, 44
Power Distance, 43, 47, 51–53, 56, 264
Price control/pricing decisions, 61, 71,
    158
Price Waterhouse, 70, 94, 104
Privatization, 25, 27, 37, 65–67
Product costs, 2, 28, 72, 149, 247
Professional organizations, 19
Professionalism, 6, 40, 48, 52, 54, 55,
    264
Profit center concept, 32, 197, 201, 212–
    214, 228
Profit split method, 199, 253
Property, plant and equipment, 106–107,
    255
Provision and reserves, 93, 117, 119,
    175, 183
Purchase method of accounting for acqui-
    sition, 107–108

Purchasing power gains/loss, 113
Purchasing power parity, 90–91

Qatar, 3, 21
Qur'an, 43–44, 53, 54, 56, 57

Radebaugh, Lee H., 5, 39, 49, 151
Rahman, M. Zubaidur, 25
Ralston, David A., 41
Rate of Return on Investment (ROI), 32,
    88, 150–155, 161–163, 165, 240
Regression and correlation, 163
Related party transactions, 33, 50, 74,
    100
Religion, 4, 8, 11, 12, 21, 39–42, 45–46
Religious mores, 5
Religious values, 4
Resale Price Method (RPM), 247, 255–
    256
Residual income, 150
Richman, Barry M., 159
Risk assessment, 10
Robak, Epsen, 250
Robbins, Sidney M., 152, 227
Roberts, Clare B., 138
Robins, Don, 171
Robock, Stefan H., 156, 208–209
Rolfe, Robert J., 10
Royalties, 79, 82, 177–178, 180, 182,
    184–185, 187–188, 191–192, 253
Ruff, Carolyn, 7, 42

Sack, Robert J., 106
Sagafi-Nejad, Tagi, 26, 27
Salimi, Anwar Y., 98, 99
Salter, Stephen B., 5, 6, 29, 40, 41, 50,
    136, 138
Saudi Accounting Association, 102
Saudi-American joint ventures. See
    American-Saudi joint ventures
Saudi Generally Accepted Accounting
    Principles, 76, 92–93, 102–103, 105–
    107, 109, 112, 114–117, 119, 136
Saudi Industrial Development Fund
    (SIDF), 77
Scarce resources, 2
Scharge, Michael, 198

Schindler, Guenter, 248
Secrecy, 6, 40, 48, 52–55, 264
Section 482 of IRC, 13, 14, 208, 237–
    238, 242–249, 263
Securities and Exchange Commission
    (SEC), 56, 115, 123, 129
Securities (stock/capital/financial) mar-
    kets, 2, 24, 25, 26, 27, 29, 30, 32, 37,
    48, 49, 61, 62, 64, 67, 95, 120, 131–
    133, 198
Sedaghat, Ali M., 26, 27
Shapland, Rick, 198
Shuaib, A., 100
Shura (team), 52, 53
Simmonds, Kenneth, 156, 208
Singaporean multinationals, 135
Soba, George H., 208
Social life, 1, 6
Social responsibility, 4, 25
Somekh Chaikin (firm), 107
Spagnola, Bob, 8
Stobaugh, Robert B., 152, 209, 227
Sturge, Derrick, 135
Sunna, 56, 57
Sutton, M. H., 129
Szapiel, Susan, 42–43, 54

Tariff barriers, 2, 155–156, 197, 209–210,
    214
Tax avoidance, 221, 222, 245
Tax credit, 172
Tax evasion, 222, 243
Tax exemptions, 76
Tax holidays, 78, 81, 82, 172–173, 178,
    182, 185, 188, 193
Tax planning, 61, 82, 171, 173, 244, 264,
    267
Tax rates, 14, 77–79, 82, 173, 176–177,
    179–181, 183–185, 187–188, 191–192,
    214, 218, 224, 237, 248
Tax treaties, 14, 78, 172, 242, 253
Technology transfer, 9, 62, 67, 171
Tel Aviv Stock Exchange, 97, 143,
    181
Temporal method, 111
Tokunaga, Tadaaki, 137
Tokyo Stock Exchange (TSE), 26, 27
Toyota, 8

Transfer pricing (intercompany pricing policies), 12, 14, 64, 71, 156, 158–159, 172, 176, 180, 186–187, 190, 197–200, 202–214, 263–264, 267, 269

Transfer pricing objectives, 14, 217–234, 237

Transfer pricing problems, 13

Transparency, 48

Uncertainty Avoidance, 43, 44, 46–47, 51, 53, 54, 56, 123–124, 264

Uniform accounting systems, 27, 34, 35, 94

Uniformity, 6, 40, 48, 52–55, 124, 139, 264

United Arab Emirates, 3, 9, 22, 62

United Kingdom, 24, 28, 124

United Nations, 21, 24

United Nations Commission on Transnational Corporations (UNCTC), 23

U.S. Department of State, 11, 66, 72

U.S. Generally Accepted Accounting Principles (U.S. GAAP), 74, 87, 92–94, 96, 99, 103, 106, 112, 113, 116, 117, 119, 127, 131, 134, 136, 138, 239, 263, 265

Usury (*riba*), 43–44, 56–57

Value-added activity, 24, 25, 36

Variable cost and variable cost-plus methods, 199–200, 238–240

Violet, W. J., 5, 40, 136

Wage rates, 72

Wallace, R.S.O., 94

Webb, Gisela, 7, 42

Weygandt, Jerry J., 113

Willett, Roger, 40, 51, 136, 244

Women, 7

World Bank, 23, 87, 130

World Trade Organization, 101

Wrappe, Steven C., 208, 228

Wright, George, 26, 27

Yasin, Mahmoud M., 47, 52, 53, 137

Yemen, 1, 44

Young, Mark S., 200

Zimmerer, Tom, 47, 52, 53, 137

About the Author

WAGDY M. ABDALLAH is Associate Professor of Accounting at Seton Hall University, New Jersey, where he specializes in international accounting and gives seminars on various aspects of doing business in the Middle East. Among his specialties is international transfer pricing for multinational corporations. Dr. Abdallah is the author of *International Transfer Pricing Policies* (Quorum, 1989), and he publishes widely in the journals of his field. He has served on numerous committees and boards and has had special teaching assignments in China, the Middle East, and Singapore.